Susan Sellers has degrees in English and Comparative Literature from the Universities of London and the Sorbonne, and has published articles on feminist theory, French feminism, women's writing and women in education. She has edited a collection of readings from the Centre d'Etudes Féminines in Paris (*Writing Differences*, Open University Press and St Martin's Press, New York, 1988), and is author of a forthcoming volume from Macmillan, *Language and Sexual Difference*. She has taught in Europe, Africa and South America, and has recently completed a first novel.

Susan Sellers, *editor*

Delighting the Heart

A Notebook by Women Writers

 The Women's Press

First published by The Women's Press Ltd 1989
A member of the Namara Group
34 Great Sutton Street, London EC1V 0DX

British Library Cataloguing in Publication Data
Delighting the heart: a notebook by women writers.
  1. Authorship
  I. Sellers, Susan
  808'.02

  ISBN 0-7043-4167-0   Y0030800

Typeset by AKM Associates (UK) Ltd, Southall, London
Reproduced, printed and bound in Great Britain by
Hazell Watson & Viney Limited
Member of BPCC Limited
Aylesbury, Bucks, England

Such queer moons we live with

Instead of dead furniture!
Straw mats, white walls
And these travelling
Globes of thin air, red, green,
Delighting

The heart like wishes or free
Peacocks blessing
Old ground with a feather

From 'Balloons' by Sylvia Plath

Contents

● Crafting

● Endings

● Women and Writing

● Notes on Contributors

Acknowledgements

Olwyn Hughes for permission to quote from Sylvia Plath's 'Balloons', in her *Collected Poems*, Faber & Faber, © Ted Hughes 1965 and 1981.

Kathleen Jamie for copies of reviews and comments on her experience of collaboration.

Simon and Schuster International for extract from Rosalind Brackenbury's *Crossing the Water*, Harvester Press, 1986, pp. 56–8.

Alice Walker for permission to reprint 'Writing *The Color Purple*', from *In Search of Our Mothers' Gardens*, The Women's Press, 1984, pp. 355–60, © Alice Walker 1982.

The editor would like to thank Sarah Lefanu for her support throughout the project and for her invaluable help in compiling the final typescript.

Preface
Susan Sellers

I spent the long summer holiday that followed my twelfth birthday writing a science-fiction fantasy in which I starred as the fabulous ruler of a make-believe galaxy *and* the captive heroine awaiting rescue. There was nothing particularly remarkable about my story – except that I wrote it entirely in code.

Not that creative writing was discouraged at school. On the contrary, our English master set us regular weekly titles; it was just that he seemed to have such a clear idea of the type of writing he wanted (a sort of cross between Dickens and Lord Baden-Powell) that I never dared try my own version of 'A Visit to the Fairground' or 'Lost in the Dark'. Instead, I rifled my bookshelves, or the 'literature' section of the school library, copying bits of poems out of anthologies, or extracts from short stories appropriate to his theme. I did once venture an especially thrilling episode from my science-fiction fantasy (in which the earthling heroine is forced to intercept interworld communications, so human beings can no longer rely on words to say what they mean), but it was marked with an 'E' grade and the comment 'disappointing work, Susan'. I would never be a writer.

For years writing remained remote and unattainable. There were hardly any women writers on my university literature syllabus, and it was necessary to consider those there were with all the distancing tools of literary theory. My own (secret) attempts to write invariably ended in the bin.

Then, in 1981, I got a teaching post near Alton in Hampshire, a few miles from Jane Austen's home at Chawton. With my students, I went to visit the house: its old-fashioned kitchen, the bedrooms with their patchwork counterpanes, the living-room with the table on which Jane Austen wrote.

The table had a peculiar effect on me. It was tucked behind the main door to the family living-room, hardly twelve inches wide, as if her writing had not merited privacy or space. The curator explained that Jane Austen deliberately left the hinges on the door unoiled so she could hide work away as soon she heard the door opening.

I think the idea for a notebook by women writers began with that table. Something about the curator's description of Jane Austen, hiding her work and cheerfully reassuming her role as mistress of the house, connected with my own childhood experience of writing, and made me think of Virginia Woolf, the 'angel' of perfect womanhood constantly nagging at her shoulder, or Harriet Beecher Stowe, asking her husband if she might 'lawfully' take a few hours from her household duties in order to write.

A Notebook by Women Writers comprises notebook-style accounts of the process of writing, from an initial idea, through the various stages of crafting, to a completed work, with a view to making that process accessible and encouraging more women to write. Contributors to the *Notebook* span a range of backgrounds and writing interests; I hope that the differences and similarities between their experiences will offer fresh insights into the nature of women's art.

Section one explores the 'Starting Points' for writing as these affect women. What has been the result of our having – until relatively recently – so few women writers as role-models? How does the pressure on women to be continually available and supportive to others conflict with the physical and mental space needed for writing? How can we, as women, juggle writing with our professional and domestic commitments?

Section two looks at 'Beginning to Write'. Where do ideas come from? Are there strategies we can share which can help overcome anxieties concerning the blank page and bolster our confidence to write?

The middle section, 'Crafting', documents the actual process of drafting a piece of work. Contributions to this section refer to writing fiction, poetry and drama, and include extracts from contributors' notebooks and examples of progressive drafts.

Section four, 'Endings', groups entries relating to finishing work. It explores such issues as 'what is an ending?' 'how do we know we are at the end?' as well as the diverse feelings that accompany 'ending', and the experience of having work rejected, published and reviewed.

The final section to the *Notebook* examines the complex subject of 'Women and Writing' from a number of angles and perspectives. Is literary language alien or intimidating to women? What are the difficulties that confront women writing about those areas traditionally regarded as outside the domain of literature – women's experience of childbirth, for instance, or the taboo of female sexuality? Is women's writing different to men's? If it is, what are the differences? And how do they arise?

A Notebook by Women Writers is dedicated to its contributors, and to all women who write.

• Starting Points

*I walk about with a mind full of ghosts of saucepans
and primus stoves and 'will there be enough to go
round?' And you calling, whatever I am doing, writing,
'Tig, isn't there going to be tea?'*

Katherine Mansfield

Starting Fiction
Carol Rumens

This is how I used to live at one time. I was in my early thirties, had two school-age daughters, and had published one collection of poetry. I worked full-time at a rather poorly paid job in recruitment advertising. My husband, as he then was, stayed at home in the week but played in chess tournaments at weekends sometimes. Every day I commuted to central London, a journey that took between an hour and a half and two hours and involved two bus rides and two trains. My husband made the children's meals and my meal in the evening. But he did very little general housework and the house was always chaotic when I got home. I used to shout at everyone and tell them to get some tidying done, but usually ended by doing most of it myself. Then I ate, then the TV went on, then there were the children to be got to bed, then there would be free time, if I only had the energy for it.

On Saturdays I took my youngest daughter to her ballet class and stayed to play the piano for a tiny fee. Then I had to take my elder daughter to her swimming class, which was in a school at the top of a very steep hill. We envied the parents we thought of as 'rich' who sailed past our slogging figures in their posh cars. A car for us was out of the question. K. grumbled if I didn't fetch her afterwards, too. I finally told her she'd have to do the whole thing on her own. (She was eight or nine.) She rebelled at that and gave up the classes though she'd been a promising little swimmer. Saturday afternoon was for shopping. We used to go to Sainsbury's just before it closed because that was when they started marking down the perishable goods like fresh fish and meat. My husband, D., always shopped with me when he was at home. Sometimes he'd carry eight bags, I'd carry four. After that we'd go to the library. We'd dump the children first in the children's library – in a different building – and though they enjoyed picking their books and browsing, they always complained we'd been too long. I suppose we must have had happy times, jokes and laughter, but as I look back on it I remember chiefly irritation and impatience, a desire for the whole thing (what? the day? the marriage?) to be over.

On Sundays I nearly always had my mother and father to lunch. They liked to come, the children liked them to come and I didn't mind. I'd spend the morning cooking unless it was a roast: somehow I managed to circulate the myth that only D. could do roasts, and he really believed it. And then, after lunch, came my big time of escape. I'd go upstairs to our bedroom, get out my novel and sprawl across the bed with it. (I didn't have a desk, not even a chair and table.) I'd read the last few sentences and wonder how I could inject some life into it. It was autobiographical, and as boring and squalid and confused as the reality. I'd have an idea, write a few more sentences, and then, suddenly, I'd wake up and find it was tea-time. I'd drag myself downstairs to do the salad.

The reason that Sunday afternoons were the best time for writing was because of the relative quietness in the room downstairs. Our bedroom had no carpet, and every noise from the living-room below came up through the floorboards. If the T V was on or the children were playing indoors I could hear every word. So it was only during the post-roast stupor, when the children were outside with their friends, that I could work.

Later I discovered a better method. I used K's bedroom which was so tiny we had been able to afford to carpet it, and sat at her dressing-table, first throwing a shirt over the mirror so I wouldn't be distracted by the haggard face of creation. I wrote a sequence of poems at that dressing-table which I called 'A Necklace of Mirrors'. It was published as a pamphlet. I've only just realised the irony of calling it that!

I even finished the novel, eventually, but no one would publish it. I re-wrote it, twice, and still no one would. I knew then that I would never again write autobiographically, and that I would completely disregard that traditional advice of veteran novelist to beginner: write about what you know. *What I knew* I found boring, trivial. I didn't know how to transform it into something interesting. Perhaps, now, I could? But the novel that finally did get published, last year, was mostly about something I didn't know at all first-hand – life in Russia. And the novel I'm working on now is set partly in the after-life. So I think I'll probably stay with what I don't know.

Though my husband at that time was doing virtually nothing to help us financially, and scarcely ever took his fair share of the housework, he was almost fanatically keen on the idea of me as a writer. He urged me on, and even liked to read my work; he was far from being a literary critic but occasionally had helpful flashes of intuition. I don't know whether I'd have been strong enough to stand up to a man who opposed it. I suspect I could have stood up to such a man: I was so angry inside in those days, it might even have released some useful energy if I could have screamed, 'I *shall* write, so there!' But I didn't have to. I also had quite an easy job, and there were times when I could do the novel at work, the typing part at least. The train journeys were good for poems. So the picture isn't all bleak. But, overall, it was a frustrating time, and I now mourn very much the fact that I was not more available to my children. I think a would-be writer should think very carefully before deciding also to be a mother. A writer does not only need a place to write in: she needs a sense of autonomy, the freedom to pursue experience. In general, wives and mothers in our society lack this privilege. Even writer-husbands (the responsible ones) are at a disadvantage, I think. Feeding your children and feeding your writing are rarely compatible.

One day I said to my husband: if I can find a very cheap room in London, would you object if I stayed there during the week and came home weekends? He said he didn't object. And so I did find a room, a very cheap room of my own (with a landlady who, as it turned out, couldn't stand the noise of my typewriter, but that's another story). I learned for the first time in my life to work in a prolonged, utterly concentrated way.

Unfortunately, it broke up my marriage and even loosened the bonds with my children, so that later it felt almost natural that I should leave home for good. I thought my teenage children could cope perfectly well, but now I realise they suffered in many ways and I feel deeply, unbearably sorry. I do have a good relationship with them now, much better than when I lived with them. They have been very generous and forgiving. I used to think my writing embarrassed them. But recently when I talked to them about the possibility of writing under another name now that my ex-husband has remarried they were quite disappointed, and I've given up the idea.

My situation now gives me more time for writing than I ever had, but that brings with it new problems of self-discipline. I find the loneliness hard to cope with sometimes. The man I now live with is out all day: the silent flat plus the blank page can be daunting unless I'm in an extremely positive frame of mind. Strange as it may seem to those who cherish the notion of isolation and a room of one's own, I worked best in the early days of our life together, when he was freelance too. We both worked at one huge table, our papers occasionally wandering across to meet and mingle. His concentration seemed to help focus mine. These were the circumstances in which I finished *Plato Park*, my first published novel. I am making heavier weather of the one I'm writing now, but then it's a more ambitious piece, and I want it to be much better than the first! I work from, roughly, eight-thirty to two-thirty, with interruptions for cups of coffee and answering the phone.

With poetry it's a different matter. I'll work on that any time and virtually any place. It has always been completely integrated into the texture of my life. I don't remember a time when I didn't write it.

By the time this is published I shall probably be in the throes of the Northern Arts Writing Fellowship I've just accepted. I feel I need at this stage the stimulus of different surroundings: I'm such a dyed-in-the-wool Londoner and I want to see what's going on elsewhere in Thatcherland. I also feel that deadlines, and the company of other people – though I chafe against both – provide a useful friction.

My great wish is to be able to afford, one day, a flat large enough to provide my children with a 'base' whenever they need it. Our current flat has one small bedroom, and the only room which can accommodate visitors is the one in which I write. So if my daughters come to stay I must either pick up my typewriter and decamp to the kitchen, or abandon the idea of work for a few days. Even at this relatively late and liberated stage of parenthood I am still pursued by the mother/writer conflict. It's not that easy to say to a friend: 'I can't see you today, I've got to get on with so-and-so' when the 'so-and-so' is a piece of creative work with no reality at all in the world beyond your own imagination. It's ten times harder, and makes you feel a thousand times guiltier, to say that to your own children. I suspect that the mother/writer conflict will pursue me in some form or another (the writer/grandmother conflict, for example?) until the day I die.

Poetry and Academe
Sylvia Kantaris

Until I was about seventeen I had no idea that there were or had ever been any female poets at all, so I had no childhood ambitions in that direction. My early fascination with the textures and rhythms of words took the form of a precocious ability to learn by heart and recite reams of verse and entire chapters of the Bible. What with that and my long blonde hair, I was a 'natural' for the role of the Angel Gabriel in my C. of E. infant school nativity play. There I was, set up on a chair, resplendent in parachute-silk, tinsel and home-made wings, my hair splayed out into a halo, but just as I was due to descend and tell my friend Janet, 'Behold, thou shalt conceive and bear a child!' I wet my knickers, in full view, and had to be rushed out in disgrace – a fallen angel. The teacher told me I was an animal.

Although my action was involuntary – the result of intense fear of being paraded (coupled with the fact that I had avoided the long trek to the outdoor lavatory at home, at lunch-time, due to the cold), I like to see it, in retrospect, as a poetic rebellion of sorts. The mind works on such incidents in mysterious ways, though at the time I was devastated, and could not have foreseen what devious routes I would have to take in order to reach the starting point of becoming a poet, let alone what daily efforts to keep a human sense of proportion and perspective would be required beyond the starting point. I still don't know why it is so important to me to mention that moment of stormy realisation that I could never be an angel, but it seems to have been significant in my limping journey towards poetry. I know there was a mulish obstinacy (mixed with extreme nervousness) in the course I took, and that reaching the starting point was partly a question of rebelling against the marked route even as I was apparently following and learning from it.

The marked route, for me, was largely academic. Not that I was born with a silver spoon in my mouth. Quite the opposite. My family background was Lawrentian without the frills. Our parents were not educated beyond the age of thirteen, either of them, but they held education in respect. There were few books in the house, but each evening my father sat me on his knee after his hard day's work making bricks, and pronounced each syllable of every fairy-tale and nursery rhyme very slowly, underlining them with his forefinger, until I grew impatient and started reading to him instead. Reading was a laborious process for my father but he enjoyed our joy, and I wish all children could have such a teacher. Our mother aided and abetted. She had ambitions for me to be a typist (having been employed as a skivvy, herself) so that, unlike my friend, Janet, I was allowed to take up a scholarship to the local grammar school. Janet's mother said education for girls was a waste of time and money. This was the general opinion in the late 1940s, and in fact I had to give up my scholarship the first year I won it, because there was a boy who supposedly needed it more than I did. So I twiddled my thumbs for a year at the top end of the primary school while waiting to take the scholarship exam yet again. In order to occupy myself, I wrote stories, even tried to write music, but painting became my main occupation. I decided to become a fashion illustrator (since it appeared to be the only opening for a female artist at the time).

When I finally got to grammar school, I was delighted to be told I had a real flair for Art, but alas I was deemed 'academic' (probably because I was hopeless at Domestic Science) and so doomed to Latin instead of Art. Latin did not appeal, due to all those centurions and legions of footsoldiers marching off to war, so I did a lot of drawing during lessons and would have failed Latin miserably but for my introduction to Virgil. I learnt most of Book VI of the *Aeneid* by heart and was entranced. Simultaneously, of course, I was exposed to many great poets, in English, French and German, but there was not a woman amongst them – not even the odd token woman in any of our set anthologies.

At this point I must make a big leap into another academic incident that seems to have been significant in my slow obstacle course towards the starting point. I was twenty-one and had started writing furtive verse – probably as a result of my frustrated ambition to be a painter coupled with my love of the sounds made by Virgil, Wordsworth and multitudes of French poets. I'd achieved a good honours degree in French, and was a post-graduate student in the Department of Education at Bristol University. I chose Poetry as my 'special option' in the Dip. Ed. course and disgraced myself utterly, yet again. I had to choose a poem and 'analyse' it, and stupidly took on Empson's 'Arachne'. It made no sense to me whatsoever but Empson was in vogue so I thought the poem must be 'great', especially since I seemed too thick to understand it. I treated it as a puzzle (which it is, of course), according to the academic methods of analysis I had been taught. Unfortunately, I added that it was totally alien to my own sense of what poetry might be about. The lecturer told me I had no gift whatsoever for understanding the first thing about poetry, suggested I get married instead of dabbling in things that were beyond me (I was about to get married anyway) and directed me towards the Novel 'option'. In fact, I had no option. In retrospect, I feel that academic poetry 'expert' did me a service, despite my devastation at the time. I learnt a lot from the Novel course, led by a woman who was mischievously anti-academic and irreverent. At that point I took up writing poetry with a vengeance, using Auden as my model. I had still not encountered any female models who were considered good enough to get onto a syllabus so, naturally, I still had no ambitions to *be* a poet. Writing was just something I could not avoid doing. It was all secret of course.

Although I had been led to believe that I had no gift whatsoever for understanding the first principles of poetry, let alone writing it, I was not wholly convinced of my stupidity. This was due to Charles Tomlinson, who had been my Tutor in Romantic Poetry (English) during my undergraduate years. I didn't even know that he was a poet, at the time, but I was well aware that his approach to the study of poetry was very different from that of most of the academics I'd encountered, and far more in tune with my own. He liked my essays. Later, when I discovered that Tomlinson was himself a poet, I was particularly interested to note his affinities with surrealism (in his graphics as in his poetry). No wonder he is so often castigated as 'dry' in our wet English climate! I spent ten years of my life working in the field of French Surrealism, and do not apologise for having written MA and Ph.D. theses, plus innumerable articles, related to French Surrealist poetry. Once you are accepted as a poet, you are led to feel guilt about having been an academic, but I was particularly lucky. Surrealism liberated me from the acadanaemia of my student years in England. I was in Australia, teaching French at Queensland University. 'Higher Research' was required of me. I think I started off by doing 'lower research', in the sense that I had to try out automatic writing for myself before I could write about surrealist poets. What a release! Automatic writing is rarely poetry, but it is a way in, a way of discovering what you need to write about. It seemed very strange to be paid an academic salary in order to divest myself of the academic stranglehold. Simultaneously I came into contact with Australian women poets – the first women poets I'd ever met. It was in that period that I started to write my own poetry, daily, though I still did not dare to submit it in the hope of publication.

'Genesis' is the title of the first poem I ever dared to try to publish. It is about the birth of my first child, in 1965. It is also about my own birth as an embryonic poet. The bravado confidence came with the act of actually giving birth, physically. I was just twenty-nine and still trying to find a balance between the strictures of academe and my gender. The Holy Sisters in the Mater Mothers' Hospital, Brisbane, treated 'public' patients like cows. In some kind of fury to redress the balance (the same old syndrome) I applied myself desperately to my M A thesis throughout the bovine period, and started on my Ph.D. when I was subjected to the same treatment again two years later, when my second child was born.

In retrospect, everything you've ever done in your life seems to have been inevitable, just because you can't help being who you are as a result of it all. Giving birth to real new people seemed astonishing and inexplicable. They say 'Push!' when you know very well that your role is to wait for the child to head out in its own time, and that 'pushing' is a fiction. I could use this as a metaphor for the birth of poems, and why not? In the act of giving birth to people, I recognised yet again that I was neither angel nor animal solely (though I'd rather be an animal than an angel). I was just human, and I wanted to write about just being human, and to celebrate it. It became difficult, juggling small children and intensive research, but my poetic career, such as it is, grew out of that collision of apparent opposites. It was all bound up with a birth into confidence directly related to the miracle of my having been able to give birth physically. Imagine! New people coming out of me! I asked if I was allowed to scream and was told it wasn't permitted. 'Only Aborigines and Italians scream' I was told. I heard them, and did one better in each case. The poem 'Genesis' was accepted and published well. Others followed. I dared to call myself a poet.

Another big leap: back in England I spent eight years as an Open University Tutor in Twentieth-Century Poetry. In order to be able to teach, I had to study, hard. I was forced to study poets I had barely read before – e.g. Rilke, whose angel-animal metaphor seems to be guiding the course of what I am writing in these notes about 'how I became a poet'. The only woman poet on the syllabus – and then only 'optional' – was Plath. In reaction, I applied myself to reading up that entire 'alternative' poetry of women – as much as was available – but was restricted to teaching about *their* work in Adult Education classes, attended mainly by women. It was a ghetto. My own poetry was in turmoil during this period. To be taken seriously, in England, it seemed women had to neuter themselves. I discovered that when I wrote specifically from a female point of view I was often castigated, even by women reviewers.

My culinary metaphors for poetry and sexuality were blamed. It is not as if I was ever domesticated into the subservient female role, but I cooked a lot of my poems in the kitchen, and obviously could not shrug off my gender, nor did I ever want to since, for me, poetry derives from the same source as my sexuality. The struggle to reconcile this with my academic training, and to find a balance, still seemed to be my main problem – including the fact that my academic work has always furnished me with a decent livelihood, whereas my poetry doesn't. Maybe the former is responsible for the painstaking slog through endless drafts of poems, and I often envy women who escaped the academic treadmill. Their poetic gifts often seem more bountiful than mine, less tortured by masculine traditions and forms.

Now that my children are young adults, I no longer have continual domestic demands on my time – though all the activities peripheral to writing poetry seem to take a lot more time than my meagre output warrants. I feel guilty when I take time off to write, and guilty when I don't. I do not feel guilty about my neglect of housework. Right now I'm sitting at the dining-room table, noting how the dust has piled up around me, but only noting it. If I were to spend the day with a feather duster, I would have nothing to show for it except a temporary lack of dust. Cleaning does not earn me money, as teaching does; nor do I find it creative, as poetry is, with luck.

Fortunately my husband is as busy with his own work as I am with mine, and I think the household chores get pretty evenly divided, depending on which of us has a spare moment (though the basic liaison work – preparing shopping-lists, remembering when family and visitors are due, preparing Christmases, doing the washing when necessary, *details* – always depends on me). I wonder whether there is something perverse about planting myself and my work in the domestic centre of the house. I think I use the dining-room as my office simply because it is the warmest room. There are problems in that work often gets mislaid or thrown into the rubbish bin by mistake in the rush to clear the table in readiness for the evening meal, but I can't write anywhere else. When I'm not teaching, shopping, performing, washing, cooking or liaising family matters, I sit at this table all day long, seven days per week, fiddling with words.

I find I write best when under pressure to do other things. For instance, when I was preparing a lecture on Emily Dickinson, I found myself writing a poem about her. The same thing happened in relation to Christina Rossetti. Sometimes I would break into poetry half-way through reading a student's essay. Perhaps this is the same old balancing act – trying to get 'blood, imagination and intellect running together' (another of Yeats's definitions of poetry; and I'm sure I know what he meant by his dictum, 'No mind can engender until divided into two.')

I need to be totally alone to write poetry. The presence of others anywhere in the house seems to sap my creative energy. Normally, I attend to letters and business matters when others are here in the house – even though they may be working upstairs or watching TV in the sitting-room. One thing I worry about is the fact that I seem to need to make more and more solitude for myself – to the extent that I am never really available, even to my own children when they come home, and no matter how much I look forward to their visits. I quickly go back into my 'retreat' in the room everyone has to pass through to reach the kitchen! (Maybe I want to be in the hub of life while keeping a distance? The same old balancing trick?) Luckily, my children are both quite as involved in their own studies as I am in my funny mixture of 'things to do with writing', but I find all work impossible when the summer influx of visiting friends starts. I want their company, and yet feel quite desperate, at times, about the interruption of the long communion with myself that I seem to be trapped in. This seems to be a feeling many writers share but rarely admit to publicly. We want to have our cake and eat it perhaps? We can't write without indulging in life, and neither can we live without writing. At least, I find myself forever at cross-purposes with myself, though the academic bit of me is quite useful for putting off friends who propose to visit me just when I'm in the throes of trying to get a poem right. I pretend I shall be teaching (real work) or that I have a deadline for a review (real work) but still have not managed to convince myself, even, that working on a poem is a good enough excuse.

Having been set up as an angel at the ripe old age of five, I have never been able to shake off the notion that I should 'look good' for public appearances, though it is a losing battle. At fifty-two, I can hardly expect to continue to 'look good', and yet the problem of how I appear, physically, and whether my clothes are 'right' or not is still a problem. This seems utterly mad, considering that most of my male contemporaries seem to be in far worse shape and yet seem not to concern themselves at all about their physical appearance, relying on their work alone to weave an aura. I wish I could achieve such confidence. Yet how can I when men are forever telling me how I *look*, often precisely at the moment when I'm trying to size up whether my performance has been good or bad? I get told I look fatter/thinner; that my hair looked better this way or that way; that skirts/jeans/high heels/flat heels suit me better than whatever I happen to be wearing; that the way I laugh creases my face, and so on. Male poets do not seem to be prey to such personal comments. I often wish I could perform hidden by a *chador*, looking out at the world without being looked at and sized up, as a poet, according to how I *look*. A well-meaning friend, intending to flatter me, once wrote and told me that one of my better performances was a success due to the fact that I'd 'looked delicious'. How very kind of him! And what if I had wet my knickers?

I do find the younger generation of males quite different. Recently, when my son and I were due to go and do the shopping in a local supermarket, I said, 'Hold on; I must tidy myself up first.' He was genuinely puzzled and asked me why I should bother. I said it was because I might meet people I know. 'Oh for God's sake, mum, you aren't defined by your appearance. Aren't you supposed to be liberated from all that nonsense?' he replied. He meant it genuinely (and for instance my daughter can't be bothered if she can't be bothered; she dresses up to look good only for fun, and when she has time). Alas, I shall never be liberated from the notion that I ought to appear to look better than I look in order to be acceptable in public. There is a lot more to this problem than seems to meet the eye, and I shall come back to it later (see p. 210), in relation to the ways in which women poets are reviewed, far too frequently, in terms that imply (ever so politely) that what they really need to put their lives (not their poetry) right is a good screw.

I was only ever an angel for one minute. My sudden fall from grace put paid to all such aspirations. The best I have been able to do is to try to stumble along inside my own human skin. I am still trying to fly, but more like a bat than an angel (a strangely winged animal, the bat). It still seems strange to me, the way that certain incidents recur in my poetry, insistently, as if to tell me something I need to know, and need to keep re-learning. They adopt varieties of masks. I don't think I have ever found any way of being completely acceptable, especially to myself.

Lady Scribbler
Carole Satyamurti

Who was it who said that the worst thing about being interrupted is not the interruption itself, but the awareness that it could happen at any time? That is certainly true for me. It has often been said that women writers are more subject to interruption that men – that they are less able to make claims for the importance of their own working time. And they usually do carry more domestic responsibilities that can't be passed on. But it is the potential interruption, the constant availability to others, that perhaps matters most, whether or not one is actually disturbed.

Unless I am working on something that is already far advanced, I can rarely write with someone else in the house – I can't write poetry, that is. Other forms of writing (such as this one) don't seem to present such a problem. Writing a poem seems to involve a simultaneous opening up and a reaching inwards – like an intense form of day-dreaming – a state a bit like madness. And there's a fear that if I am interrupted, I'll fall apart and not recover my 'normal' self; or that what I'm groping after, that elusive form I'm trying to make more substantial, will disappear.

For the same reason, I don't like anyone, even my daughter or my partner, to look at a poem before it is finished. It feels too private before that. To write a poem, it has to be possible for *anything* to spill on to the page in the process of drafting, but the finished poem represents a choice about what I am prepared to show. I have a positive pleasure in tearing up the drafts when a poem is finished. It feels like a clearing of the head ready for the next poem. Perhaps I lose the opportunity of storing up lines I haven't used for future use, but I know I would never look at those drafts again, and I hate being cluttered up with piles of paper. In general, I love throwing things out; I want there to be nothing anywhere in the house that I don't positively value.

I am lucky in having a job that allows me one, or sometimes two, days a week at home. I use that time for writing poems, and do my marking and teaching preparation in the evening, when my family is around, which is anyway not prime writing time for me.

My ideal circumstances for writing are ones where the time available has no externally imposed limit – where I don't have to stop in order to get the shopping, answer the phone, get a meal, be sociable, etc. etc. That means going by myself to a cottage in Suffolk owned by a friend of mine who lives in Canada. There are no close neighbours and no telephone. The house is comfortable and well equipped – not least with lots of books – but it isn't exactly someone else's home, so it isn't full of personal objects making claims on my attention. It feels like a perfect place to work in, and whenever I have gone there (for up to a week at a time) the writing has gone well.

Something else that is special to me about that place is that, although I have borrowed friends' country cottages before, that is the only one where I have not been frightened at night – afraid of being looked in on, attacked in my bed. That is very much a woman's problem, and one I am rather ashamed of. But it is partly realistic, and I feel very angry about it – as though there is no possibility of being genuinely alone; the potential male attacker is always there too, occupying head-space. In the Suffolk cottage, that feeling is at a minimum.

I admire people who can write in their heads. I can't – I have to have a blank sheet of paper. The sight of the paper reassures me that there could be – will be – a poem. I write on a large table in my bedroom, overlooking the street. In front of me is a row of dictionaries, a pot of pens, and a rack with paper etc. in it. There is a lamp, and a pink-leafed plant, and nothing else. It is important to me – in my life generally, but especially in relation to writing – that there is order. Everything in the room has to be in its place. I envy people who can write surrounded by a chaos rich in the possibility of discovery and new conjunctions. In principle, that seems creative – allowing one's surroundings to develop their own life. In practice, I can't stand it!

I started writing poetry seriously when I was forty-three. Before that, I had written sociology and a bit of journalism. And in the ten years before I was forty-three, I wrote perhaps half-a-dozen poems, the first of them arising from the pain of a failed love-affair, full of raw emotion and very little art.

I didn't know anyone who wrote poetry or fiction, and although these were forms I valued highly as a reader, it didn't occur to me that I could write 'imaginatively' myself (I use that word a bit uneasily, because I think that the imagination is, or should be, active in sociological writing too).

I thought that poetry was written by Real poets – people, men usually, who had English degrees and knew other Real poets. I subscribed to the T L S and to P N Review, and the literary world I perceived through their pages did not seem one that I could ever be part of. The other people who wrote poems were the Lady Scribblers, a patriarchal stereotype that I had absorbed against my will – the middle-class, middle-aged woman who expressed in bad verse all her secret griefs and desires. I certainly didn't want to identify myself with that!

Yet writing creatively was something I had always wanted to do – the most important thing. Perhaps I didn't attempt it for so long because I dreaded finding out that I was no good at it. I don't understand myself why I left it so late – or what made it possible to enrol on an Arvon poetry-writing course in 1983, having written so little.

That course changed my life. It was five days at Totleigh Barton with two practising poets and fifteen other people who wanted to learn about writing. The impact of it was comparable to a sudden conversion experience, or to falling violently in love – in fact I did fall in love with one of my fellow course-members, and have often wondered if I would have done if I had met him at the annual conference of the British Sociological Association.

Everyone there was serious about writing, and the tutors took seriously the task of helping each of us to write better. They were encouraging about the pieces I had brought, and very critical of the poem I thought was my best one, which was both hurtful and exciting. I hardly slept during those five days. I remember vividly everyone who was there, how they wrote, what we talked about. At the end, I got on to the train at Exeter knowing that to write poems as well as I could was what I most wanted to do, and that I would give all my available time and effort to it. I had begun to learn how to see what was wrong with my own work, and to find a way of thinking about poems.

In the years since then, I have been lucky in my association with the man I met on that Arvon course – first as a lover and then as a friend, but always as someone with whom I can discuss what we both write, and think hard about it. To have a constructively critical response to everything I write, rather than having to rely only on market forces in the form of acceptances or rejections, is immensely valuable. I have been lucky in my current partner, who is unfailingly interested in, and responsive to, what I write, and in other friends with whom I exchange poems. I think it is in the nature of poetry that the process of sharing it brings people into a relation of intimacy greater than is the case with other kinds of writing.

The 'Double World' of Writing
*Hélène Cixous**

I have always wanted to write. Even as a child I couldn't live without books. Later, of course, I began to write myself; I had children, a job, but none of these things ever stopped me from writing. When it's a question of life and death one always finds time to write.

I don't like to write if I'm not on form, if I feel tired for instance. Writing is a constant battle, for which I need all my strength. If I feel tired or a bit under par I stop writing immediately.

I write in the morning. In fact what this means is that I begin writing at night, in my dreams. I start writing very early in the morning and only if I know I have the whole day ahead of me. I write all day without stopping, often for three or four days at a stretch. Obviously this creates problems. When I really want to write I try to organise long periods of time completely protected from the intrusions of my professional life.

Sometimes I feel as if I have a double life. There is the world of my professional activities and relationships, and the other world of writing, which accompanies me everywhere, gradually taking shape within me all the time I am occupied in other things and cannot write.

*Hélène Cixous' contributions are based on a tape-recorded conversation with the editor.

Present Words, Past Stories
Jeannie Brehaut

Starting to write meant getting over my childhood and adolescence. Sorting through all the different and conflicting versions I had of me in the world and trying to strengthen the ones that gave my writing self time and support.

As a child I had a lot of other people's garbage in my head. There is no other way to describe this. My parents' lives were cluttered with untold stories; I wrote down a lot of what they told me. The stories were strangely unmoving and flat once I got them on paper.

I started writing about two children, Eli and Marcy, strange, unconnected kids who live with their father in a farmhouse on the edge of Canada. The three of them are waiting for the return of their mother. She left a year ago without saying anything to anyone and she still hasn't come back. Eli and Marcy will do whatever magical and crazy things they need to do to be released from her power. At the same time, more than anything, they want her back.

It's hard to combine writing with the need to work. What I do is waitress. I work between forty and sixty hours a week. I'm able to work mostly nights which is good. It's morning-time, or whenever I first wake up that I write best.

I sometimes sit down at the typewriter and think, 'I'm not going to be able to do this today', but then I wait and I usually can. I like to come to my typewriter with my head as empty as possible. I don't read anything or listen to the radio or any music until I've finished that first stretch of what will hopefully be an outpouring. When I'm on holiday or can afford to cut back my restaurant hours then I work every morning and that's the best.

My thinking and planning for a piece of work follow me when I start writing; I try to trust this process. Right now I need to write about Eli's arrival in the city and what I'm full of is another person who has lit all the candles, put them inside a cupboard and then closed the door.

'Now that's done,' she says, 'that's that.' I don't know how this ties in with Eli. I write it down because that's what I'm full of this particular morning.

When I'm working well I have the physical sensation of being sunk quite deeply inside myself, I'm oblivious to the room I'm in and anything going on outside the window. Somewhere I know everything about my characters and their stories. The new way I feel when I work, if I'm happy with what I'm writing, is that I'm being listened to. There's no one in the room but me and I feel calm and listened to very attentively as I say aloud what I've been typing. How I receive my own stories before I show them to anyone else is important. I like to read my work aloud in writing groups when I'm ready and my work is ready. Sometimes I submit work for publication before showing it to anyone else.

Last summer I took part in a six-week residential writing programme at The Banff Centre in Canada. I learnt a lot. Established writers came to visit us there and we were encouraged to show them our work. We were a group of twelve participants and we lived and worked on the second floor of the building. In the basement visiting writers posted their appointment times and if we wanted to talk to them or show them our work we were asked to sign up. I put my name on almost every list. I wanted to show everyone my newly-born first chapter of my novel. One woman didn't like what I'd written so far. She really questioned what I was doing, whether my characters were true enough to care about, whether or not I emotionally understood what I was writing. I'd never shown anyone writing that was so important to me before and had it received so badly. I was devastated. I spent the whole night sitting on the side of a mountain crying.

I think this was one of the most important things that has happened to me so far as a writer. After a while I could look at it like that. I abandoned part of that first chapter because every time I worked on it I felt uncomfortable. There was some truth for me in what this woman had said and I argued with her inside my head. This helped me to develop my characters further. Something else I realise was that my chapter was too young to show at that stage. I was looking at my chapter full of excitement for what it was becoming; the writer I showed it to saw everything it wasn't. The work was like a promise at that stage and I expected her and my other readers to see it this way also. I'm tough about my work and who I'll show it to now. This is protective, not unfriendly. I always think carefully about the sort of feedback I need at the time before deciding to show an early draft.

When I'm doing a lot of shifts in the restaurant I sometimes find it hard to keep the story of Eli and Marcy moving. I always want to write about their lives and I have a strong feeling of both of them but when I'm tired or over-charged from working I can't always focus on my characters and pick their voices up. I remind myself there is no race involved in writing – either against myself or what I had initially thought of as my deadline. These days I'm trying not to make predictions. All this is left over from my performing-bear childhood and it's not easy to shake off.

I long for a time of open-ended space to write in, maybe two waitressing shifts a week and money from publishing or a grant. Still I know what I'm writing now is what counts. Whether it's a page a week or a hundred. As often as I can I put my pen to paper; try to focus myself and write.

Stretching to Fit
Sue Stewart

The starting points for work are silence, warmth and a room of my own. I made a study for myself about five years ago and I still swim in it, in the expansiveness of it. It encouraged a professional attitude as nothing else could; almost as if I had to produce poems worthy of it, prove I'd earned all that yardage.

I always wrote, and always wanted to be a writer, but it took some time to develop stillness and confidence – the two prerequisites for any creativity to flower. I was like a jumping-bean on a hot tin roof for most of my twenties, and it took long painful years to learn how to relax. I've always admired the naturally serene but the calm I feel now, which allows me to work, is one I've trained myself into.

For ten years – five before, five after university – I worked at dozens of jobs, from the eccentric to the dull, ever hankering for something 'other'. The three years as a student changed things irrevocably, just as I had dreamed they would: I felt as though I'd been let out of a tiny box into a vast arena of learning, of knowledge and ideas. After graduating though, I went to London and got the cramps all over again: working in publishing and a variety of stop-gap jobs, living in bedsits, shared houses.

After the grind of these years I'd learnt to appreciate the space and stillness of the countryside, and the possibility of having a room just to write in. The making of a study had become as much a symbolic as a practical act. It was a statement of intent, a final commitment: also a declaration of preparedness, so it had to happen naturally, in its own time.

At first I worked on the kitchen table, or in John's study when he wasn't using it (not difficult as he works mornings, I afternoons). The kitchen table was comfortable, even comforting, in a historic kind of way. It was an old oak table, a bit battered, and it swallowed the endless drafts uncomplaining. John's study was another revelation altogether, and I was encouraged by his openness in lending it out so freely. Working there, though, did eventually begin to have a strange effect on my work. I wasn't writing in his voice, but I wasn't writing in my own either. I hadn't found it, because all the walls threw male echoes. I was in a never-never land, trying to play the triangle in the middle of a drum roll. What compounded this difficulty was that John's poetic voice was so different from the one I felt I had to develop, both linguistically and rhythmically. For instance, adjectives and adverbs were beheaded on sight, and lines frequently began with a stressed syllable. This works dramatically well for him, but in my own work I wanted to loosen the linguistic belt, and find a different rhythm.

Once I'd made my study, the writing underwent a sea-change. All the discipline I'd striven for – the paring down of words to the bone, conciseness, starkness – held me in good stead as I began to work at the style, find my own voice. I was lengthening the lines, letting the air in, working in an entirely new way. The surreal had crept in, or rather, emerged from its corner. I felt able to give more free vent to the intuitive, the weird, the lateral. Also I was reading an enormous amount of work by contemporary women poets at this time, and learning valuable lessons from them: that obliquity and strangeness can be used to good effect, for instance, and that meaning in a poem doesn't have to glow like neon. I still concentrate more on women poets, partly out of a natural affinity and partly because a dispro-portionate number of our poet friends are men, so I like to redress the balance.

We live between two beech woods, so I'll often go for a walk before settling down to work. There are pheasants and squirrels in the woods, and I see a deer about once a year. This peace and quiet has a healing effect, as does the fairly isolated life we lead here. The woods seem to remind me that 'there's always time'.

I tend to write intensively for a few months then take time off to do other things. I'm kept pretty busy with workshops (especially in schools), readings, reviewing and editing. Money – its lack – rakes in the usual problems each week, as it does for most writers (and probably many readers, and half the population of England): I keep waiting for a boat to come in, but haven't figured from which direction.

Writing has to accommodate all the daily jobs: looking after a fairly remote country cottage demands at least a semblance of organisation. We try to restrict our shopping expeditions to once a week, and frequently fail. Chores such as washing, ironing, house-cleaning and cooking pale beside the more enjoyable rural jobs: chopping and stacking logs, laying fires, weeding the garden and vegetable patch, mowing the lawn. We divide these up fairly, according to strength, inclination, and which one of us is working the hardest on a piece of writing.

'Room of calm, room of thunder . . .'
Medbh McGuckian

Evening, four minutes after eight. I sit down at my desk for the first time. Birds because it is April and the boys still full of life till the birds stop. John is wearily closing doors and shovelling coal. I go to see if I can settle them a little. Their bedrooms are on the first floor, my 'study' is the return room beyond the bathroom between the main floors and above the kitchen at the shadowed back of our Victorian semi. So most of my working life is spent in the servants' quarters, either upstairs or down, which must be how I want it, and often satisfies me, but sometimes drives me to despair and a masochism of marginalisation. The sun which makes most love to the front windows pays me a brief visit downstairs and has just slid behind Cavehill on my right, a very masculine jawline. Early this morning, it coloured the forty shades of the most feminine mountain in my world. I will check now if teeth have been washed, and John, though neglected, has a paper or beer or television in return for my silence.

Near me I have a box full of old love-letters in case I am reduced to writing a novel, and a small white bookcase with only the books I am reading or might refer to, plus three box-files of my poems, photocopies or carbons. My desk is an old teacher's table from the school I used to work in, with education beaten into its grime, like me. I have improvised an extension with a barley-legged table to clear some of the mess, but it's never tidy. It wobbles from being held together by precarious screws in the wrong places, also like me. The three tiny drawers are jammed with old diaries, new paper, passports (I have at least three), old tickets, pens that don't work, unused Christmas cards. There is a box of to-be-answered letters, supposedly my 'In-tray', poems from people, mostly women seeking encouragment. Sometimes I will answer these from my official study across town in the University, when I'm not interviewing students or answering the telephone. It is impossible to write poetry there. Here, I can turn the sound of the telephone low and hope the door will not open. At this time I should be reading Beatrix Potter to my children, but that would mean another half-hour sacrificed. The radiator is lukewarm, the boiler chugs like a barge below.

It is two minutes past nine. John is taking a noisy bath, the birds and boys continue. I will write no poems till they sleep, though I can write this. I will do the dishes in the morning. We have few visitors, so this time, eight till ten, is mine. Since I begin a poem so late, they are all night-poems. If I am free in the mornings when my three-year-old goes to nursery, maybe they will be morning offerings. A night out means no writing for that day. Sleep, proper sleep with dreams, is vital to my work, so I need to retire early, unless a poem demands to be finished. The house is difficult to run, but my babyminder helps. There are evenings I am too tired, too depressed, too disturbed by news I've not watched, to do anything. I need the combination of solitude with the family atmosphere, I need to feel well, without a headache or cold; birth and death disrupt me, also hormonal changes. Although some people write better if they are unhappy, I have to feel content and secure; the weather influences me, the season, I write little in the summer.

A Strong Story-telling Impulse
Emma Tennant*

As a small child I used to wander round the garden telling stories to myself aloud, and I think one of my motivations for writing is simply a strong story-telling impulse – like people say of someone, 'so-and-so is musical'. I was often alone as a child and I suppose the stories were to make up for my sense of isolation, though I also think there was the drive of something which needed to be said. After that there was a blank, since it didn't occur to me that this impulse could turn itself into a typewriter or pen; then, in my early twenties, I got a job on a magazine and started doing reviewing and odd bits of writing. My editor asked me to try a short story, and although she didn't think it was good enough, she was very encouraging. I think I was twenty-four when my first novel *The Colour of Rain* came out. I wrote this more or less straight off in about ten days. I think this broke some kind of barrier, since after that I decided I had to be a writer. For the next six or seven years I wrestled with structure, accumulating a great heap of unfinished manuscripts under my bed, until finally I met someone who gave me a formula I could work to. I think a lot of people are put off for life by the difficulty of organising material; I know I might never have had the confidence to continue if someone hadn't stepped in to help.

I think it's very hard to write if you have small children. Sylvia Plath was reduced to writing at four in the morning, and her incredible fatigue undoubtedly contributed to her final breakdown. Of course many women have children and jobs as well, and I think as far as writing in these cases is concerned it's first thing in the morning that counts. Even if you only get half a page down by the time you have to leave for work or children are awake, there's a sense in which the rest of the day can take care of itself: you don't mind as long as that half page

*Emma Tennant's contributions are based on a tape-recorded conversation with the editor.

is down. Then, if you're lucky, you'll be able to come back to it in the evening, and correct a bit, or have a thought or two about what the next day's bit will be; again, if you're luckier the next day, you might find that everyone is out and you can do a bit more. People are sometimes taught on creative writing courses that you have to get an awful lot down, and of course this doesn't mean anything at all, and some of the best writers are pleased to get a few hundred words down a day.

Permissions
Nicki Jackowska

Although I am, as it were, beginning at the beginning with the conditions, the ground of writing, I fear there will sneak in here fragments from 'Beginning to Write', 'Crafting' or even 'Endings' – since it's entirely possible to have as one's ground the end of something else. I may, for example, find it necessary to have near at hand a postcard of Leschaux, a fragment of Nottingham lace (under the telephone) and a list of words:

    ABOVE THE TREELINE
    THE ISSUE
    THE HERO
    CLUES

which constellation took place in the making of the poem 'Cutting', and thence grew a limb, a demanding/expansion or spilling of the poem; so the fiction waits, is conceived and has these few scraps as its only visible foundation. As Brodsky said: poetry and fiction is born of rubbish. (I immediately think of Stanley Spencer's 'Resurrection' where it is the dustman and his wife who are reborn and friends offer cabbages.) Also Yeats – 'the rag-and-bone shop of the heart'. I stay close to these scraps of potency and so now, at this moment, is the gathering of the material for my current novel (in progress), *From the Terrace.*

There are two – no three – parallel tracks here, and they influence and speak to each other: my landscape, my page of words, my head – the state of all of these is important, but overseeing the lot is VIGILANCE/ATTENTION-SPAN. I must keep the widest, most sensitive antennae twitching and fidgeting away, in the dark or the light, whether I know where I'm going or not. To make the connections, to gather the elements, to proceed.

But let me take a step back again. My landscape is composed of the page of words and my head. The page of words is composed of landscape and my head. My head is composed of the page of words and the landscape: plus history, loves, friends, anticipations, fragments, music, physical condition.

I need alcohol.

I need music, of all kinds.

I need to have access to outside sources of energy, instantly if necessary. I often ring someone up not to talk about what I'm doing at all, but to shift my head – shift it anywhere.

I have a cassette/radio which I can turn up very loud and I have a large room with a bay window which lets in light at different angles. This bay window is important. It is as though the room bulges, leans into the street with the fullness of what I am doing. It is also as though I extend a hand, issue an invitation to the world at large – a tentative saying 'I am not entirely separate – this window extends greeting – I am, almost, half-way out'.

There's a lot of muddle surrounding the question of self-indulgence, individualism (in a pejorative sense), isolation. I am, with my letters, telephone and my room full of reminders, in touch with the whole world by keeping solitary hours. I am not isolated. In writing most deeply from myself, I tap all human sources. The problem is to get there, to touch them oneself, track them and channel. The personal and universal are most intimately interconnected. This is also a political, though subtle and hidden front-line, where one broaches the question, re-shapes the life, addresses the human. And in doing so, propels forces through and on to the page. This is always an act of faith – and an act of love whatever the subject. It is always a political act in its concern for all people.

No, I don't have this thought in front of my nose when writing. I write selfishly, obsessively. But this thought or faith *supports me*, is a condition of 'starting point', without which I would not arrive at the beginning of the act, or the journey. As essential as my chair (three cushions), my bed (in the study also and separate from night and shared sleep), my marble bowl with dried flowers, my plastic lampshade (fifty pence), my deep red velvet ex-theatre curtains (recent gift), two tables (I must always have an alternative) and the presence of this particular street. My neighbour with her walking-frame struggling to the Labour Club for her Guinness.

But that is only now. If I were in another house I would gather *something* to say hello to. To endure through the mammoth changes that *I* will need to endure in the course of the book. I write when I have gathered enough pieces.

My daughter, Laura, is seventeen. She nourishes me. I steal some of her energy! We need always to have access, I think, to adolescence (in ourselves). I think I will grow to be an eccentric old lady in this house with a parrot – though my friends may stop me, unsettle me – and here's the contradiction. I am drawn also to Hebden Bridge, to a wilder edge, and there I take a spirit that needs none of these things – write in the woods, Gorple rocks, the raw life of the town. My thanks to Colin I met there, for such openings.

I ride the tension between familiarity that holds but can also bind, and the wilder unknown that can inspire but can also turn into chaos and decay.

And all this is still a condition and a ground.

I also pace and am irritable. I wear loose clothes. I need the work to dance in me, or to dance the work.

In sole charge of a house, I'll frantically clean one of its darkest corners, then clean nothing at all for days. I never clean my study. The dust is important. To clean my study would be to expose all the areas of the room (my head) and I don't need that. My poems lurk, furtive and ambivalent. I pull out only what serves, the half-spoken.

Space, time, dimension, angle are all on the move in this room.

I am close to a man who can meet all the stations, though not always at the same time. He lives in Lancashire. We exchange nonsense and also important, potent fragments. And silences. I don't organise. Sometimes I creep through a thicket, sometimes I hack it down. Last night I dreamed the lion was let loose from his chain and we must run for cover. This room isn't safe. But I need safe areas somewhere, or the whole lot's on the go. I read the *Radio* and *TV Times* and watch 'Tutti Frutti' and often write poems in front of the television. It is essential that I can light a fire in winter.

I'm sure there are no useful formulae here! At root I am saying – permission, give yourself permission to be *large* enough, to take what you need.

I have to keep on remembering what I can be.

(Now, as I break the script and fry up bacon and eggs and make tea, I see it's one-thirty, I'd promised myself I'd go buy plates from the bric-à-brac shop, clear out the cat-litter, wash clothes before Tim comes. Decision – work for one hour more. So is the day constructed.)

Nourishment from letters, fragments, reminders and contacts. Essential backdrop, as theme. Gathering. Held. Over-night Stop.

To write about something, it is essential to be able to see the extraordinary in people.

I have to fight a tendency to over-explain.
Sent by David Rose, heard on the radio

At best one's voice will contain something of what one/it is. Undiluted truth is virtually unsayable. We need the vehicles, mirrors? Containers? And we need to select the right ones, that most clearly serve the purpose.
Letter from N J to D R, 29 February 1988

Merchant of Words
Amryl Johnson

> I am a merchant of words
> turned to stone in the spotlight
> defiant
> before the barrel
> of any pen

Those are the final five lines of my poem 'A Merchant of Words'. Nothing has changed. The sentiment remains the same. The poem was written a few years ago. I am still a merchant of words. I still earn my living by my pen and by teaching Creative Writing to undergraduates and teachers on secondment at the University of Warwick. I still lead writing workshops in schools and colleges and with adult literacy groups. And I still acknowledge the passion I feel for words.

'Words are the most powerful vehicle you could ever have at your disposal', I remind my students.

When I am not out inspiring others, I am at home putting what I preach into practice.

At some point, the transition took place. At some stage, I became aware of the way I begin the day, the preparation involved, the motions I go through from the moment I wake until I begin my writing. I dare say that at this point of awareness, the ritual became a fairly precise one. From that moment on, every aspect of preparation became important and not just a prelude. I do not regard myself as disciplined. I live my life within a flexible framework. There was a time when I could say, 'my writing day begins at seven' or 'my writing day begins at nine'. That was while I lived in Oxford, before I bought this house and moved to Coventry. Nowadays, my day begins as and when. As and when I get out of bed and as and when I get down to it. It may be down to owning a house and finally having a lot of space to myself. It has resulted in this manifestation of freedom. This is my house and I can do as I choose. This has little to do with inertia. I am an Arian. Friends and acquaintances say I manifest the most extreme traits of my sign. Dynamic? born leader? creative? impatient? Is that what they mean? I have always been afraid to question them too deeply in case they tell me it is the less positive side of my sign they were referring to.

Okay, so my day begins as and when. If the dawn chorus is particularly vibrant, during spring and summer, this could be as early as six o'clock. Otherwise, as late as nine. I suffer from bouts of insomnia (is this an Arian trait?) and, freedom to do as I choose in my own house aside, the occasional late sleep is always welcome. When I awake, regardless, I do so with a feeling of exhilaration. From the moment I open my eyes to the world, I am full of enthusiasm.

The dining-room also serves as my study. When I push open the door, the room is still darkened. An awareness of the ritual brings with it recognition of the room as a sort of shrine. An altar. On better mornings the sun filters the maroon and grey striped weave. I open the curtains realising that what I am performing is an unveiling ceremony. Somewhere in my mind, the word 'dawn' registers. This marks the beginning. I am in control. Light streams through the nets on to the thirties furniture bought to compliment the house. It falls on the sideboard, the dining table and chairs, the Welsh dresser. It falls on the plain brown carpet inherited with the house. Yes, and the freesias. There is always a vase full of freesias on the table. As I walk into the room, their fragrance sometimes comes to greet me. Not always. At other times, they are like a breath being held. Released only when I have opened the curtains or when I sit down at the table. At some point during the day, I will look at the freesias to see if any flowers have faded. I have tried growing my own (is this another Arian trait? Blind optimism?). The chain reaction fascinates me. As I remove one dead flower, the next bud along the stem opens. As one dies, the next lives. It is as if strength or life is being passed on. When I lived in Oxford, I had a cat. Midnight died shortly before I moved here. Even though I thought of getting another one, I seem to spend so much time away from home these days, it would not be possible. The hazard of living on your own. And new neighbours don't necessarily appreciate the commitment. Something about freesias, with their fragrance, drawing me to their attention while I am working, soothing, stroking, almost comforting me, fills a sliver of the emptiness left by Midnight. Their perfume is alive and stirring.

I am an addict. Aren't we all, to some extent? Tea! My day begins with several cups of the beverage. I use powdered milk in tea and coffee. I have done so for years – to the horror of a few visitors. With the first cup, I sit in contemplation, sifting the correct amount of milk into the mug. The silence is superb. I stir the granules, watching them dissolve. I am, perhaps, a little too relaxed. Almost concentrating on the faint scrape of metal against pottery.

The dining table is seven foot long, taking up half the length of the wall I will be facing while I work. It is, like all the other walls in the room, plain white. Unless I happen to be entertaining, the entire table is taken up with typewriter, dictionary, notes and the full range of stationery. The table is untidy. There are only three pockets of order. The fruit bowl, the vase of freesias and the space around the anglepoise lamp. Once or twice the sense of ritual becomes so intense that I clear the table and set about polishing it before settling down to work. Some considerable amount of time is spent working polish deep into the grain. As a rule, this is only ever done when I am having a lunch or dinner party.

When I can afford to do so, I will probably buy myself an Amstrad. Every writer I know seems to have one. A curious selection of people who aren't writers seem to have one, also. I have owned this portable manual since 1978. Nowadays, the ribbon direction change is held active by a metal twist. One of the springs went a long time ago and I never got around to getting it fixed. The key which holds the number one and asterisk is so twisted, it no longer works. For almost a year now, I have been using the lower-case 'L' as a substitute. Asterisks are put in by hand. Also, the key guard is warped and no longer fits. Consequently, I am able to follow the movement of each character from the moment I press the key. These eccentricities make the typewriter very much my own and, consequently, difficult for other people to use. It is an old friend. An aid, an accomplice. When away from home, I am loath to use other people's typewriters. I always seem to make far more mistakes than usual. Nevertheless, accuracy has been one of my strong points. The generous supply of Tippex, both liquid and strips, at my elbow as I type this bears testimony.

So I sit stirring that first cup of tea, casting a critical eye over the chaos on the dining table, basking in the fragrance of the freesias. All the while, my thoughts are ticking over. It is as if a clock in my head is slowly moving onwards. Every forward movement takes me through the process of sorting my thoughts, deciding how I am going to harness the inspiration, tackle any development in the story-line. How am I going to shape my working day? I cannot drink scalding tea. While it is cooling, I will nip upstairs to the bathroom and brush my teeth. A little later in the day, I will take a bath and get dressed. Depending on how the inspiration works for me, how well I am able to get on with my work, I may well spend the best part of the morning in my dressing gown. If the morning has meant a particularly early start, I will have three good hours before the post arrives around nine-thirty. Three hours in which to get my thoughts rolling before the intrusion of post being forced through the letter-box. There is always a letter or two. I do not have breakfast. The first meal of the day is around twelve o'clock. The evening meal is taken as and when. As and when I get around to it. Sometimes, I have just one meal a day. Once a fortnight, I fast. Just tea, coffee, herb or mixed fruit tea, grapefruit juice and Perrier water for the day. I feel I owe it to my body. Also, I seem to work better. I feel more alert after a fast. There was a time when I could go for three days, perhaps longer, without food. But my body no longer responds well to any prolonged fasting. Some of my best early writing was produced during those periods of abstinence.

Sometimes I work well into the night with few interruptions. Other times I work fitfully. Half-hour breaks for washing dishes, phone calls, personal letters, doing the laundry, shopping. I do not have a timetable for these things. There is no note on the calendar to tell me that as it is Thursday, this gets done or that gets done. I sometimes feel that I lead my entire life around inspiration. In the middle of a sentence, I may suddenly leap to my feet having decided the time was right to go out and do some shopping or write a letter to a friend. Out of term-time and not leading workshops, I may stay in for days, writing and doing this and that around the house. I like living on my own. I very much enjoy my own company. Perhaps, when you spend time creating characters and situations, you are never truly alone. You could never be alone.

Unless I happen to be away or there is something at home infinitely more pressing, I feel very guilty indeed if I am not able to do at least a little writing. I feel as if I have failed in what makes me, essentially, me.

In an article for a magazine a few years ago, I wrote, 'I am either zooming across the sky on my broomstick or else I have crash-landed. Friends have to pick me up, dust me off, and set me back on it again.' The analogy is still a precise one. I am either sizzling and blazing a determined trail or else it feels as if I am ashes in a breeze. So here's one fiery, temperamental, perhaps slightly eccentric fire sign ready to move on to the next stage of her creativity.

Unwordy Skiving
Marcella Evaristi

In order to keep this day clear for writing, I decided to cancel a Parentcraft class. I made the decision lying in bed very early this morning, and prominent amongst the muddle of this-way-and-that feelings, prominent amongst the to and fro-ing, was a definitely pleasant sensation. Now it's very odd for me, very rare, to experience any feeling of pleasure at the prospect of writing. It's an excellent development, this pleasurable anticipation, for I am continually berating myself and disappointing myself because I am not prolific. No, it's much worse than that. Not Prolific could be quite noble and unwordy; it could involve taking five painstaking years to write an exquisite novella. (I have just noticed an interesting slip of the typewriter – writing *unwordy* instead of *unworldly*. *Unwordy* describes me rather better. I shall keep it in.) No, I disappoint myself because I have an appalling response to the sentence 'I shall begin writing now'. Appalling, I feel sick, I want to postpone, I shadow-box with irrelevancies whilst only half listening to myself, I delude myself, and I play truant. It's a banal kind of truancy too: it's skiving without kicks. This problem feels deeper and more desperate than just the 'normal' discomfort of facing the blank etcetera. I feel I should be truanting from other things in *order* to write, and I feel a loss because that's how it used to be. Writing as compulsion and transgression – sexy and satisfying. I wonder if this is fanciful. In this section of Starting Points, I must be *specific*. This is not the place for Loss and Transgression, the Truant and the Despairing Self.

I did start off specifically enough, though, when I told you I had cancelled a Parentcraft class in order to write this. I am consequently missing out on a tour around the labour ward and a relaxation class and some other aspects of preparation for the event. Still, it's good that the Pleasurable Skiving Factor is helping me towards the typewriter rather than away from it.

I have just telephoned the hospital to tell them I can't make it. It turns out I can be shown around the labour ward on Wednesday instead. I was thanked for my consideration. I was told that it was nice of me to phone. As a truant, I am a total wimp. It occurs to me that this has always been the case. I remember leaving school one lunch-time to go to a disco in Sauchiehall Street called The Electric Garden. I remember looking at the place with its neon sign from the top of the bus and finding myself incapable of getting off. I just went straight home and told my Mum I had a headache and she was very nice about it, she felt my forehead whilst my stomach contracted with guilt. She wrote me a note. Failed Ruby Tuesday:

> Don't question why she has to be so free . . .
> She's going to tell ya it's the only way to be!

Huh.

Specifics, specifics.

I am a freelance writer so I cannot complain about how my day job exhausts me. Children until now have not made claims on my time and energy. This is coming to an end. These days I am constantly being told to savour these last weeks of independence, but you can't pre-empt these things can you? It's difficult, lumbering around, exhausted by ten in the morning, trying consciously to feel like a Free Agent. Besides, I don't feel like my own person, I feel thoroughly inhabited.

When I do write, I write in the front room of a ground floor flat in Glasgow, my typewriter on a table in front of the window. This is where work mainly happens, though sometimes (some of the best times too) sometimes when I am writing fast and happy-furious I retreat from the front face of the house into corners, to bed, or to kitchen warmth. This feels like burrowing into straw.

I always used to write straight on to the typewriter. Although I'm not very fast and rather inaccurate, I've been writing on the machine since I was fifteen or so. Of course, I was really inept then, but I loved the *idea* of it. Quite often I would start typing something, then, fed up with the frustration of making so many mistakes, I would change to longhand, which would allow me to get on with what I was actually writing. Around this time I did a touch-typing course but gave it up after about three days. After all, *my* typewriter activity had nothing to do with the attainment of secretarial accuracy, nothing to do with offices or dictation. (Catch Ruby Tuesday in the typing pool!) No, my adolescent heart pounded before the picture of the writer at the portable, ashtrays overflowing, bourbon/wine/black coffee at the ready. I stared at photographs of playwrights on the back covers of Methuen playscripts. In my scrappy collage of excitements, the portable typewriter had its place amidst Simone de Beauvoir, the Citizens Theatre, black polo necks, Mary McCarthy, Edna O'Brien, James Cameron and Mary Quant brown blusher for cheekbone effects on white faces.

Writing longhand was fine but it was arty in an old-fashioned sort of way. Banging away on the machine was somehow radical and anti-establishment (as they used to say). Still, it can be too easy to parody the aspirations and fantasies of our younger selves while deluding ourselves that our present maturity has freed us from any such self-consciousness. We still have to imagine how we are. And, to be fair, my typewriter preference did have something to do with a growing sense of craft. My own handwriting was perfectly fine for letters and diary entries, but anonymous typeface was good for distancing and judging my stories and poems; it helped along the feeling that fiction was something to be *worked* at. From very early on, I felt that when it came to writing, the sincerity of my feeling was not enough. My overflowing waste-paper basket was a cliché, but it did bear witness to effort, rewrites, seriousness. This is not to say that I didn't write self-indulgently, I'm sure I did, but the therapy of the activity didn't just come from 'getting it off my chest' but from honing the feeling into something shaped. I think at sixteen I thought longhand was for amateurs. (Given my typing proficiency I was also – like many others – extremely grateful to ee cummings. though that phase passed too.)

In May of this year I wrote myself a one-woman play and I wrote it very quickly and by *hand*. This extraordinary longhand precedent happened as follows. When I found I was pregnant I gave up smoking completely. Normally I chain-smoked at the typewriter. Fags were just part of the kit. All-night sessions required *stacks* of cigarettes; wimping around with a couple of packets and a resolution to ration myself was pointless. The resolution to write was in itself massive and painful and discipline-devouring enough without complicating the issue. To choose a time like that to worry about the weed would be insane. I was already suffering the cold turkey of giving up writing-postponement – to ask more of me would be like nagging someone who was drying out about their cellulite.

But I had taken my last drag on the way to the chemist to collect the result, that result was positive, so there could be no half measures. I knew I was an all or nothing smoker. Smoking during pregnancy could lead to premature birth, and given my addiction, especially around deadlines, this baby, unless I stopped, would be due Tuesday week. So that was settled. To the amazement of all who knew me, I stopped. I wore a halo of a billion brownie points. I had never been one of those who were constantly trying to give up. I think I'd tried once, about ten years before, and had managed a month. An acquaintance talked of herself as being 'an addictive personality' and I remembered thinking, 'Yip. Me too.' For the main struggle in my life, as I've said, the main continuous and bloody battle was on the word front, and it took all of my energy. Similar story with drink. Of course you can't write when you're pissed the way you can write when you're chain-smoking, but alcohol can loosen or help relax if used judiciously. That's the point of course. It's easy to misjudge this one and totally bugger up an evening set aside for work. It's a small step from the drink which deadens the premature dampners and downers which stop you getting started, to the drink which fills you with such delighted conviction that you're on the right track that you confidently postpone the whole endeavour. (Can make for a terrific evening of course after having depressed yourself for days in the company of dreary sober old Self-doubt.) And there *are* advances you can make with drink. Booze gave me the courage to kill off a character once, and it was the right decision. Anyhow, pregnancy meant these sometimes delicious and certainly dubious aids to the artistic flow were out.

I did believe that I would not renege on the cigarette decision, but at the same time I could not imagine writing a play without a cigarette. I supposed such a thing might happen eventually but I had no idea how long such a massive turnaround of habit and association might take and I was committed to producing the goods by a certain date. I was going to perform the thing myself after all. It said so in the publicity brochures.

Now manoeuvring myself into this do or die position was nothing new. I often bullied myself into action, steering suicidally close to the wind when it came to deadlines. I would plan and fret and make endless rather abstract notes and then write in a manic rush, fiercely concentrating, oblivious of everything else. I would end up black-tongued and wrecked but high and happy that I'd finished, that finishing *was* a possibility, and I would try to hold on to this proof so that the next time I would not hammer myself so.

I was aware, you see, that my method was a bulldozing cliché to put body and soul through; the lack of sleep, the tarry coffee, the fags and the whisky and the wine. But as long as it produced the goods, I had left it too late to care. By that stage of the pressure there could be no other consideration except finishing the script. And in the middle of this mess and panic a small patch of joy appeared, a joy like nothing else in the world, mad though it sounds. There existed a plateau where confidence and concentration, judgement and imagination, each in their (at long last) proper proportions *made it happen*. Achieved the trick. I actually imagine it like that circus trick where plates on sticks, whirling precarious and thrilling, are risked and saved again and again by a last minute sleight of hand.

Had I been writing this last year, I'd have maybe just described the manic rush and its reckless essential-seeming fuels. But I think there is more to it than the discovery that I could give up smoking without a career change. (Though I could not bear to use the typewriter at first. I curled around notepads, and clutched pencils, terrified to let my hands dangle above the keys.) Of course the fact that I could write without the Manic Kit was important, but my route to the Plateau had to be reassessed. My old strategies were proving as useless as they were masochistic. So there I was, contemplating my subterfuges and their increasingly diminishing returns, when I discovered that I was myself increasing threefold. I was expecting two babies. A boy and a girl, I happen to know. A Baby Kit.

I am back to the typewriter again, or as near as my abdomen allows. My body has quite taken over, the smell of whisky disgusts me, I rarely crave a fag and I am quite incapable of doing an all-nighter even if I wanted to. My cravings are for ice cream, Italian amarena cherries and a private income. Of course I am terrified that with little money and two babies my writing will crumble away like a Farley's rusk, but then I cheer myself up with the thought that writing's a bastard no matter what your circumstances, that I was capable of finding the business impossible when I was childless, and so perhaps the reverse will be true. How I will cope practically, I really do not know. My study has gone already. The books have moved out and the bunnies have moved in. The babies have got A Room of Their Own, and I am working in the front room. But I have to come clean on this one. I never enjoyed working in that study I had wanted all my life. The view on to the back garden was uneventful compared to this view of the street that I'm looking at now. So, babies apart, I write here by preference, playing truant from the Duty Room, which itself no longer exists.

The Journey Out
Rosalind Brackenbury

Starting to write something begins with the pinprick of an idea, far back in the mind, that grows until it seems to have filled all the available space. But actually getting down to work, to write, to deliver it? I know I need movement; since schooldays, cannot sit down and think at a desk, in front of a typewriter, but use walking, swimming, running, digging the garden, having a massage, something physical in order to get going, in order to still and silence something restless, to deal with the physical, be immersed in the physical world, before beginning to abstract what is there, take it quite coolly and rationally from its shell, see what *it* is. There was always a sort of torture about sitting at desks, with the world going on outside the windows, all light, fresh air, variety and movement locked out, and everything stuffy, stale, immobile, locked in. By not focusing on it, the idea grows in my mind. Swimming is ideal, tires the body quite gently, cools and assuages the mind. Walking by the sea, now that I live quite near it, with my eye on the horizon and on close, found things like shells and bits of flotsam. Going round and round the Botanic Gardens, visiting favourite trees. When the idea I have is fully formed enough, or when I can begin to hear the 'voice' of it, how it sounds, quite clearly in my head, then I can face the desk or table, the typewriter or blank page, and begin. I may potter about for days, beforehand, and now have, at long last, the time for doing this. I walk round the room between sentences sometimes; and then again, once it is all under way, can sit and type for two hours without moving. I never work consecutively any longer than this, but need a walk again, company, a change of view, something completely different.

How strange, to write these idiosyncratic things, these movements evolved now over decades, the oddities of an irregular working life.

A description of myself starting to write could sound like this: I jump out of bed in the morning – or lie for a long time immobile but not asleep. Stand in the middle of the kitchen floor with a mug of tea. Pace around the house. Go upstairs. Forget what I have come up for, go down again. Go outside, walk round the garden, stand in the garden staring back at the house. Go in, run upstairs again. Manage to clear an empty space at my work table, throwing bills and letters into heaps on the floor. Stoke the stove with peat. Go out into the street without a coat, take out the rubbish, walk up and down. Come in, make coffee, carry coffee up to work-room, stare out of window. Go out for a longer walk and then rush home. Cross the street for no apparent reason, several times. Back in the house, walk in and out of rooms, pick up the telephone, decide against it. At last, stand at work table staring at typewriter and paper. Sit down suddenly, roll paper into typewriter. Write perhaps one word. And then more; tugged at still by thoughts of coffee, alcohol, cigarettes, sex, and by the fear that there still may not be anything to say, I have begun.

There is nothing like it, the pleasure of being launched again, of the unfurling and uncurling of ideas which seem to stretch themselves further and further with exercise. I have still not quite worked out what makes it feel so hard to begin and yet so pleasurable to have begun, but guess that it is a mixture of fear of committing myself to something this big yet again, the isolation that writers do suffer from, and feelings left over from the past that I am courting disapproval from doing this selfish and even onanistic thing. But lately, I have found ways of combating or getting round these feelings: working in close proximity with another, or others, working straight into notebooks or looseleaf pads, longhand, cheating just slightly the feeling that I am 'really' working. I like the added looseness, ease and relaxation of this, and increasingly do odd bits of writing, like sketches, whenever I find I have an empty few minutes somewhere. Then, the writing flows, without the extra pressure that this has to be 'it'. After years of working straight on to a typewriter in an empty room, I find it gives me a sense of being able to play, doodle, sketch, try things out, which is good.

It's hard to know what ideal conditions are when you have spent a working lifetime doing other things – looking after children, tidying up houses, doing paid work – and writing in the interstices, always manically, always with a sense of time passing. I have, in fact, only very recently arrived at what feels like the ideal situation – enough time, uninterrupted, not just to write but to think about it, potter about with it, dream about it. So if the description above sounds more like that of a dog let off a lead rushing crazily around a field sniffing everything and not knowing where to stop, than of a sensible person sitting down to write, that is probably why. But although I have spent twenty years involved with my children and running a house, I have not had to take full-time employment of the sort which can dull and exhaust a writer and make it quite literally impossible to write, and for this I am thankful. My children, who both have disabilities, have not stopped me writing, and neither did the fact that I was for a long time married. In fact so much of these experiences has gone into the writing that I find it hard to imagine what my subject-matter might have been, had I been 'free' all this time. So, even if I have not had 'enough' time, I have had time, made time, snatched time, used the time I had; and have almost always had the sense of a rich brew bubbling away into which everything went, and which never was really off the boil. I do not want to consider writing, ever, as something which makes me hold apart from life, but which rather involves me, is about going in at the deep end in all sorts of ways, is not an either/or. Deciding to have both life and writing has sometimes been tiring, often difficult, but never impossible. Always, one feeds the other and this has been so, really, for as long as I can remember.

I am still scared by the vista of uninterrupted time, and the slow unrolling of thought that this affords. Having started out writing for about one hour a day, when my first child was asleep, I find having enough time quite strange. It takes getting used to. What will I write if I no longer have to go at it like a bull at a gate?

I heard tell of a monk who said that for half an hour of apparent praying, he achieved perhaps half a minute's real prayer. Real writing flourishes with space around it, and I am only just beginning to feel what that is like.

So, yes, a desk, a room, a house of my own. But I also write, increasingly, in notebooks, in cafés, in odd places, in other people's houses; wanting a fluidity and ease of access that is different from a particular desk, view, or typewriter. I started this in France, where the typewriters do not happily take to writing in English, and you can run up some strange looking conjunctions of letters. I value freedom to move about – I go to saunas and heat up my brain. The Finns are right, it is a great place to think in, and the best ideas come when you are dashing between sauna and cold shower. When I am writing concentratedly, I give up thinking about what I am wearing or if there is anything to eat in the house and tend to want to shut people out. As soon as I have finished, I become social, frivolous, want to buy clothes and go out to things. After a couple of hours of writing, I want company, long to meet another human being. The balance between being alone and being with another, or other people, seems to be crucial. Writing alone is really quite lonely, and we are social animals and depend upon each other. My ideal is to be able to spend creative hours alone, and then to meet up with somebody who is extremely interested in what I am doing and on the same wavelength. I have set this up with my next-door neighbour, who is a painter, and we meet nearly every day for a few minutes to talk about how work is going, have a laugh, share the news. In fact, throughout my working life I have benefited a great deal from the company not only of other writers – even half an hour's 'chewing the fat' on writing making all the difference to a day spent otherwise alone – but of visual artists too. Somebody painting in the next room is quieter than somebody else typing, and hearing a painter talking about her work, different but similar, is stimulating in a different way.

In writing groups which I lead, and in the small group of women with whom I have been writing and talking about writing for about three years, I tend to use the time to sketch things out, begin poems, try out approaches, using the safety of knowing my audience, trusting their ability to say 'that's terrible' or 'that's going somewhere', to laugh and even to cry at what I write. This is a great help – gets me past blocks, gives immediate feedback. Curious, too, the difference in writing in a room with others, after years of working alone. The avoiding actions appear as what they are – ridiculous, but shared – and we get down to work more directly. It's a limbering-up, exercise time, time for trying things out with people you trust; different from sitting down 'cold' in front of a typewriter, and I recommend it.

Getting started has for me an immense energy and delight about it; it is like falling in love; it is perhaps a time of falling in love with your own creation. It's at once easier and harder than the rest of the work – easier because of the freedom and sense of adventure involved, harder because of the feelings that accompany that first plunge in. It is the start of a journey, but you know that all the hazards of the journey are there to discover. It's a renewal; yes, the old energy is back, the ideas are flowing, the doubts are banished again. It's a commitment, to several years, sometimes, of work. It's the moment at which I imagine the perfection of the finished work, which so often gets lost in the doing.

Sending Everyone Away
Sue Roe

I thought I was going to get started on this yesterday, but it suddenly seemed very important to buy a television. This is what happens: it is like going on holiday – you had better get absolutely everything done before you go, because the idea that you will be coming back is unimaginable. I can renew my road tax at the same time, and buy a new coffee pot because the old one fell to pieces in the washing-up water. And anyway, I can't do a thing until I get a new supply of typewriter ribbons. I'm on the last of the reserve supply, and I'm sure it won't last the weekend.

The Office Supplies shop is closed on Saturdays. There is a three-tiered queue at the post office, and they have stopped making red coffee pots because everybody's kitchen is now apparently grey. 'It's the new colour,' the assistant in Importers explains, looking a shade unconvinced. 'It did use to be red, at one time,' she adds, sympathetically. 'I'll come back when I've found a typewriter ribbon,' I say. She looks confused.

I go everywhere in the town looking for Office Supplies shops. Every single one is closed, including the important one down an alley and up some stairs, that only the real connoisseurs of office equipment know about. I go to Habitat. It seems it's true about the red coffee pots. They have black, white, gold, silver . . . But no red ones. It will take away a whole important patch of colour on the top of the fridge if I don't get one. I am beginning to get annoyed. Typewriter ribbons. Priorities.

There is a juggler on the pavement in front of W. H. Smith, with a red plastic nose, making people laugh by dropping all his coloured batons and appearing to be astonished that they fail to stay up in the air. I wonder if he had to learn how to do it properly first, in order to work out how to make a mess of it. It seems unlikely. There is a crowd of children, standing in a circle . . . I don't stop. 'Do you have typewriter ribbons?' The assistant points mutely to a shelf. I go over.

There is none faintly resembling the ones I have learned through bitter experience are the only ones my typewriter will accept. There is a 'young man' hanging about trying not to be approached. I confront him. I ask him if he has any typewriter ribbons like these. (I have brought one with me : I hold it out.) 'No,' he says resignedly. 'No.' He looks at me as if to say, Well, that's it, then. 'But who does?' I implore him. 'Somebody must . . .' He tells me the name of a shop, and how to get there. It is already a quarter to twelve, the shop might close at twelve, I had better hurry. As I make a bolt for it, he says, helpfully, 'If you find yourself at Waitrose, you've already missed it.' This is obscurely encouraging.

As I hurtle along, I pass another branch of Importers. There is a red coffee pot in the window. I skid around on the pavement, then go crashing into the shop. It's no good. It's only £4.99 with a free bag of coffee, but it's just got a filter, no plunger. I say I can't decide: its redness *is* important, but I wanted one with a plunger. Anyway, I've got to get to the Office Supplies shop. If I don't get the typewriter ribbon I won't be able to get started on this over the weekend. I can't write in longhand, the ideas don't come. I once told somebody I couldn't write because I had run out of typewriter ribbons (this happens regularly) and he said, 'Well, you've got arms, haven't you?' which made me realise how he thought of me: as a huge, chimpanzee-like creature, brandishing an enormous (five, six feet long?) pen. The door of the Office Supplies shop has a notice on. It says O P E N. I am not convinced. I read the small print. 9 a.m. – 5.30. *5.30*? But they surely won't have the right ones . . . 'I'd better have about nine,' I say. I don't want this to happen again. I take some erasers as well. These are not the right kind, but he assures me they won't stick to the ribbons, like the last lot. I have to believe him. Good. I can get started, now, as soon as I've bought the television.

I go into a television shop. 'There are big ones and little ones, really,' the assistant (Ricky, it says on his badge) explains, kindly. 'Everything in between's a bit of a dead area. You want a big screen but you've got a quite small room, you say. I see. Tell you what: shut your eyes, imagine them big ones aren't there, and the little ones look bigger.' As I am shutting my eyes, something else occurs to him. 'Roughly,' he says, tentatively, 'very roughly, how much . . . doyouwanttospend?' I look away. He looks tactfully away. 'That big one over there,' he says, encouragingly, 'is £399.' It sounds an awful lot of money. What I really need is a bigger room, it suddenly occurs to me. This floors him. He is thinking rapidly.

Suddenly, he points to a little hi-tech box in a corner. 'Of course,' he says, 'this one's got tele-text . . .' Text. This reminds me of something. Text. Text. Writing. It is nearly one o'clock and I haven't even got started yet. 'And when I say it's instant,' he is saying, 'you'd be amazed, but this is what I mean. Here. Come and look.' He picks up a remote-control panel and points it at the set. A list of bright green information is instantly flashed off the screen and another flashes into place. 'At the touch of a button,' he says. But I don't think I want tele-text. I quite like leafing through the newspaper. I don't think I would want to be able to point a small box at a bigger box and have a list of things like Presidential Elections; Tory Party Conference; Rapist Brutally Murders Three Women; Becoming Cloudier instantly flashed up. It all sounds completely meaningless, presented like this. I like to read the actual story.

I retrieve the note that says, 'replace coffee pot' from the bin. I put the road-tax sticker in a place where I can't avoid noticing it and try to remember whether it's all right to stick it on *before* the renewal date. I throw away yesterday's local paper, which I bought for the T V programmes. I fit the new ribbon and eraser. Something is annoying me. There is a very empty feeling gathering its forces in me, now that I have come back here and shut the door, now that I am ready to start. I do not want to sit here thinking about getting this piece of writing started. It is sunny. It is Saturday. Everybody else is out having a good time. Why should I be excluded? I ring up a friend and complain that I have told everybody to go away so that I can write but now I want them all to come back. I can't stand the isolation. I am sick to death of being alone, writing or no writing. I continue in this vein for quite some time. She says, 'But Sue, you can't write in the middle of a cocktail party.'

We decide to drive out to Monks House, where Virginia Woolf lived. She is charmed by the simple austerity of it, which I always find obscurely depressing. I am glad to be there with her, though, because she is a painter and is fascinated by the relations between tones of green, both inside the house and out. This arrests me, this problem of the greens; I am stopped in my tracks. My head begins to stop spinning around the problem of this writing I should be getting started. My mind averts its gaze; allows its attention to be diverted, calmly. We study a photograph of Virginia and Vanessa and I am absolutely transfixed, as I always am, by the spectacle of Vanessa's big, cow-like eyes, by the concentrated passion in them. Virginia is aloof: her eyes are averted; too small.

Jean says, 'But she was never actually present, was she.' We decide that this is not only a difference between sisters: it is a difference between writers and painters. She says, 'As a painter your object is there before you: it is there. All your senses, all your powers of concentration are focused on this object and on the attempt to transfer it on to the canvas. With writing it's totally different. Your mind is not on an object, your mind is . . .' We peer in at the writing room, at Virginia Woolf's table, her chair, the plain, unadorned room with the plain cream walls, the complete absence of distraction or decoration . . . 'Well, what *is* it on?' asks Jean. 'It is everywhere, it is pulling down threads, it is connecting . . .' I say. That's it: that's the trigger. For the first time, writing seems as though it might be even more exciting than painting. There might be more going on. There might be an exciting simultaneity. It would not be sufficiently tactile; writing is never sufficiently tactile. This is the aspect of it that maddens me. But mentally, it would be very exciting. Very exacting.

I decide to stop worrying about the fact that I don't feel quite authentic. There might be a reason for this: if Virginia Woolf was never actually present, then perhaps nor am I. This would explain my failure to purchase coffee pots and tele-text, that kind of thing. When I decide this, the difference between the greens becomes yet more complex: I can see further gradations, subtler tones of light. The sky is softly in motion. As we make our way up the road, a van pulls out ahead of us. It is exactly the same shade of green as the Monks House sitting-room. 'Monks Van!' we shriek, a shade hysterically. While this is going on I am thinking, what have I got to say, anyway? What have I got to say, that someone else might want to know? I tell Jean about the van I saw rounding the corner just along the coast from Dublin, after I had been to see Joyce's Martello Tower. I try to recreate the effect of its ordinariness: something about its incredible authenticity as a van created the same effect, at that moment, as ordinary things have on you sometimes in childhood. Jean says, 'You had the actual experience of the van, rounding the corner. You felt it, just like he did: the actual experience of it.' There is something important going on here, but I am not quite sure what it is . . .

That evening, I read Anita Brookner's new novel and think, why do I bother, I'll never write like this. It is something to do with painting, this gift, she clearly knows everything there is to know about composition. I get a bit drunk. I cook some pasta which I flavour (by mistake) with dried lavender. I listen to some loud music. I go to bed.

This morning, I decide I have had quite enough of being alone. I will telephone some friends and invite them to supper. They can stay over and tomorrow we can go and look at Monks House. Or the West Pier. As I am getting up, I am thinking, but that would take up the entire weekend. I am beginning to hear the odd voice in my head; I am sure that the strangeness of yesterday had something obscurely to do with getting started. Yesterday was full of triggers, the thing to do is to get some of them down. I bath quickly. I pull out some clothes I can move about in: my white shirt that feels like an artist's smock, some rather odd trousers. I make tea, not coffee (tea is quicker) and grab a biscuit. I will do my make-up later. I put on some rings instead, so that at least one bit of me looks reasonably festive. I kick the phone off the hook. I pick up the notes I had begun to make yesterday, before the last typewriter ribbon began to run out. I read them. There are some things here that might do for Section Two. The thing is just to start. Just start anywhere. Say what happened yesterday, just start telling a story. Then out of that, if it is working, will emerge . . .

Just before I start, I decide to be even cleverer about the phone. I turn the volume right down and put it in a cupboard. I wedge it under a pile of pink towels. Because this is the moment, now, I do not stare out of the window. I do not write down my random thoughts. I do not sketch out a plan. I resolve that I will not need a second cup of tea. I do not read a few letters first; read a novel first; type out neatly one of my own stories first, just to get me in the mood; I do not get drunk instead. I just start telling the story.

I need complete solitude, now, complete quiet. No interruptions, no noise, no interventions. A knock at the door, now, or the sound of someone's radio will send me mad. It is a completely closed world. Though there are people close to me who function from time to time as muses, no one else can enter, now. If I put the writing aside, having once begun to get it started, I will need to 'hold' the illusion of this state. Everything else I do will be peripheral until the piece of work is finished. Just tell it, I say to myself. Just tell it.

• *Beginning to Write*

Behind Me – dips Eternity –
Before Me – Immortality –
Myself – the Term between –
Emily Dickinson

Writing *The Color Purple*
Alice Walker

I don't always know where the germ of a story comes from, but with *The Color Purple* I knew right away. I was hiking through the woods with my sister, Ruth, talking about a lovers' triangle of which we both knew. She said: 'And you know, one day The Wife asked The Other Woman for a pair of her drawers.' Instantly the missing piece of the story I was mentally writing – about two women who felt married to the same man – fell into place. And for months – through illnesses, divorce, several moves, travel abroad, all kinds of heartaches and revelations – I carried my sister's comment delicately balanced in the centre of the novel's construction I was building in my head.

I also knew *The Color Purple* would be a historical novel, and thinking of this made me chuckle. In an interview, discussing my work, a black male critic said he'd heard I might write a historical novel someday, and went on to say, in effect: Heaven protect us from it. The chuckle was because, womanlike (he would say), my 'history' starts not with the taking of lands, or the births, battles and deaths of Great Men, but with one woman asking another for her underwear. Oh, well, I thought, one function of critics is to be appalled by such behaviour. But what woman (or sensuous man) could avoid being intrigued? As for me, I thought of little else for a year.

When I was sure the characters of my new novel were trying to form (or, as I invariably thought of it, trying to contact me, to speak *through* me), I began to make plans to leave New York. Three months earlier I had bought a tiny house on a quiet Brooklyn street, assuming – because my desk overlooked the street and a maple tree in the yard, representing garden and view – I would be able to write. I was not.

New York, whose people I love for their grace under almost continual unpredictable adversity, was a place the people in *The Color Purple* refused even to visit. The moment any of them started to form –

53

on the subway, a dark street, and especially in the shadow of very tall buildings – they would start to complain.

'What is all this tall shit anyway?' they would say.

I disposed of the house, stored my furniture, packed my suitcases, and flew alone to San Francisco (it was my daughter's year to be with her father), where all the people in the novel promptly fell silent – I think, in awe. Not merely of the city's beauty, but of what they picked up about earthquakes.

'It's pretty,' they muttered, 'but us ain't lost nothing in no place that has earthquakes.'

They also didn't like seeing buses, cars, or other people whenever they attempted to look out. 'Us don't want to be seeing none of this,' they said. 'It make us can't think.'

That was when I knew for sure these were country people. So my lover* and I started driving around the state looking for a country house to rent. Luckily I had found (with the help of friends) a fairly inexpensive place in the city. This too had been a decision forced by my characters. As long as there was any question about whether I could support them in the fashion they desired (basically in undisturbed silence) they declined to come out. Eventually we found a place in northern California we could afford and that my characters liked. And no wonder: it looked a lot like the town in Georgia most of them were from, only it was more beautiful and the local swimming hole was not segregated. It also bore a slight resemblance to the African village in which one of them, Nettie, was a missionary.

Seeing the sheep, the cattle, and the goats, smelling the apples and the hay, one of my characters, Celie, began, haltingly, to speak.

But there was still a problem.

Since I had quit my editing job at *Ms* and my Guggenheim Fellowship was running out, and my royalties did not quite cover expenses, and – let's face it – because it gives me a charge to see people who appreciate my work, historical novels or not, I was accepting invitations to speak. Sometimes on the long plane rides Celie or Shug would break through with a wonderful line or two (for instance, Celie said once that a self-pitying sick person she went to visit was 'laying up in the bed trying to look dead'). But even these vanished – if I didn't jot

---

*Ironically and unfortunately, 'lover' is considered a pejorative by some people. In its original meaning, 'someone who loves' (could be a lover of music, a lover of dance, a lover of a person . . .), it is useful, strong and accurate – and the meaning I intend here.

them down – by the time my contact with the audience was done.

What to do?

Celie and Shug answered without hesitation: Give up all this travel. Give up all this talk.

What is all this travel and talk shit anyway? So, I gave it up for a year. Whenever I was invited to speak I explained I was taking a year off for Silence. (I also wore an imaginary bracelet on my left arm that spelled the word.) Everyone said, Sure, they understood. I was terrified.

Where was the money for our support coming from? My only steady income was a three-hundred-dollar-a-month retainer from *Ms* for being a long-distance editor. But even that was too much distraction for my characters.

Tell them you can't do anything for the magazine, said Celie and Shug. (You guessed it, the women of the drawers.) Tell them you'll have to think about them later. So, I did. *Ms.* was unperturbed. Supportive as ever (they continued the retainer). Which was nice.

Then I sold a book of stories. After taxes, inflation, and my agent's fee of ten per cent, I would still have enough for a frugal, no-frills year. And so, I bought some beautiful blue-and-red-and-purple fabric, and some funky secondhand furniture (and accepted donations of old odds and ends from friends), and a quilt pattern my mama swore was easy, and I headed for the hills.

There were days and weeks and even months when nothing happened. Nothing whatsoever. I worked on my quilt, took long walks with my lover, lay on an island we discovered in the middle of the river and dabbled my fingers in the water. I swam, explored the redwood forests all around us, lay out in the meadow, picked apples, talked (yes, of course) to trees. My quilt began to grow. And, of course, everything was happening. Celie and Shug and Albert were getting to know each other, coming to trust my determination to serve their entry (sometimes I felt *re*-entry) into the world to the best of my ability, and what is more – and felt so wonderful – we began to love one another. And, what is even more, to feel immense thankfulness for our mutual good luck.

Just as summer was ending, one or more of my characters – Celie, Shug, Albert, Sofia, or Harpo – would come for a visit. We would sit wherever I was sitting, and talk. They were very obliging, engaging, and jolly. They were, of course, at the end of their story but were telling it to me from the beginning. Things that made me sad often made them laugh. Oh, we got through that; don't pull such a long face, they'd say.

Or, You think Reagan's bad, you ought've seen some of the rednecks us come up under. The days passed in a blaze of happiness.

Then school started, and it was time for my daughter to stay with me – for two years.

Could I handle it?

Shug said, right out, that she didn't know. (Well, her mother raised *her* children.) Nobody else said anything. (At this point in the novel, Celie didn't even know where *her* children were.) They just quieted down, didn't visit as much, and took a firm Well, let's us wait and see attitude.

My daughter arrived. Smart, sensitive, cheerful, at school most of the day, but quick with tea and sympathy on her return. My characters adored her. They saw she spoke her mind in no uncertain terms and would fight back when attacked. When she came home from school one day with bruises but said, You should see the other guy, Celie (raped by her stepfather as a child and somewhat fearful of life) began to reappraise her own condition. Rebecca gave her courage (which she *always* gives me) – and Celie grew to like her so much she would wait until three-thirty to visit me. So, just when Rebecca would arrive home needing her mother and a hug, there'd be Celie, trying to give her both.

Fortunately I was able to bring Celie's own children back to her (a unique power of novelists), though it took thirty years and a good bit of foreign travel. But this proved to be the largest single problem in writing the exact novel I wanted to write between about ten-thirty and three.

I had planned to give myself five years to write *The Color Purple* (teaching, speaking, or selling apples, as I ran out of money). But, on the very day my daughter left for camp, less than a year after I started writing, I wrote the last page.

And what did I do that for?

It was like losing everybody I loved at once. First Rebecca (to whom everyone surged forth on the last page to say goodbye), then Celie, Shug, Nettie, and Albert. Mary Agnes, Harpo, and Sofia. Eleanor Jane. Adam and Tashi Omatangu. Olivia. Mercifully, my quilt and my lover remained.

I threw myself in his arms and cried.

Building Words
Carole Satyamurti

If I haven't had time to write anything for a while, I get the feeling of tenseness and ill health that is perhaps similar to what athletes describe when they are not able to exercise. That is not necessarily because there is a particular poem pressing to be written, although sometimes it is. I just seem to have a need to write, to repeat the experience of making something from nothing, of seeing something shaped out of an inchoate mass of ideas, words and images.

Sometimes a poem starts as a faint shape in the mind, an impression of a sound – a rhythm perhaps, or a tone of voice, like a conversation heard in the next room where you can't quite distinguish the words. Then a word comes to the foreground, or more than one word, and the subject for the poem becomes clearer, ideas start to come, and work begins.

At other times, I have time set aside for writing and nothing occurs to me. Then I sometimes use a deliberate device to get started. For instance, I stick a pin (or usually, a finger) in the dictionary four times, then I stare at my four words for a while and often a picture or an idea comes to mind. Or I might write down a list of words as fast as I can – whatever comes into my head – until one of them makes me pause, and I have the germ of an idea. I did that once in the garden of the Suffolk cottage, and one of the words on the list was 'indefatigable'. As I sat there, a cow wandered round the corner of the house and I watched her pulling up great tufts of grass and chewing, and the word 'indefatigable' seemed to apply to her – 'indefatigable eater'. I called her Evita to rhyme with eater because a slightly jokey tone seemed to suit her – the more I looked at her, the more preposterous she appeared, both the look and the idea of her. The poem became a celebration of her cow-ness, but tinged with sorrow that she should have such delicate, dancing ankles, yet be weighed down by motherhood and milk. She came to mean more than just a cow.

57

I love notebooks, and carry one with me always. I especially like French notebooks, with spiral backs for easy turning, and squares instead of lines. In my handbag-sized notebook, I write images, incidents that have caught my attention, snatches of conversation, words, subjects – anything that strikes me as possible material for a poem. Sometimes I jot down something that has made me angry – some piece of injustice I have observed, or a piece of insensitivity on the part of an official, or a thought about the times in which we live. I would love to be able to write poems out of such anger, but I have tried, and so far the resulting poems just have not worked. I recently spent three months working on a sequence of poems which was based on the idea of the *Herald of Free Enterprise* as a metaphor for the enterprise society. I feel angry about all those lives needlessly lost at sea largely because profit was put before safety. And about all the people whose capacities are wasted and stifled in a society which also puts profit first. But the poem was not particular enough. It was too much trying to make an extended point, putting forward a view. And even when I realised that and tried to remedy it, I couldn't make it live. I couldn't do justice to the subject. I still feel upset about that, because it seems to me that the failure was a deep one – that is, the problem was not one of technique; it was one of grasp. I was not big enough for the subject.

'Emotion recollected in tranquillity...'
Medbh McGuckian

A poem doesn't begin with an idea. I would have no idea how to write a poem beginning with an idea or having an idea in it somewhere. That may account for so many people having no idea what my poems are about, since they are not obviously about ideas. This is not very helpful, but in my experience it is no good waiting for an idea to come into your head for a poem, because even if does, it is unlikely to be any good.

There are ideas as I'm writing this because I'm trying to think communicatively rather than creatively. When I begin to think creatively, ideas take a back seat. The original instrument or raw material to be worked with or abandoned are the words or phrases that come into my head, arbitrarily, ready-made or half-made, something overheard, something on the radio or television, something said with a child's sense of novelty. I build the poem from such scraps of language and bind them together in a form that I can ultimately name as embodying an idea or expressing some personal experience. The poems are to cover and warm empty spaces like rag-rugs or quilts with primitive colours, they stem from the same protectively decorative animal instinct. They are more to be admired than useful to others, but primarily useful to me for clothing the raw or bare consciousness. They shield me from basic harsh reality, which they jazz up and present as food is arranged or flowers vased. The pleasure is in the arrangement or the vase, though this is often its own statement. If I find I can't arrange them, I have to wait for my mood to alter or lift. I can wrestle with a bunch of words for hours to no avail, the next night a cloud will have moved and the words go to their natural places as if without me. I avoid the absolute blank page in a way since I have the relief of the store of words in my head, though the first line is always critical and decisive, as is the first word.

What I do begin with necessarily is an *emotion*. If I am dull or dead to feeling I might as well not bother. It doesn't have to be a noble or exalted feeling but it usually has to be intense to make a poem powerful. A light feeling, like being glad to be alive, or relieved some anxiety is over, does contribute – I am not always on a continual high or low. But the best poems push up like bulbs from anger, desire, despair, fear, shame. Afterwards, I might dismiss it as trivial, to be distressed by this, or excited by that, but at the time the feeling is heightened and permanent, demanding to be recorded.

I don't think feelings are ever simple or uncomplicated, they are often ambiguous, which makes for the tensions and contradictions in my poems. A recent poem began from a state of resentment against two separate people who seemed to be siding together in opposition to me, a mood of paranoia which soon passed. My distress at being hurt or betrayed was, however, the intiation of the poem. The images embody a suppressed bitterness:

> Spring skims the garden with his wintry eyes
> Their electric-blue centres stained
> With a little pale blood
> So they look brown in photographs.

The balance or choice of words is a way of counterposing my attitudes. When I use 'garden', I am usually the passive, receptive soil that the season has power over. Someone I would normally have expected warmth from has glanced at me coldly, I begin with a positive and break out of it. The date of the poem was an uncertain March, I was unsure of everything. The figure becomes more Macbeth-like during the stanza. Electricity fascinates and terrifies me. The blood-stain is an apparent understatement but its indictment is definite because of the veiled allusion to an early description, by a female journalist, of the attractiveness of the youthful Hitler. Brown and blue are among my favourite antinomies. I reversed it all – if there is evil in the best person, then there must be good in the worst, and all our judgements are biased because they take place in time, like snapshots. So even as I'm saying, good and evil are inextricably mixed, I'm trying to stand apart from that platitude as a narrowness, which the full poem ultimately resolves.

The Paranoid Defendant
Marcella Evaristi

There is a sense in which you don't know what you are writing until you are writing it. Of course, the preliminaries of theorising and pre-plotting and looking out of the window do contribute in a strong unconscious way. They are part of the job. (Consequently, it's very difficult to answer honestly when asked how long something took to write. Three weeks and three years could be equally true.) But there comes a point when all this 'Notes Towards' stuff has to stop, and you just have to start.

Anywhere.

With anything.

Otherwise all the analyses and the defining of goals can just end up short-circuiting you.

Tell a story. Or ask yourself what happened next.

Overcoming a block for me is often about overcoming a ridiculously stern intolerance of first ideas. (If only I could stop being so hard on myself, I think; let myself play around with my thoughts.) 'Ideas' for a play tend not to be great or terrible *in themselves* anyway. I mostly hate Stage One of writing where you can still change your mind about your subject; perhaps great unconscious strides are being made but what it feels like is neurotic shadow boxing.

So . . . bully or trick yourself however you can into Stage Two. I find it sickeningly difficult. It feels as if I have a highly suspicious jury inside my head whose strictures I would dismiss out of hand when applied to other writers but their judgements on me and my work leave me cowed.

This is a jury which constantly transforms itself. Sometimes it is po-faced and Stalinist. I can see they are on the look-out for the reactionary and the frivolous. They think themselves salt of the earth, it's an excuse for their own dourness. I stand before this jury and try to defend myself. (I am annoyed that my voice has become rather tremulous.) I say that I believe radicalism consists of asking the right questions rather than providing the right answers. I talk about 'uncovering absences'. I mutter that the truth itself is radical: that we should trust it to be so. I up my volume and try to declare that I'm not interested in producing chinese poster art, in agit-prop.

When I mention Jean Rhys and Elizabeth Smart they look vindicated.

I use my preference for Wilde above Shaw to prove my case; they look at me as if I was comparing washing powders in the suburbs.

I warn that the wrong kind of populism in the arts can lead to philistinism; anti-intellectualism in the guise of unpretentiousness; but my sentences cluster in polysyllabic lumps and I have to stop. Pull myself together. Surely I'd argued that lot away a long time ago? And sure enough the jury fractures and reassembles itself.

Nothing puritan about Jury Two. They couldn't give a bugger whether I was populist or not. I try to look them in the eye and explain my concerns, but I get to talking about the moral basis of fiction and I'm getting tangled up again. They think they can smell the rat of prudery. While *I* can imagine one of *them* beginning a sentence with 'I'm not a feminist but . . .' They yawn when I mention Neruda.

I try to talk about accessibility and art, but I can hardly be heard.

I change the subject. When I say I'm Glaswegian there's a flicker of interest but it's over in a flicker, like all fashions.

In front of this lot, I've grown a chip on my shoulder. (Where were you, chip, when I needed you? Jury One would have patted you.)

In front of this jury I feel like the first of the immigrants to make it to university.

I feel European to their Englishness.

I feel their sneer at the vulgarity of commitment and I disagree.

I feel like I'm writing one of those Personal Manifesto poems that are mostly more satisfying to write than to read; I laugh, and the jury disappears.

Getting the jury to disappear for long enough to let you begin, that's the trick. That beautiful moment when you click into Work Proper and that woman with the depressingly defensive self-justifying catch in her voice finally shuts up and the self-consciousness goes, time speeds up and you lose yourself in the work.

Another Way of Seeing
Nicki Jackowska

Beginning – does one ever stop? I mean the work of focusing, choosing, connecting and gathering.

I have four collections of poetry and three novels in print. Currently, a new collection in progress and the start of a new novel. I see it more as a series of overlaps, the one feeding the other. The poem 'Cutting' providing an essential core-trigger for the novel *From the Terrace* (with the linking, under-pinning theme of Resistance and all the questions this calls to itself.) And even the silence is part of the continuum, the so-called fallow period. Even the silence feeds the voice.

I haven't written much over the past two years. Largely due to the ending of marriage, a regressed cat, learning not to pull in surrogates. Learning to re-shape my world. Learning all over again that there's always another way of looking at it.

So the start is the building-up of impression and experience, the forced landing somewhere new.

Let me talk about work-in-progress, and work backwards. I wanted a new book that would be very close to home. Not in the sense of autobiography – this isn't. I start with something I know since that gives me the original and authentic spark (like Michelangelo's painting of god giving life to Adam). It's that *original* moment. Thereafter is fiction, one is always, always inventing from then on. So although I locate my character Maggie on the threshold of a house very like my own, she is already on the move and changes shape under my hands. For example she is much larger than I am, and the house opposite has changed its shape as I write of it. This novel needed a large coloured box to grow in. In there I put fragments, finished chapters.

Here are my clues, what I call my 'constellation'. The clatter of this 'gathering of parts' is the noise of the book beginning:

• my neighbour left a huge parsnip on my doorstep. I didn't know

63

it was she who left it – nor that this brown and bulbous object was indeed a parsnip.

● in the house opposite the upper room is uncurtained and I am often able to see events which *may* be . . .

● a man in Cornwall, thin, moustached, keeps a ferret. Hunts at night with a gun, a poacher. He is transformed into Jake, chained in this street, poaching on women?

● resistance to taming.

● '*secretti di due, secretti di Dio*' ('the secrets of two, the secrets of God') – old Tuscan saying, quoted by the Tavianni brothers.

● photograph of Hotel Bellevue, Leschaux, near Annecy – another Terrace. Another Cutting?

● the patron patrols his terrace – as Maggie does hers.

● conception in the mountains, above the treeline.

And so on. The ingredients begin to mix, begin to influence and interact. I am both director juggling the pieces, arranging the events, but also a helpless witness of their autonomous inspiration. (Language lives.)

When to interfere? When to hold back? When is it my voice and when a voice that speaks through me, or out of the elements I have arbitrarily placed here?

The holding and relinquishing of control.

The Islanders is my most recent published novel. It began with a single image, that of the island – the specific geographical location of the Isle of Wight whose shores are rapidly eroding. It is also a metaphor for the island of self, family, nation. Again I decided to set it at a time when I was the same age as my character – so that I could capture the *flavour* of growing up in the fifties. Thereafter it is fiction – except that I know how this feels! How they all feel. For each, I try and enter the skin. We are all, at times, macho, out of control, victim, gypsy, spinster, mute, liar, infidel, vagabond, saint.

I mapped this book carefully and knew the overall shape as I began. There would be three sections: the first would establish the lives within the 'enclosure' with a hint of shifting restlessness; the second would be Caroline's break-outs and her 'crossing the water'; the third, a necessary return to find all was not as it seemed, an exorcism, a touching upon the undersides of that idealised and ordered life. Her witnessing the stories beneath the surface.

In each case, each section, I wanted the language to evoke the quality of the experience. This linguistic change and control is threatening to some people (critics? reviewers?) who want the language to play second fiddle to the 'plot'.

I have another intention altogether. The story I tell must bring the reader close to the raw edge of experience – whether ecstatic, edgy, bland. I'm not interested in creating fiction to pass the time of day. If there is discomfort, so be it. How is it possible to read an account of the bleak experience that much adolescent sex can be, without a shiver? I consider I have failed if I do not make my reader shiver, and draw close to the heart of it. This applies to experience of liberation and joy, as well as the sordid and the raw.

I wrote poems for many years before writing novels. I watch for the moment of ignition, and also create it. One waits and one acts to keep one's writing alive. I work from an idea, or a single word. A doodle, an improvisation – or a carefully crafted piece where I may be following a subject-matter very closely.

The poet is witness, hunter, spy – of language and life together. Is what she wants to be, what is necessary. Potentially, everything is interesting enough to make the beginning of the new poem which is also, at the same time, another link in a larger work. I am prepared to use anything – fragments plucked out of other poems, T V, music, objects, postcards, a particular look between two people, lines on a face. The detail can be as monumental, as full of potency, as the 'grand idea'. And in fact the latter is deeply embedded in the former. Love hovers beneath each surface, within each cavity. You have to dig. And when I say love, I mean revealment, release. The poet/poem unlocks the world from its prisons of habit, failure, that-which-is-less. I write when I encounter the world without fear, prepared (or desiring) to see what is there. And sometimes it is necessary to write oneself through to that encounter. Sometimes I need to write of disguises in order to hint of what lies beneath. You can't always get to the heart, but knowing there is one, matters.

I've just read this over – it sounds all very energetic and optimistic. Here's a quote from Ann Nietzke:

> And nobody could write about Danny the way I might if only I had the courage to fail. Someone no doubt could write it all more perfectly, but no one can say what I have to say unless I say it myself. It's the doing that counts . . .

So I have talismans also, for sending the failure, the fear, packing. We can refuse our own reluctance as though it were a person – 'Be gone, I don't want you,' – and write because to not-write is worse. And because of that unique individual angle that each of us brings to the common hoard.

The enthusiasm of finding a chair, or a table discarded in the trash, discovering beauty where others looked away.

Letter from Tim Shaner to N J, 29 December 1987

Clues
Rosalind Brackenbury

Where do ideas come from? I think of the beginnings of each of my novels and can spot their conception: an image, as if from a dream, something strong, vivid and worrying, something that puzzles me, hangs about in the mind, will not go away; it is the answer to a question not yet asked, it persists with the accuracy of the unknown future, it is what *will be*. It becomes the pivot of the book. How obvious this is to readers, I don't know – perhaps sometimes, in the writing, it becomes nearly invisible. But it is the matrix, from which all the rest is spun out. It may be a person, an event, a thing, a feeling, but once it is there it irritates, there is no getting away from it. Any novel I have started without this 'it' at the centre has been dead, merely an exercise. It's not reasonable, cannot be planned for, is elusive, obsessive, uneasy, surprising; may break surface several times in several different forms over a span of months or even years. Once I've recognised it, it's as if it has begun to work in the open. It drags unlikely things in its wake, makes strange connections. Sometimes it seems to come from the outside world – a person glimpsed in a crowd, a story someone tells me, a detail, like glittering glass in a handful of sand. Sometimes it surfaces in dreams or in the time between dream and waking. It wakes me up, makes me suddenly alert. But I think that the connections are strong between the outer and inner worlds, that what we pick up in the outer world corresponds strongly with the inner. The images, words, fragments, are all part of something, and the 'something', the completed novel is as far as I can get, each time, in understanding the whole. And no sooner have I finished one quest, as often as not, than another begins. It is a process, in which individual pieces of writing are visible parts. I write to try to understand these things, to make explicit the buried connections, to draw in the story, the sequence, from which the initial idea may have come; like the drawings of archaeologists, filling in, guessing, extrapolating, where the shards have not yet been

67

found. I write to try and make sense of my own time, my own life. I pick up what floats towards me on currents whose force and direction I do not know – and write from here, if I trust my intuition, which I would define as a sort of fast and seamless thinking. Sometimes it feels like going far out on a limb, not knowing if anyone will be able to follow. At other times it founders in banality, seems to be a blind alley. But the next clue, the next fragment, sooner or later always appears, and I have begun to learn to trust the process.

Listening to the Truth
Hélène Cixous

When I'm writing fiction, I begin with the inkling of a thought which is in the process of unravelling itself in front of me. I set off after it, trying to hear all its minute gradations as it works itself out. It's as if I am trying to record something in the process of being born. I listen, with all the ears of my body, trying to write it down. And my phrases are almost always insufficient, at one remove from the truth. I go over my phrase again and again, each time trying to get a little closer, until I am as close as possible to the truth of this thought. It's slow, painstaking work. But there is a model. The model, or example, which is my own thought, is there, before me.

I work progressively in this way, fragment by fragment, until I am as close as possible to the truth. What guides me is the call of what I have to say. In my most recent work of fiction, *Manne*, for example, there are many different themes and motifs. What joins these themes together are the questions: of loss, separation, reparation – the innumerable mysteries of life which preoccupy me and whose variations are infinite. What I'm searching to record is the particular music of these themes according to the character or text I'm working on.

I don't begin with a phrase, the phrases come, joining themselves together musically in the service of my theme. I use language rather as I imagine a painter uses colour. I must paint with accuracy. My singing must be in key. And language helps me to achieve this. It has its own song, its own system of signifiers and phonic associations, its own cultural and poetic memory, it brings its own treasures, its own patterns and harmonies, which work together as I write.

Round and Round the Graveyard
Sue Roe

The difficulty is in finding access to a finely tuned, poised and precarious channel of yourself which contains all your tools, all your raw materials. All you need is paper, a pen or typewriter, and yourself, but yourself is the difficult bit. There is an area of your perception that needs to be brought into play again. You will have kept on catching glimpses of it – out of the window, the colours, the forms, the light are suddenly transformed, the frame contains a painting, you have a keen impulse to capture this sense of things having been transformed . . . and then it is gone. The whole thing is so maddeningly elusive.

The combination of things you are trying to tap combines the gathering-in of some focus on the senses with an obscure stance of detachment, so that you feel at once stretched to the limit and also, in a strange way, already split. You have already destroyed something. You have already begun to cease to tell the truth, there is already an everyday kind of responsibility, a normal kind of common sense, which you have already decided to relinquish, in order to make the attempt to meet a new and entirely obscure responsibility. I have to remember that only I can do it in quite this way. I have to remember that I have no idea what I will produce and that there is no reason on earth why it should not be good. I feel quite shaky; I am hovering on the edge of something . . . This does not mean I have forgotten how to do it, I tell myself. Henry James probably felt like this when he was searching for a starting point for *The Golden Bowl*. Virginia Woolf undoubtedly felt like this when she began *The Waves*. If you were about to begin on something that turned out to be magnificent, it would probably – even then – feel like this at the beginning.

I don't think I have very much to say about the conditions for working. You make time. You make a space – though I find I always write in exactly the same place in the house. I wrote one of my best stories on a Sunday morning wedged between a miserable Saturday and dreading what I was going to have to do on Monday. I was so angry that I started throwing things around in my head and breaking them – as it were – and suddenly the things I was relating began to tip over into a place on the page that I had not been able to make them occupy in my mind. I was quite merciless. I just went on and on writing about amputations and deformities until I got to the place where I was able, suddenly, to tell the story of what had gone wrong. That seemed like a good technique: follow the tangents, if they continue to obsess you, and eventually you will find yourself back on course.

Writing my second novel, *Masquerade*, I walked round and round the graveyard. Round and round and round I went, reading the inscriptions on the stones and hoping to find some kind of clue. The suspicion that I was probably going slightly mad was troublesome, but you have to hang on to the feeling that this piece of writing is at least as important as anything else in your life. You may well need a room of your own, a good typewriter, a good night's sleep, an exciting or a supportive relationship, complete solitude . . . Who knows where the first words come from. What you do need is an exceptionally good idea, and this may prove extremely difficult to define until you are a good way into the project. When I wrote a story recently, I began with two starting points: an episode in my local Pakistani grocers', and something I was desperate to say about Picasso's late nudes. After about six drafts I finally sacrificed the bit about Picasso, and the story began to fall into place. You have to make sacrifices, but Picasso had been important – I'm still not entirely sure how.

Another way to hit on a starting point is to read. I like reading about painting, and novels about painting – Eva Figes' *Light*; Gabriel Josipovici's *Contre-Jour*; A. S. Byatt's *Still Life*. Thinking about painting is always a good beginning for me. I start writing when I am forced to remember that I have no idea how to paint properly: I have to go back into my own medium. Or I do a different kind of writing: I write letters to friends who are writers, even to friends who are not writers – anecdotal letters, telling stories, in an attempt to galvanise my story-telling faculties back into action. I think back: what was it that triggered my first novel, the poem I think is probably my best poem?

It is so difficult to answer that question, because such a complex network of events and psychological forces triggers a piece of work. There is, perhaps, a moment in which all these forces coalesce, a moment which in retrospect seems to be the heightened moment at which the idea 'took' . . . You are waiting for some change . . . I remember the evening of one damp, black day in August. I had been watching the way in which the sea and sky seemed, that summer, to be so tightly wrapped together, and that evening I drove to the edge of a cliff and watched the sky open out to display a whole range of shades and vibrations: layer upon layer of spread, resonant colours, and just the sight of this happening was the starting point for a new poem, because something that had been very flat and bleak and dormant suddenly opened up, to reveal – as it were – all its contents. You find analogies, metaphors, for what you want to say, and then you can begin to say it. It is as though you are looking for an obscure kind of 'permission'.

A moment comes, I think, when you suddenly and starkly 'see' – painted all around and ahead of you – the things you have been thinking about, transcribed into a single image. It feels like something of a revelation, but you also know that you have been waiting – and watching – for this moment: it is a revelation, but also a reflection of your ideas. What you could not have anticipated is precisely what this moment would 'look like'.

Another way of experiencing this pivotal moment might be in a moment produced by the imagination: it might not be necessary to *literally* 'see' the moment or image in which the work appears to be encapsulated or previsaged. I had two moments like this, prior to writing the novel I have just finished. I can't remember which came first, but I retained both in the novel, in a kind of transcribed form – this feels appropriate for this particular novel, which has dual or parallel themes.

The first came after, I think, several evenings in my study in which I simply sat at my desk and doodled and imagined, and read and idled and despaired of ever writing anything again. (I think this must have been two or three months or so after having finished the previous piece of work.) I had been reading all of Elizabeth Bowen, and some bits and pieces of Henry James and George Eliot (in the back of my mind I knew I wanted to write something quite 'weighty', and something about history). The person I was living with was in another room, working on something he was concentrating on, and I was anxious not to disturb him, but this anxiety was making me feel very tense and strung. I looked in on him to ascertain that he was still working, then very quietly returned to my desk and wrote, in longhand, a piece about a woman in evening dress looking silently in at a doorway – leaning against the frame – and seeing a man in a dressing gown or smoking jacket slumped across a leather-topped desk, having slammed down his fist in anger and despair. His face was broken in pieces and the entire scene had an atmosphere of something immaculate and poised and precious having been shattered to smithereens. There was some notion, here, of the effort to create a 'beautiful life' having been fractured under the weight of the attempt . . . something like that. There is a moment something like this in the novel, though the scene is described differently. After the description of this scene in my notes I knew that I had previsaged one of my central characters' collapse, but not the sequence of events that would take him to this point, nor indeed anything else about him. This is the moment at which one of my central characters in *Masquerade* first 'appeared'.

The second 'vision' happened while I was in Paris, in the middle of the night. I knew I needed a week in Paris in order to begin this novel, so I spent a week just trailing about in the streets – just walking and looking, eating in restaurants, trying on clothes, buying junk-shop trinkets and not writing anything at all. I stayed with a friend who was out at work all day, and felt that this was an unfortunate compromise: I should either have been in company, or alone in a hotel room . . . (Later I did spend a week alone in a hotel room, and what I wrote there did go directly into the novel.) This question of seeking out a situation in which you will feel very alone is, I think, important: I find that I need to go through a period of desolate isolation before anything begins to be triggered.

On my last day in Paris I bought a collection of old knives from a junk ship, and spent the evening with some friends in a local restaurant drinking rough red wine and eating, I seem to remember, ice cream laced with liqueurs (I think this was – bizarrely – the patron's speciality). It was an evening which felt warm and vibrant and convivial, after my solitary days. That night I woke in the early hours to a narrative running in my head, which told the story of a woman and her child getting off the métro and walking to a shop very like the one with the knives, to choose some gifts. The child was transfixed by a case full of lead soldiers, which had not been in the actual shop (at least, I had not registered them). The mother and child were talking, and I got up and recorded the whole of their conversation, without translating it into English – I wrote about six pages.

When I got home, I tried to turn this dialogue into a short story, but I couldn't seem to find an appropriate ending, and it wouldn't translate, so I put it aside, knowing that even if the novel I would write next didn't include this scene, it must nevertheless contain the elements or germs of the fiction I was about to write. It was not until I was a good way into writing the novel – some two or three years later – that I could see just how many of the novel's themes were in fact contained in that early, imagined scene. But – as with the earlier scene – it was the atmosphere of this incident – an atmosphere of ominousness or premonition – which seemed important, and seemed to encapsulate some anticipation of a beginning.

Openings
Emma Tennant

I think it was Henry James who said he liked to 'walk up' his characters, and in some peculiar way walking seems to release characters swimming into my mind. My two most recent novels, *The House of Hospitalities* and its successor *A Wedding of Cousins*, are both novels of character, and in each case the germ was a character I felt I'd invented and got to know. I'm particularly attracted to different aspects of women's character, but I don't think I get drawn to a character on her own so much as to the idea of there being quite a babble of them, and of them interacting with each other. Often, I find I'll write a crowd scene followed by another crowd scene as characters rush in from all directions, and I have to be careful of this, as it can be boring to have one crowd scene following another.

A number of my novels begin with a situation, and often this has been a situation I've wanted to express in feminist terms. At the moment I'm working on a novella called *The Strange Case of Ms Jekyll and Mrs Hyde*, and here I'm trying to transpose the exclusively male world of Stevenson's original and bring it up to date. I began by looking at the structure of the original to see how it was laid out, and deciding, for instance, that there were too many sealed documents in it, and that anyone now wanting to find out the truth about the deprived single mother Mrs Hyde, and Ms Jekyll trying to keep her head above water and hold down her prestigious job in a London art gallery, would not look for a written statement, but to more modern means of communication instead. So I decided to leave Ms Jekyll's confession on her answering machine, making it an allegory of what London and England are like now: with this terrifying split between the privileged and the deprived.

For *Queen of Stones* I went to *Lord of the Flies*. What kinds of myths are girls brought up on which could lead to the murder of a victim?

75

What kinds of fairy-tales penetrate girls' psyches, and what kind of girl would the scapegoat be?

In *Wild Nights* I wanted to describe the atmospheric and psychic effects on a child of the relationships inside her house. I tried to get as far away from realism and remembered detail as possible by going right back to the time when my house seemed huge and my Aunt Zita came to stay: discovering a strange, forgotten landscape that had nothing to do with the colour of my parent's sitting-room or what time I went to bed. My Aunt Zita was rather fiery, and the way I as a child and then poetically came to see her was that she was permanently surrounded by a flickering flame. Here, I think the writing process was to do with trusting memory and imagination, however strange or far out these might seem.

Skeletal Poem
Sue Stewart

I need to feel quite still in myself before I can begin to write. This pretty much rules out sitting at my desk if I'm elated or depressed, unless the feeling can be subsumed in some way. It's not that I wait for the perfect state of mind (if I did I'd be disappointed), just the attentive state necessary to catch those few precious words that might make up the skeleton of a poem.

Once the first draft is down, the real work begins. I wouldn't balk at twenty drafts if necessary (any more and I have to ask myself if I'm flogging a dead horse). Some poems come after only three or four drafts, like a small strange gift. I see the drafting or crafting as essentially an act of love, a homage to the language. If you love a person, you know his or her likes, foibles, idiosyncracies; a poem demands the same affection, the same alertness to hints, nuances, quirks.

I enjoy working on a sequence of poems, taking one theme and developing it in diverse ways. I have to prepare myself for the marathon though, not the one-minute sprint. I wrote a sequence called 'Book of Hours' (twenty-four poems, one for each hour of the day) in a very intensive six months, but the idea had been simmering for a while, and I continued to fiddle with odd words for some time afterwards, so a year would be a more realistic estimate. I felt rather lost when it was finished. The Hours had felt like a family of poems, full of sibling rivalries and excitements. An occasional poem by comparison felt like an only child.

I need to take a break from time to time, to freshen up. At one point I'd begun to feel so hooked on the one style that I feared I'd slip into a sort of self-parody by force of habit. After a break, though, I found I was concentrating more on metre; the 'tricksy' or punning element had abated; the convolutions were less laboured.

Study of form was another important stage for me, and by a stroke of luck I did this at the right time, when a little confidence had been gained and a voice was beginning to come through. Otherwise I think I might have become bogged down by technicalities at the beginning and let form be the boss instead of the guide.

I don't have 'blocks' as such, but there are certainly fallow times when poems won't come through. Feelings of emptiness and word-lessness often follow a long, concentrated period of work, but I remind myself it would be very mercenary to expect poems to rise with every sun. I don't feel the Muse deserts, just that she waits for a proper reception, for fertile ground to cast seed on. I once wrote a poem called 'The Muse Comes to Call', trying to get across this feeling and something of the comedy of the situation.

I need to care about a theme, or insincerity creeps through and betrays me on the page. Some themes I seek out, others suggest themselves. One time when I was stuck for an idea I sat at my desk and stared out of the window, hoping. I wondered after a while if I ought to move the dead bluebells from the window-sill so as to better my view of the lawn, the gate, the lane and the universe. I thought not; it would be an interruption. More hours (it seemed) passed, until the penny dropped. The eventual poem, 'Bluebells', I've shown in the 'Crafting' section.

When trying out a new form I don't expect a poem to come of it; if it does, it's a bonus. It's usually only when I've begun to approach the form with a sense of ease, of familiarity, that I can relax enough to let the right subject find it. I was playing around once with some words for a villanelle, and wrote the first poem, a rather ponderous piece which ended up in the waste-paper basket. Then a second, in a child's voice, about sexual abuse. Then a third, about Lucinda Love, a trapeze artiste whose husband gets wind of her infidelity half-way through their act: her life, as it were, hanging in the balance. This was the one that worked best, I felt, because it used the repeating lines and the rhyme scheme to heighten and embroider the humour, albeit black. And I'd got used to the form. Too used to it, in fact: after a couple more villanelles I got hooked on rhyme and had to kick the habit.

Sometimes a subject I might never have thought of presents itself via an outside source. I had a letter from an editor a while back, asking for fairground poems for a new anthology. I had loved fairs as a child but grown to dislike them at puberty, so I didn't want to take the jolly approach. I wrote 'Gypsy Sarah', about a young girl at the fair whose menses have just begun: careering down the switchback, she is already beginning to retreat into a private, dark, supremely female world. Sarah is also the name of an old Romany gypsy I used to visit on Morecambe Prom!

Pencil on Lined Paper
Amryl Johnson

I don't remember at what point I stopped saying, when asked what I did, 'Oh, I write,' and replaced it with, 'I am a writer.' I am not certain but maybe it came with being published. *News for Babylon* was the first anthology which had my work. Finally, I could take myself seriously, or, more to the point, I now stood a chance of the world taking me seriously.

Whether it is poetry or prose, my first draft is always handwritten, in pencil, on lined foolscap. Depending on the feint, I may or may not use double-lined spacing. The major benefit attached to this method is I find myself being able to take advantage of long coach or train journeys. I have a stack of bright red hard-cover notebooks (with black corners). I use these for first drafts. When I am travelling, I take the current one with me. Strangely enough, I find it impossible to read a book while travelling but creative work presents no problem. With that first draft, I never cross out, I erase. Even though it obviously slows me down, I find it much easier to collect my thoughts when faced with a tidy page. Crossings-out leave my thoughts in a maze, shriek chaos when I glance at the page. Perhaps, more importantly, I experience difficulty in reading my own writing. So much takes place during the process that I do not necessarily stop to remind myself about the various stages which follow on from the initial inspiration. Now and then I become aware of the slowing-down process, of stopping to erase a word in order to replace it with a more suitable one. And I am only sometimes aware of following my thoughts through the pencil as it dips and flows. I do not follow every word. No, of course not. But I certainly follow every sentence. I have to. Words are, in themselves, so totally devoid of colour that I am naturally always anxious that the picture I am presenting is an accurate one. While I translate my thoughts into words on the page, this question is constantly circling through my head – do these words successfully capture the vision I want them to?

Curious how far the inspiration can sometimes take you. The germ, nucleus of the original thought may get lost as the idea grows and changes shape and direction. I would like to think that I practice what I preach. I would like to think that when I encourage my students to understand the importance of not discarding any idea but keeping it in a closet for possible future use, I do not neglect to do so myself. Inspiration may come from an idea which, for no particular reason, stabs at my brain. It may come from something seen or overheard, a voice, a gesture. A conversation may also have registered sufficiently to spark the imagination. Even if I feel unable to do anything, sooner or later I will make a few notes. These notes will be about the quality of the voice, gesture, etc., which caused it to remain in my mind. In other words what made it (them) so special. I will file it away in my 'wardrobe of ideas'. Every now and then I sort through the file to see if there are any ideas I would like to try and develop. An idea which may not have registered during one occasional 'sort-out' will very likely do so the next. So I hold on to ideas. I never throw them away, no matter how long the time-lapse.

Ideas are divided into two categories. The ones which get committed to file for later use, and the ones you know instantly you'll be starting work on, as soon as you finish the present project. These ideas I carry in my head while physically working on the current project. I may carry them with me for days, weeks, months before committing them to paper. All the while the situation will be developing, the characters growing. When I am finally ready for them, they are well rounded. This applies to poetry as well as prose. I approach both facets of creative writing in the same way. The germ of an idea gains credence in my thoughts. Later, it will be translated into a poetic form or into prose.

Drama is a vital element in my work, be it poetry or prose. I like to feel that something is taking place. I like my work to sound exciting. In the same way that one idea may lead to another, may grow into something more profound, more concrete, so also do I build on sounds and movement, putting in expressions, mannerisms, developing the characters. Sometimes scenes, entire stories, are acted out in my head. I very clearly visualise scenery, first of all, who and what I place in that scenery, the conflict and how the characters respond to it. This, to a larger or lesser degree, is my approach and the format of everything I have ever done or am ever likely to do.

A few years ago, I experienced a mental block. It lasted for almost a year. Although full of ideas, I found it impossible to put them into words. Every attempt to put pen to paper proved fruitless. I could not find the words, right or otherwise. Whatever I wanted to say simply dissipated the moment I sat down to translate my ideas. I found it impossible to overcome the hurdle. It was one obstacle which refused to be vaulted. Discussing the problem with a friend, he thought for a while then came up with what he felt was a solution. The conversation went more or less as follows:

'Do you keep a diary?'

'No. Not in years.'

'Why not go back to it?'

'I haven't kept a diary since I was in my teens.'

'Try it and see how it works. It might well be the solution. Might be a way of overcoming the block, getting you back into the swing of things.'

I tried it. It worked. Curious situation. It was like learning to walk again. For almost a month, the factual side of my life was painstakingly documented. That month proved to be the most disciplined part of my life since school and university days. For almost an hour every evening I would sit to recall the day's events. At first, I was very conscious of what I was doing. I was very aware of the fact that I was deliberately bringing to mind certain things I had experienced during the previous few hours in the hope that it would help me to do the same with things that I imagined. After a while, I became less aware of the precise purpose of the task. I became less nervous of it. It became less of a chore and I relaxed into it. After the first two weeks, I would attempt a paragraph of creative writing directly after writing up my diary. Gradually, this paragraph lengthened. The entry in the diary became shorter, and the short story, chapter by chapter, grew longer. As I've said, learning to walk again. After those first tottering footsteps, your confidence and your strength grows. I gave up the diary. I no longer needed it. I was able to concentrate totally on my creative writing. I believe the mood (some might say the Muse!) created, through putting those facts into words, left something in its wake. A wisp of determination which grew stronger by the day. It was like a rusty wheel. Difficult to move, at first, but with regular oiling soon began to turn and eventually to spin again. Overcoming that mental block resulted in a reclamation of self and, equally importantly, self-respect. Form and art form.

When certain things happen in your life, the mental block for example, it sometimes leaves you blatantly grateful for other things once taken for granted. English was my best subject at school. These handwritten first drafts may well be a habit from those days. Who knows? For that matter, who cares? Those days when I was forced to keep a diary made me aware of the essence of soul. This was what I was able to capture by harnessing my inspiration and putting it down on paper in my own handwriting. This was my style. A vitally important part of ritual. It was my seal of identity.

I have not arrived at my zenith. I certainly do not feel that I am at the top of the mountain. However, I have most certainly arrived at a point where I can say, yes, I am reasonably content with the way I am saying things. Reading through work recently completed, I find I am getting closer to saying things the way I would like them to sound. I am becoming more fluent, more confident. Mercifully, I am still in transit. Still arriving.

And that will do for beginnings!

Looking at the Source
Nina Sibal

It's good to look at the source from time to time, to wade back through the chaos and confusion through which the writing has percolated. One shouldn't do it too often. Who knows, it could stop up the source. Might bring bad luck, putting a magical process under the microscope. But still.

You see the final body, neatly, or not so neatly – what did my last critic say? – in place, arrayed in modern garments, with well-chosen accessories. An earring glints, hair is shampooed and set, and that's the novel, oh after the tenth draft, proofs corrected, text printed, reviewed, maybe even read. But when I begin to take off the layers, one after the other, going faster and faster through the flesh, until I reach the chattering bones of the skeleton inside and still go on, where do I reach? If I'm lucky, the Void, the empty space at the centre of the wheel. I'm not there yet.

Susan Sellers suggested that details of how I organise working space and time, where and when I write, the physical conditions of writing, might be of interest to you. Everything in this area clusters around time: how to grab it from a schedule of a full-time job and a well-stocked household of a husband, two growing sons and a wide-eyed dog, all of them loving and interacting. For I'm not escaping from them at all, not 'getting away' from them into my writing. Time retrieved from a chock-full life. And time spent and forgotten, its usually strong and biting edges vanishing, the alternate possibilities of its usage no longer relevant, as I sit hour after hour, just waiting. Not for something to happen but simply waiting. For words to form, for the story or chapter to begin. It can be agony, and is always distinctly uncomfortable. And at the end of these 'waits' I am very exhausted, as if I have lived intensely during that period, several people's lives. In a sense as if I have been on a long journey somewhere else and am now returning, tramping and tired, my brain tied up in tight little knots, longing for the wool to unravel, for the flow, even just a trickle, to begin.

I could tell you more about environment. I write in a room at the top of the house, either in Delhi, or in my mother's house in Dehra Dun. But I think I could write anywhere. I can cope now, through long, frustrating practice, with interruptions, most of them created by myself, since I am obsessed with household details: when the rubber-plants must be tied, who is grinding the meat, if the pump which gets water up to tanks on the roof is not working. I long to push all this away during the four hours of work which begin in the early morning, before I set off for my office, to float on top like a buxom ship, my round dove-breast cleaving unsplattered through the waves, but I cannot. They reach up and grab me, break up my thinking, spiral away my imagination – but still I write.

Furniture, I suppose, is important. A large desk with lots of space for books and papers, since I use a lot of references, and notes made on scraps, envelopes, invitation cards with smooth ivory backs (why waste them), or even orderly notebooks; a chair with a straight back but spacious enough to permit me to sit cross-legged and meditate when I need to draw up and concentrate energy; and, most important, a bed. For various uses. One of them is, for lying in wait. Eyes closed, body relaxed, entire being ready and concentrated, like a panther sitting for hours at a water-hole, ready to spring.

The other very fertile place for me, is Dehra Dun, where my mother lives; a small town full of retired people and busy lime-stone quarries, where mysterious murders take place from time to time. We visit people, and the ideas come bubbling through. Not many of them have become stories so far, but who knows. My mother takes me along one morning – beautiful winter sunshine, the smell of leaves in the air, everything moves much more slowly here – to visit an old friend of hers, recently widowed, who lives alone in a big, empty house. A buffalo and three cows in the out-houses, who are much more work than she and her aged gardener can handle. Two entries from notebooks relate to this visit.

Story. Woman here, empty house, but how beautiful, she is planning to pay with a cow the debt of the man who is dead. These are the sacrifices to our ancestors. 'Jayashree's mother lost her son in this house. Sent him here to work, and then he ran away . . . Well, he was not an unkind man, my husband, I do not know what happened.' The rich widow. Emptiness of the house. But was it happy when he was here – what is happiness? – this life is constant interchange. Jayashree's mother. The cow, the widow's attachment. Describe the garden. Class connections. How did the boy just disappear?

Story. Old lady, a fighter, alone in a large echoing house. Picks up the clothes in the bathroom, wears them in darkness. Goes back to her room. And suddenly she is covered with hundreds of little red ants. Bursts into tears, such as she has never cried before.

This man is not an idea, he is very palpably human. Not particularly good-looking, skimpy beard camouflaging a lantern jaw, very kind and good-humoured. A young man. That's the important thing. A young man who, one day, looked across a room with a curiously intent, fascinated stare at an older woman, and she caught the look. Then, for days, it is not me, it is a woman in the story, I have to find a place and a setting, a plot and a series of dramatic incidents to hold them; I place them in the tea-gardens of North-East India. For days I cannot push her away, I move in a miasma of strong physical attraction for this young man, I'm sure he notices, but I don't care, I don't even make myself ridiculous; and you know why, because it's not really me at all, I have given myself up, been captured, possessed, by this other woman, who is in love with this younger man, and must surely, surely, come to a tragic end. A vague idea of the plot which will hold her begins to work itself out in my mind. Gradually I forget about the real young man with the lantern jaw. Another, an equally real fellow, who does different things, who has an ancestor who went to China and married a Chinese wife, takes over.Notes begin to appear about the tea-gardens, and I am longing to go to the North-East to see for myself (Who will go, me or the other woman?).

About seventy-two tea-gardens in Darjeeling hill areas which provide employment to 75,000 people and support population of four lakhs. Value of annual tea output Rs 70 crores. Production loss because of the disturbances about Rs 4 crores.

Notebooks are the place for pronouncements. Not the fascist ones of dictums to impose, here, look, this is the truth. But Zen-words, which float to the top on their own, and come gradually together into sentences. Crafting must work from that same place where the Zen-words start; unknown place. The novel gives enormous freedom, the question is how to use it. By all means, plot, structure, characters, words, incidents. After all, *nobody* must get bored, not you nor I. But they must come only from this place. Fed, surely, by the old, tough meat as well? I have read and listened. This baggage of technique, how other people did it, I carry with me.

What glory, what indulgence, to write a notebook. For the 'I' to be fully me, myself, and not the character in a work. But then, the funny thing is, when I come to write even notes, where's the difference? The line is very thin, where I end, and Rohina, or Krishna or Arjun or Mark Tully take over. Whether it is notebook or novel. After all, characters come from the same place – me, as well as the others.

The element of the unexpected, the character who bobs up carrying his or her own story into the middle of a careful narrative. Or, why does a prayer-wheel travel from the lake-shore to the top of Mount Kailas just as I am lying in my bed one morning, suffering from a viral fever, and thinking of nothing – certainly not of the plot of my new novel *Bodhisattva*. Turns out to be the best twist of plot possible in the context. But of course, I didn't think it, it happened.

To be open to these things which just happen. Truth does not come from pursuing it. It comes from just sitting. What is the process by which I select one 'truth' rather than another? Surely there is a selection, of words, sentences, whatever else populates the novel? Maybe I don't know this process. Maybe it would be dangerous to know.

Something akin to meditation. Opening long channels to the Buddha-nature inside, watching what comes up. I must not be too greedy, try to grab it, but just let it be there and, casually, almost inadvertently, let it gather.

I don't want anaemic petals fallen from the tree. Withered leaves. How sentimental, sad and nostalgic. I want the life of the tree in my books. The energy and passion of being alive.

Symbols. They enter the novel, swell, get refracted, in mostly unpredictable ways. The best symbol is probably the one you don't even notice or register as a symbol. I wonder how the earthquake in *Bodhisattva* will turn out. It is so much a part of the plot: structural faults in the plain north of the Himalayas, connected to nuclear testing sites, the geology sections. But I find that my 'Notes' ground it, with a logic which the novel will probably never see.

Quotation from a geology textbook:

Tectonic earthquakes may also be associated with the displacement of blocks of the lithosphere as a whole, as well as of the crust. They are therefore the deepest type, their . . . immense energy accumulated and released . . .

'If the moving of her personality'

'Collecting together'

'Accumulation, saturation, explosion = satori'

Underwater earthquakes or seaquakes are a special variety of earthquake. Those that generate tsunamis, or seismic sea waves, often have catastrophic consequences.

'Lake Mansarovar, the Holy Lake, will overflow, spread all over the plain, source of the four great rivers, the sub-continent will be affected. Dry up? Polluted? Poison large numbers of the population? What is the nature of this evil?'

I have to write from the inside out. There is no other way. Constantly breaking up the blocks. As Krishnamurti says, dying each moment, not just at the end of the day when I go to sleep. That is why earthquake is such a perfect symbol. No way to separate my writing from my life, except that writing catches the pieces as they fly. Necessary that they fly.

That the earth quakes.

Considerable debate about whether the large central section of *Bodhisattva* shouldn't appear separately, as a novella entitled *The Dogs of Justice*. It is an interesting, self-contained story about Shehnaz Ali Khan, who is quite close to the pain inside my heart. Not much relationship in terms of plot to the rest of the story, except that Shehnaz is the mother of Rohina, who is perhaps a central figure. A woman working towards enlightenment. I even offer it to my publisher, to consider for separate publication, and then retrieve it hastily, it is too close to the emotional structure, and must go in the novel. The swelling of desire, and its desolation. One of the central 'appearances' which moved the Buddha to leave his royal home and set out in search of enlightenment. It must therefore be here in *Bodhisattva*,

Shehnaz, suffering and lost, the only legacy which she gives to her daughter, to show from her own life the torture of desire. Will Rohina be prised away from attachment?

Nothing gave me so much trouble in terms of structure as the ending of my first novel, *Yatra*. I must have written it about ten times, wanting to pick up all the threads which had worked themselves through the book, knotting them up neatly, pointing the long shot forward, to the future. But it just would not happen like that. The novel seemed to resist an ending. Maybe one day, in some novel, I will have the guts and the inclination to leave the narrative in mid-stream. Simply withdraw. After all, why not?

Anything I do and am shapes my writing. Being a bureaucrat eight to ten hours a day affects my writing principally through the interaction with people. My identity at present is a bureaucrat, not a writer. The automatic distance this gives might even be good for writing. Lonely but good, always to be a watcher, even as you shape things.

Do I feel guilty about not contributing to the world? 'Words make nothing happen.' Is that why I choose a bureaucrat's job – to cover all areas? Like the man who did not believe in superstitions and magic but still had a horse-shoe over his door, just in case the believers were right.

I find the period between the ending of one work and the beginning of another most difficult. As if I need the circus-net of writing to hold me as I fall into each day, letting me get to the next. My version of a drug-habit? A way to survive joy and despair? Of being alive?

To float, somehow, on this terrible contradiction.

• *Crafting*

I write two pages of arrant nonsense, after straining; I write variations of every sentence; compromises; bad shots; possibilities; till my writing book is like a lunatic's dream.
Virginia Woolf

Not inspiration, practice.
Rebecca Harding Davis

Into the Labyrinth
Sue Stewart

I work directly on to the typewriter from first draft to last, and have no notebook. I get through sheaves of rough paper, some of which is donated by a friend with a colourful sense of humour: blue, green and yellow sheets marked the seasons one year. When a poem is finished I gather the drafts together, staple them and date the top (completed) poem. For some poems the drafting can be labyrinthine, for others a clear run, so I've taken four – 'Sleeping On', 'Hansel's Birthday', 'Inside Wolf' and 'Bluebells' – to show something of these differences, and in each case I'll show the completed poem first.

SLEEPING ON

There is no truth in your book of splinters:
the pages hinge on a faulty recall
of a rusting spinney, timeless gold-leaf.
The sycamore key is long faded, locked
in the humus of a fictional wood.

True, my door is open to the brave:
the deathless spider, more at home than I,
her limp hammock straddling my virgin posts.
Mice soon lose their fear, avoiding only
my breath as they propagate, ransacking
the house as their parents did before them.

But if I can help it, I do not dream.
Brambles know my ways, and comfortable oaks.
And I theirs: the creak of February joints,
the exact angle they allow the wind.
There'll be no gust let through, him in its wake,
no quickening, or sluice-gate lids opening

as the final chapter breathes to a close,
not the look of eyes that have known me or lips
the colour of mine, so recently met.

'Sleeping On' was rather unusual in that I didn't have a clue what it was about when I started it. I was trying to catch a mood, a feeling of melancholy and patience in an other-worldly setting, so I began by just writing a few lines, playing around with some words to see what would come. The setting focused slowly as a spinney, a branches' lean-to, humus on the forest floor. When an oaken door and spiders turned up, I found what I was looking for: Sleeping Beauty. In the final poem, by a sort of mirror process, I wanted the identity of the sleeper to become clear only as the poem progressed, ending on the definitive fairy-tale kiss (or denial of it). In this way I hoped to humanise the voice, make it closer, more personal, rather than simply an identifiable character, an 'other'.

Once I'd got the first draft down I tried to strip childhood associations from the story, and see it from a different angle. For instance, what if the Princess, coming out of her long sleep, had lost her reason? She was after all waking from a coma. If she had woken, would she have known about it? Or would sleep have so enveloped her that waking seemed like dreaming?

Or perhaps the Prince never arrived. In the story, he was saved only by impeccable timing. The 100 years expired just as he approached the brambles, which then gave way for him. The implication is that he was punctual because he was perfect and could read the signs – the right man at the right time. What if he'd been the right man in a hurry, or is this a contradiction in terms?

I wondered what the deeper meaning of the fairy-tale might be, its psychology. The curse on the Princess had come from the thirteenth fairy, the 'uninvited' one at the feast. If we take the Jungian premise that all characters in dream or myth represent different facets of the personality, what are we to make of this thirteenth fairy? Does she represent all that is unacceptable, repressed, 'uninvited' in the Princess – that is, her subconscious, or shadow self (or, to use the Jungian term, her animus)? And does the Princess need to accept the animus in order to have a balanced psyche, an integrated life? Is the Prince as her opposite a further symbol for animus, a second chance as it were, and does his kiss signify resolution?

Many other interpretations could be offered, but what I wanted to do in the poem was the opposite of conclude; cast doubt. I wanted to leave the Prince's arrival in question. The Princess says he did not arrive, but her series of negatives at the end reinforce the ambiguity, a case of protesting too much. It also, hopefully, prompts the question: how does she know what 'didn't' happen, in such detail, unless it did happen?

But this analysis didn't begin the poem, or even propel it: it rode in tandem, very much on the back seat.

The first draft looked like this:

```
1st draft
```

Sleeping On

In my book of gold-leaf there are no secrets. *but splintered*

embossed contents
The ~~pages~~ hint at ~~a~~ memory, *a rusting spinney,* its
~~where like attracts like~~ the branches lean-to *an active* ~~feat~~
~~offering no more than privacy.~~
                                            sycamore's
The ~~skeleton~~ keys ~~of the sycamore~~
are long faded, ~~locked in the humus of a forest floor~~
~~Now the burnished page waits for my impression,~~
~~the saving grace of Thursday's child~~

locked in the rustic mould: humus on the forest floor.
                              taken
While my ~~door~~ is always open to callers:
the ~~a~~ spider ~~has made one corner all her own,~~ *More at home than I,*
its angles glossed over ~~and over~~
just as I'd turn in the page's corner
rendering ~~the~~ paper weaker each time until
~~it resembles not so much wood, thinly spliced, as silk~~

her   *webbed*   *virgin*
~~and the~~ ~~mice and spiders labour under and over,~~ *ng my*
~~great~~ hammocks ~~of webs~~ straddle ~~the~~ (four) posts,
The mice have lost all fear, avoiding only my breath
as they propagate.

~~I do not dream~~

If I can help it, I do not dream:
~~though the picture book assails me~~   *know my ways,*
~~inescapable~~ The ~~with barbed-wire~~ brambles ~~and~~ overgrown oaks.
There'll be ~~no~~   ~~A~~ breath of fresh air pulling him in its wake   *the*
no ~~then~~ a quickening, ~~the~~ sluice-gate of my lids opening,
not the look of eyes that have known me,
or lips the colour of mine, so recently met.

*And I theirs:
enough to ignore
the ancient rendering
The proposed
rendering it
only their
creaky joints*

*And I theirs: the creak of their joints, the
exact angle they allow the wind*

I decided on the series of negatives at this stage, and got rid of all the tatt in the first and second stanzas. The second draft honed in on the first stanza:

2nd draft

[handwritten draft of poem:]

Splinters: with

There is no truth / In In my book of gold-leaf are no secrets.
gold-leaf / The page splinters, on its own memory, hinges on lean-out only
a rusting spinney, its branches' lean-to.
an active privacy.   is
Its   The sycamore's keys are long faded,
locked in the rustic mould,
The humus on the forest floor.
a

Further drafts shaped the piece, and by the fourth I'd decided on a syllabic count of ten. I left the metre to itself until the fifth draft, when I marked it down. This was retrospective, as I wanted to see if any natural pattern had emerged. By the sixth draft the poem was almost finished.

Dilemma over one word in the second stanza led to a seventh and final draft. I decided eventually on 'limp' so as to add to the inherent connotations of the line.

The second poem, 'Hansel's Birthday', rather took me by surprise because Hansel and Grethel had never been one of my favourite stories. I found myself jotting down 'Grethel Rethinks' on my pad of up-and-coming ideas, but thought it could wait. I left it there, wrote the second poem in the fairy-tale sequence, 'Cinders', and started to think about the third. I wanted to see what I could do with the Little Red Riding Hood story, but Grethel was still trying to get through. I reached for Grimms'.

The story, compressed, is this: Hansel and the orphan Grethel are twice led into the wood by Hansel's father, a poor woodcutter, and left to their fate. But Hansel leaves a trail, first of pebbles, then of crumbs, so they can find their way home again. The second ruse is unsuccessful, as the birds eat all the crumbs, forcing the couple to roam the wood in search of a way out. When they come across a hut made of bread with

barley-sugar windows and a roof of cake, they can hardly believe their
luck, and fall to rapturous eating. Thus the spiteful fairy traps them,
and a series of adventures begins. They steal the fairy's wand and pipe,
and metamorphose into new forms in order to trick her: Hansel
changes into a lake, Grethel into a swan, Grethel into a rose, Hansel
into a fawn ... I was hooked. Thing was, they were having so much fun
I wondered how it compared with their rather monotonous 'happy-
ever-after' life, so I decided to take this approach in the poem:

HANSEL'S BIRTHDAY

Restless in the night, I find you harking back
to the old days of making do, on the hoof.
Dawn is a hunter and you run the gamut,
a fawn who limps his arrowed dream to my lap.

If I told you I'd baked a cake you'd mimic
the lake's transparent smile, make castles vanish
in mid-air like sand running free, running out,
and relive the barley-sugar's matchless kiss.

You were happier then, with berry and shrub,
chafing the plaited rushes of your lead.
Or piping the witch's tune, her five-mile step
no match for my stillness, the coiled entrapment

of a rose. Were we children when I, as swan,
skated the surface of your spilt mind's-eye?
Now your fingers dislodge a pebble as white
as a moon or scouter's palm your crumbs flew from

and I wear red to match the florist's bundle,
tempting you nearer the party by tugging
your voluminous sleeve, adopted sister,
familiar wife, as full of love as ever.

The first draft, by comparison, looked like this:

1st draft

Hansel's Birthday

8   Restless in the night, I find you
9   supping the water's edge at seven.
11 Dawn was a hand's span and you ran the gamut;
10 again a fawn / limping the arrowed dream
5   to my ready door.

8   If I told you I'd baked a cake
8   you'd mimic the lake's glassy smile,
11 silencing the Adam's apple of your laugh.
9   Our castle in the air's a soaked heap
8   of sand, running dry, running out.

12 You were happier in t~~he nuts and berries~~ *our tenderberry* time,
11 I pulling the plaited rushes of your lead,
11 *piping* or ~~catching~~ the witch's tune, her merry dance
10 no match for my stillness, the entrapment
11 of a rose. Were we children when I, as swan,
10 skated the surface of your spilt mind's-eye?
10 Such pride! Now your fingers loosen and place
9   crumbs on the path like ~~sand grain~~ / a scout's trail
5   to ~~be~~ find or be found. *by a slice of moon.*

9   And I, ~~pleading with~~ *tempting* you ~~to come~~ in from the cold,
11 tugging at your sleeve like a little sister
9   as full of love as she's always been.

I wrote down the syllabic count to see if there was any pattern trying to break through. I decided to go for the eleven-syllabic line and let the metre sort itself out for the moment.

At the sixth draft I decided to use rhyme. I'd been wanting to make more use of imperfect or dissonant rhyme for some time, liking the idea of its subtlety, and I felt this poem could use some structure. In some cases this meant changing the whole line, so as to incorporate rhyme whilst maintaining the syllabic count. By the seventh draft it was shaping up:

7th draft

Hansel's Birthday

Restless in the night, I find you harking back
to the old days of making do, on the hoof.
Dawn is a hunter and you run the gamut,
a fawn who limps his arrowed dream to my ~~door~~. lap.

If I told you I'd baked a cake you'd mimic
the lake's transparent smile, ~~have~~ make castles vanish
in mid-air like sand, running free, running out/,
~~Even talk of bread or barley-sugar hurts.~~

~~and~~ You were happier then, with berry and shrub,
chafing the plaited rushes of your lead.
Or piping the witch's tune, her five-mile step
no match for my stillness, the coiled entrapment

of a rose. Were we children when I, as swan,
skated the surface of your spilt mind's-eye?
Now your fingers dislodge a pebble ~~creamy~~ as white
as the moon or (the) crumbs of your scouter's trail
and I wear red to match/~~you~~, still the ~~hero~~
tempting you nearer the party by tugging
your voluminous sleeve, ~~the little~~ sister)
as full of love ~~and plans~~ as she's ever been.

[handwritten marginal annotations, partially legible:]

and would relive / you still taste
retrieving the matches / ...the barley sugar's fainttest / kiss

artist / faintest kiss

on/our/at / from.

a

scouter's palm you crumbs flew from / palm

track / cipher

the florist's / bundle,

turtle-dove / intended / devoted wife,
and blameless / guileless

adopted

You voluminous sleeve like a turtle-dove,
adopted sister, full of love as ever

·—|·—|·—|·—|·—|·—·

Then I came back to metre, putting asterisks against 'faulty' lines. I decided to leave these as they were because they had their own pattern. For instance, line seven was strictly speaking not-on, being a mash of iamb, trochee and monosyllabic feet. But it had its own rhythm: te TUM TUM, te TUM TUM, te TUM TUM, te TUM. Others that clashed were lines eleven and fourteen, which ended on three monosyllabic feet. The stress, though, seemed to be quite fruitful as it added a lumbering quality to 'five-mile step', a slow motion one to 'spilt mind's-eye'. This was more good luck than good management. At this stage I had to remind myself not to become a slave to form. I think I could quite easily have become over-zealous, so I tried instead to hold to the spirit of the poem.

No such strictures for the next poem, about Little Red Riding Hood – who was patient enough to wait until I'd finished with Hansel. It seemed to find itself very easily and went through only minor changes after the first draft.

I think at the back of my mind was a feeling about the wolf, that he might not be evil, or bad, or even hungry; and that Little Red Riding Hood might, similarly, not be saccharine, or helpless, or foolish, but that some effort at unification was being attempted in the story, and that the only violence was that perpetrated by outsiders, instilling fear. The wolf was, perhaps, another 'animus' figure, threatening only to those who refused to acknowledge him in themselves, or, in this case literally, themselves in him. The grandmother, of the old order, is afraid and colludes with the outsiders to escape. Little Red Riding Hood, being young, is fearless, and elects to stay with wolf to the death. The potency of her red hood suggests a sexual symbol and alludes to blood, reinforcing the tension between her youthful fertility and her wilful imprisonment.

The completed poem:

INSIDE WOLF

I lose a shoe on the way in, as sign – my one
mistake – then teeter on his tongue's root
and dive into cramped air, counting the pillars
of bone that arch and spool like a cocoon.

If I lie flat and stretch out my splayed feet
I can touch his ribs, play the concertina
of their breath. And then I know happiness,
held in a minor key or, as now, drumming thumbs
against the taut and ivory skin of their brow.

His panting chest has me to handle, dead weight
in the adjacent room. I squint straight ahead
but can't decipher one red from another,
untangle threads of satin warp, aortic weft.

And this is as I would have it, though a voice
tunnels from the other side, reassuring me
the hood is intact, that I am alive,
my grandmother also. They have plans
to make me fill his belly with stones,
drag his heavier heart to a glottal stop.

But wolf and me are in this blood bath
together. He arranges knowledge in a swan-song,
music I'll not let him suffer alone.
As womb is grave, I'll not come out
though the gamekeeper and granny
call over my body, each to each.

This was the first draft:

I ~~lost~~ my shoe on the way in , as sign: my one mistake
~~like all the best heroines, and there~~
~~the similarity ends.~~

his tongue's root

~~Hostage to fortune,~~ I teetered on ~~the brink~~
then dived into red air, counting the pillars
of bone that arched and spooled like a coccoon.
If I lie flat and stretch out my splayed hands,
I can touch his ribs, ~~feel their quick beat~~
feel the concertina of their breath.
And then I know happiness, cramped
in their ~~major~~ key, drumming fingers ~~now~~
        minor
against the taut skin of my brow.
His panting heart has me to handle,
~~almost a~~ dead weight in the adjacent room.
I squint straight ahead ~~at the middle distance,~~
but can't decipher ~~one red from another,~~
~~his aortic weft to my scarlet thread~~
        ~~snaking through~~

aortic weft ~~or scarlet~~ thread. warp
And this is as I would have it,
though hollow voices reach from the other side,
reassuring me the hood is intact, that I am
alive, my grandmother also. They have plans
to make me fill his belly with stones,
to drag his/heavier heart to a glottal stop.

But wolf and me are in this blood bath
together. ~~His night howls seer me~~
~~His~~
~~I'll be his~~
His moans run through me like a harp,
music I'll not let him suffer alone.
~~If this womb be my grave also,~~
As womb is grave, I'll not come out
though the gamekeeper/ and granny
call over my body, each to each.

Finally, another poem which went through very few changes. It was the first poem I wrote after the Book of Hours marathon and I think this had something to do with its easy lope. Relief, or something like it, sighed behind the lines. The finished poem:

BLUEBELLS

The bluebells have other ideas
waking limp from their pointed dream,
the analysis of vases.

Their ragged tint is more telling
than the restless prose I wrap them in,
comforting each one
as I snip its sticky fuse

stretching the flora like fingertips
to the east and west of windows,
frayed lips easing down
to kiss the sill.

They crave the teapot,
a larger pool to lean from
where tanin homely as loam
fosters their lilac sheaf

my kitchen's bulb
warming the surface
as a sun might.

The first draft sprawled a bit:

its triumph gifted triumph

And the bluebells, limp overnight,   *wafer*

~~as I am~~ from the pointed dream,

Their heads too low   ~~the heavy arms of sleep~~ folding   *the slow*

in upon themselves ~~to find a corner~~

a context   ~~where the probing stops.~~

a play without context

Their ragged tint is more ⟩

telling ~~dreamy~~/than the restless prose

I wrap them in,⌐ talking to each

as I snip its sticky ~~scent~~   ~~curves~~ *Jule*

~~using the curves,~~

the stretching flora/   *like my fingertips*

~~reaching~~ to the east and west

of windows, frayed lips

easing down to kiss the sill.

They last longer in a teapot,

a larger pool to lean from

I whispered   the ~~faint~~/tanin hue ~~reminding them~~   *echoing*

an echo of the damp loam ~~I plucked them from~~

my yellow anglepoise

~~like a~~ streamlined daffodil

my kitchen's bulb → lighting up the surface

~~as~~ a sun might.

I was trying to lengthen the lines too, but curiously enough, by the last draft, I found they were dwindling naturally towards the end of the poem, finishing with Old Faithful, the two-foot line. It was almost as though the lines had a good stretch at the beginning of the poem, as the bluebells 'woke', then collapsed inwards, to a reflective ending. I decided to leave the poem in peace, and consider it finished.

The Woman in the Tower: Notebook
Rosalind Brackenbury

Here, I've taken the chronological development of one novel, which came out as *The Woman in the Tower*, as it appears in my journals of the time. It surprises me to find, on re-reading, how much work I did on this book, and for what a long time I lived with it.

I think its roots were here:

Jan '77: I go on with the novel (*A Superstitious Age*) and imagine in brief flashes another, made up of fragments, pure, clear, real, plotless, or with the plot *not stated*, a world of relation and movement without beginning or end; yes, I must do this one just for myself, just for the pleasure of it.

And again:

Realisation – that this book is in the margin of the other, typed one, & if I have a true and unselfconscious voice, it's here. I see a possibility of using this idea for another book, the free, fluid, ideal, diverse, differentiating one. Which will tell no story but be in the margin of the story.

At the time, I was reading a lot of French fiction, and I think the idea of the *marginale*, or the text existing beside the official text, fascinated me. I was also trying to get away from the novel as it is supposed to be written; my previous novel had seemed to me to be a 'proper' novel – constructed, rather than evolved. (Incidentally, the 'proper' novels are the ones which have brought me 'success' and any money which I have earned from writing.)

Oct. '78. The strong idea of a novel. Two people talking about a third and thence about themselves. But with the characters not just single personalities – somehow to be open, flexible. The idea of one person as a substitute for another. I want a controlled but

103

loose link between 2 or 3 stories. Hearing just 5 minutes of the
Truffaut film last night, I think now, the novel *is* for telling a
story. The story is what's compelling & I want to do this stripped
of all that's extraneous and that I've so indulged in. But who tells
it, and how, is essential. I write this all down fast on Sun.
morning after breakfast as it feels I must hang on to this
conviction I had early a.m. – of how to do it, & that I can. Dare
to do what's unfashionable, just because I want to dare some of
the insights poetry gives me. Can I tell a simple story so that it
compels, in the way Truffaut does, for example? He says 'They
did not meet for 15 years' and one feels all the poignancy of it.
(Thoughts: 'She said you were the one person she wanted to see.'
'Did he love her?' And 'What do men feel? Is it qualitatively
different?')

I think I was playing with the idea of the seemingly innocent
question, or phrase, which opens up the story. I wanted, not
complexity of plot, but simplicity, with a complexity of feeling. As the
novel stood, in the end, it included two stories, two love-affairs, told in
such a way that they intertwined. And I think in the 'flashback'
love-story, I achieved some of this simplicity.

Back to the journal:

1.   The basic story.
2.   The two who discuss it. One is having a love-affair and wants
to know – what happens? As if she can extrapolate from another
woman's life.
3.   Made up of conversation, one at a time telling the story, to
catch the compellingness, 'once upon a time', of narrative. Keep
narration simple. Relationship between two speakers? This v.
important – a growing mutual trust. It occurs to me that they
might love the same man. Where women's relationships with each
other fall apart is in this situation; can one go beyond it?

A thought: all men are either husbands or brothers, i.e. the
relationship is either allowed or incestuous, inherently.

Start with little 'given', see what grows. Don't be afraid of this
one, of open-endedness, of it being 'a woman's book', telling
what it's like when men aren't there. I want a sort of generosity
between them.

(Is it possible to love two men? If you have enough energy.
What is usually limited is not love, but energy.)

Now I want to start, but no time left today. Perhaps I'll let it build up and intensify in my head, and jot only.

Here I see the usefulness of the journal to me, to work things out when I did not have time to write at more length. These notes are like signposts, showing me where to go next, so that when I next sit down to write, I have some idea where I am going, and do not have to start 'cold'. I see here that my original idea was to do with women loving the same man – an idea which I have explored in later novels but that what took precedence in the end was a story based on the historical difference between what could take place in the 1940s and in the 1970s: the similarity of situation, and the changing mores and possibilities.

Nov. 7th. '78. The novel — or will it remain a story? Sexual obsession opening up into a different kind of love, freed of the culture's patterns. I envisage a long, slow development in her of the ability to feel. (Sleeping beauty motif.) At the end, she's alone.
Distancing. Teilhard de Chardin's idea about evolution & the great changes between generations. She's a person in transition, evolving. 'Realistic' passages – about her falling in love with him, sex, the telephone etc. 'Detached' passages – seeing her as an isolated creature, as though under a microscope. What is her relation to the culture that produced her? What I want: that one should both believe in her & care about her as a real person, but see her not just as an individual but part of a whole changing scene.

Dec. 5th. Thinking of K. 'Live it through.' '*Be* stuck.' 'You *are* time.' I hear her voice so clearly – have to evoke her for myself – but still have her voice and her words & that extraordinary, no, unique view of life which means no escape, but strength. Thoughts of writing about K's attitudes to life and love – the debate being I suppose about whether one suffers in silence or not. Starting with her in hospital, working backwards maybe through the scenes, our relationship, hers with F., mine with M. But too soon perhaps.

Here, I notice the merging of my own theories and wishes about what sort of a novel this could be, the tone etc., with an actual real-life story, belonging to someone who was close to me. The 'too soon perhaps' seems to mark some unease about actually tackling this. The closer the fictional comes to lived experience, the more scary it gets; here I feel close to the cutting-edge, and feel both alarmed and elated.

Oct. 29th '79. A log fire, and Dinu Lipatti playing Bach. I get out my bits of writing, get closer to the knowledge that I have to dare, scare myself, do what's frightening me – to write the story of K's and my friendship, the 2 love-affairs, love and death; to write it plainly, without censorship – that would satisfy – to take the risk this music does. This evening sat with my head under a towel breathing in Friars' Balsam, feeling it all stream out of me, what I need to do. Of all the things I've done – plunge in there, closest to the dangerous truth. *Time*: I will give myself two hours a day.

Nov. 9th. Writing, in the attic (a good idea, private and undistracting). I go on, trying not to think about censoring myself, being acceptable, writing for an audience.

Dec. 11th. Done about 90 pp. but still find it bitty – each return to it difficult – tho' I'm saying things I want to say about women waiting & the whole 'in love' scene. Interweaving K. & 'I' in the present, he and she in the past.

Jan. 19th. '80. I work on, past p. 120 – don't know where I'm going exactly, but trust the writing for the moment.

Jan. 24th. Finished, or came to the end of, K's story. A sense of relief and peace about that. Last night came back to find M. sitting up a bit pale and weary looking but entranced in my book – 1st time for a long time. He says he likes it very much, that it's quite different from anything else I've done, that it *is* a novel in its own right – this surprised and delighted me.

Feb. 8th. Sent off the M S to Richard, thinking he won't think it does as a novel.

Feb. 26th. Talked a.m. to R. who loves *A Time To Speak* and wants to send it to Harvester. This again terrifies me. Where is the pleasure I used to get from such acclaim? I'm afraid again that this may be fantasy, a false turning, not my real way. Why? What is all this fear, I wonder? Intimately linked with 'what will people think?' and 'getting it right?'

Jul. 16th. Harvester interested in *A Time To Speak*. Why so much unease about it?'

Aug. 14th. Harvester have reservations about A.T.T.S. because of lack of money.

Jan. 15th. '81. Frisson of excitement as I unwrapped A.T.T.S.
from a parcel from Richard – saw my first words again. Never so
clear a knowledge of what's right for me. Henry Miller's remark
that a book one has written is a skin sloughed. What I want to do
now: develop K's story, move further if necessary away from the
factual truth – somehow less 'I' and more 'she'. It is her book.
Express the truth of what comes beyond the question – 'how to
get out of this impasse?'

Winston's remark yesterday that any novel that doesn't attempt
to say something about love & death is of necessity on a lower
plane than one that does.

Jan. 20th. Today at Waltham with J. She settled to draw from the
upstairs window at the back, while I worked on A.T.T.S.
downstairs at the table, a big wood fire lit in the hearth.

Feb. 3rd. Thoughts for novel (working here with J. today)
1.   Cut letters considerably, interspersed with comment.
2.   Move on to: his evasiveness – develop theme of Hyde in
London & how he affects their life – buying the house in town –
the whole story (uninterrupted?) till his death, her illness.
3.   Leading up through all scenes of me and her – going back to
her in hospital, the change of emphasis, death into life, upbeat at
the end.

Windy, changeable day here. I've just walked out in sun and
come back in a shower. J. talking of painting representationally
(as she's just done, from my porch) & then going home and being
able to abstract from the original *through* the first painting to get
what she wants. With the novel, a sense of all the balls up in the
air at once, various components all to be juggled. Tension,
excitement – will I be able to? Sureness underneath. Lovely
working here together, in harmony, both trying for something.

Mar. 5th. The novel in the post.

Mar. 13th. Richard writes me a gloomy note on the state of
publishing – things don't seem hopeful for A.T.T.S. Tolstoy's
conclusion that the only thing that matters is to write 'the truth'.
How hard – when at each step it seems one is uncovering a
different truth, discarding an old one that no longer fits.

Oct. 8th. Thoughts about A.T.T.S. – 2 years on from where I
started it:

1.   Simplify. Tell the story as directly as possible. Present time, hospital, 'Thomas and I' – up to restaurant scene and Mr Flynn.
2.   The love-story – right up to Hyde and the stroke.
3.   Present time again, the love story, ending at Christmas. I want it as clear and minimal as possible. Keep going, and finish this term.

Nov. 16th. And now – 10.30 – I've just finished the rewrite again of A.T.T.S. & it's quite a different book from before, because I am in it, & I've done the bridges with the present time relationships and I hope someone else likes it as much as I do! It seems to me to flow now & to have an assurance about it that it lacked before – in what I've put in and what I've left out.

Dec. 11th. Harvester 'seriously considering'.

Nov. 1st. '82. The T L S review of *The Woman in the Tower* 15.10.82 makes me see that I have actually achieved what I wanted in that book. But don't want to do anything now that doesn't have that intensity of lived experience. No more fabricating.

I hope that this conveys some of the experience of writing this particular book, From the 'idea' stage through many tortuous to-ings and fro-ings, rewritings and reconsiderings, right through to eventual publication and reading reviews. In picking out these pieces of journal, I can see clearly what mattered, and matters, to me: trusting my own thinking and purpose, being supported by other people, having enough time, not giving up when the going gets rough, working on a piece beyond the place where I feel easily satisfied with it (or nearly) or think that it might 'do'. My early unease about publication was, I think now, to do with the book not being really finished – it evidently needed that further rewrite, although it was painful to realise it at the time.

What happened to this novel once it was finished? I sold it to Harvester Press. I made no money out of it at all. It was well reviewed, and I had more letters and general response to it from individuals than to any of my other novels. It is now out of print, and unattainable. I have one copy of it left in the house, which I have lent to people until it is completely dog-eared. The American publisher who fell in love with it is out of a job. It is, I think, my favourite of all the books I have written, and I am glad to have done as much work on it as I did.

If I had not kept the journal, I would probably have forgotten much of this process, for with the book finished and in print, this skin was sloughed. What remains, always, is beginning on this same process all over again.

I Hope You Don't Think I'm Being Too Personal
Marcella Evaristi

My radio play, called *The Hat*, evolved very curiously. In the winter of
1985 I was suffering from insomnia and exhausted. I was living by
myself and, because I was unhappy, in the middle of a bleak marital
separation, I was desperate to work. Imagine the phrase 'She threw
herself into her work' was a mirror; well, I cherished and polished it
but it refused to reflect me. Tiredness was part of the problem but not
its heart. The problem was the man and myself. I felt no desire to write
autobiographically 'about' it. In fact I castigated myself for being so
bound up with love. Love, love, love. I was proving Byron right. *'Twas*
my whole existence, when it came down to it. Love and betrayal and
sleepless nights and despair. And I cringe to write it now just as I
cringed from writing about it then. So, turning away from this cloying
personal world and mustering my intelligence and my resilience, my
humour and my sense of a fulsome whole world 'out there', mustering
all that, there I was, with all of it mustered, staring at the ceiling, quite
incapacitated, very scared. And very awake. I tried reading; I faced a
different version of the same problem. I couldn't get involved with the
'out there' books. The factual, the historical belittled my concerns
without firing my enthusiasm; whilst the brave books of the heart
telling of human need and passion and loss – the sore, ordinary,
important stuff – those books belittled me even more. Now I think, fair
enough, that time was for mourning, it was too early for my story to
become *another* story. Hardly surprising the damp Kleenex didn't
magically metamorphose into Marcella's miraculous novella, from
pain to prose-for-posterity in the twinkling of a red eye. But that's
now.

So there I was, as I said, wide awake and staring at the ceiling;
reading was out, working was out, and there were hours to go till
morning. So I began to draw and it kept me sane. All right, if you're
wincing at the near-madness talk, it *felt* as if it kept me sane. The

drawings were like cartoons with the odd sentence floating underneath. Wry but not sentimental. The gaps between the words weren't painful, for the writing was no more important than the images. A girl in a cloche hat and the words 'Crispin never liked my hat'. Crispin. Not a name to break your heart over in real life. Heartbreak in inverted commas. So when Crispin sets the story going by rejecting the girl in the cloche hat, and she tries to be brave and worldly and her 'mustering' business is all focused on her hat, you are quite happy to follow her. Writing/drawing the story, I was sort of off the hook. Passing the time with a doodle of a demi-monde world where a jilted girl's see-if-I-care night ends up with her sleeping with one man and then another. ('Imagine that' – is her only comment.)

The second man assumes she is a whore and leaves money by her hat. He had seemed like a new beginning, and this had silenced her in his company, which had contributed to the misunderstanding. This experience doesn't cause her to overdose or phone her friends or even tell us what she feels. The little face just looks at us from under the rim. The few words tell us what a strange night it has been and that she has resolved to keep it under her hat.

I went back to the story again and again. I worked on the drawings, and reduced the words to the minimum. Within its modest terms, the thing worked. In the middle of the mess, there was something I was pleased with. (Minor key. Keeping my hand in. Reminding me of childhood, the excitement of crayons and cartridge paper.) As for myself, I didn't overdose either, though I did phone my friends and, indeed, told them how I felt. Eventually, the insomnia went. The marriage healed. Other projects were embarked on.

Later I was asked if I had any ideas for a radio play, so I was raking around for one. I had done radio plays before but they were always adaptations of my stage plays. I'd never written for the medium directly, as it were. The Hat kept nudging other ideas away. Yet I kept thinking I must be mad trying to turn an eccentric little cartoon, an illustrated *very* short story, into a radio play. One aspect I thought I might pick up on was the way the heroine's hat changed its appearance depending on her mood, on how she felt herself judged. At times the hat was a pathetic little carbuncle, at other times it was wonderfully raffish. But that's not much is it? I thought. Yet The Hat would neither go away, nor would it become a play. Its aspects were all out of proportion for a play. I didn't see the two men she slept with as characters for instance, I couldn't see them *becoming* any more than they were. I wasn't interested in an arbitrary picaresque adventure. I needed a story.

The setting was to be Paris, 1920. Marianne, the heroine, became an artist's model; Crispin, the artist who leaves her. Marianne has been the model for his acclaimed collage and the picture after she has been dismissed begins to transform itself from a Dadaist collage into a naturalistic picture of a girl wearing a hat. When Marianne had changed into a more outrageous, less clinging creature, the picture began to approximate to her old image. New plates on sticks appeared and the play began to take shape. In the surreal world of the play, the objects surrounding Marianne came to life; she talked to her mirror and confided in her hat, then realised what she was doing, then wondered if she were going mad with jealousy. Crispin had a new, less 'needy' lover. A model, too, called Katya:

Marianne: (To her hat) Please. I beg you. Please don't speak to me. In other circumstances, perhaps, but not today. I must be clear-headed.

Hat: I am very glad to hear that, I can tell you, You always angle me best when you're feeling in the least certain about anything. But you're confusing 'clear-headed' with *bare*-headed. Please come over here and collect me.

Marianne: Be quiet!

Hat: Of course. I am afraid I misunderstood you. I thought you realised we suited each other perfectly, but no, of course, Crispin reviled me so you are happy to let the wind take me. Fine.

Marianne: Silence! Do you imagine I am the kind of woman to be bullied by fabric? Ha ha ha!

Hat: As you wish. I'll face rejection perfectly well, unlike some not a hundred miles from here I could mention. Loyalty, when unreciprocated, does sit so badly on the truly stylish. Forget it. Walk on. The likelihood is that I shall be pounced on by some wonderfully unconventional creature who will have no qualms at all when it comes to pure-chancing on a hat/ a Kat/ya Katya.

Marianne: Ha. Just let her try to go home to my old home wearing you. Crispin hates you. She'll get no compliments for all her unconventionality.

Hat: She won't care.

Marianne: She won't?

Hat: Not in the least. And Crispin will love/that/that/Katya.

Marianne: Oh damn his eyes! His almond-shaped long-lashed kingfisher-blue eyes!

Hat: Oh flock and linen, I've lost her! Psst! Please! Marianne! I'm choking with dust. Please, don't cry but I was so hurt, please don't walk on! I'm inching towards the gutter.

Marianne: Hold on. There. Let's sit down here, at this table shall we?

Hat: Makes no odds to me where you sit, now that I'm firmly on your head again.

Marianne: You've changed your tune now that you are no longer abandoned.

Hat: Well, that's only human.

Marianne: You think you're human?

Hat: You think I'm talking?

With the benefit of hindsight, I can trace much of this back, not just to the original story, but to the emotional atmosphere of writing that story. I can see that a great deal of it was 'there' from the beginning. The drawings and little story were a way of keeping things 'on hold'. My sense of incapacity when it came to the public, political 'out there' world is figured in the play through the hat's perspective on the world. He is explaining the journey he has taken to his present 'camp' style:

Marianne: What on earth is happening?

Hat: On what level?

Marianne: Mother of God.

Hat: If you ask what's happening near to hand, you've asked the right hat. But if you're asking on a wider level about world affairs, then I'm of no use to you.

Marianne, you must understand that two years of Crispin's path from indifference to unrelenting dislike has corroded me politically. Fact. The solidarity of silkworms. The economics of cotton. The plight of Panama. I still care, somewhere. But I have been so hurt, I cannot focus on *anything* that far away. I feel as if I have been dunked in some dreadful liquid and I've shrunk to half my size and that quite incomprehensibly I'm the only one that's realised. To everyone else I'm the same.

I can see that for the play to come into being, certain things had to happen. Distancing factors had to come into operation, so that the 'truth' of the world experienced could breathe and not be suffocated with autobiography, with literal facts. The complex narrative that evolved was – apart from its own aesthetic justification – also essential for the pain at the play's centre to come clean, to admit itself. (With dignity, I suppose, or style.) At the same time, Marianne's pain – and that of other characters in the play – the fact that the fate of a character was an emotional 'issue' for the audience, this caring, I think had the effect of militating against what one critic accurately described as being the pitfall of 'surrealist' plays:

> A surrealist play, much more than a surrealist painting, always runs the risk of a kind of brittle harshness which gets its kicks from its sense of its own inscrutability.*

When it works, and you look back on a piece, it all seems rather inevitable, I find. Which is right, of course, you *shouldn't* see the joins. It is odd that the joins are ultimately invisible to the author as well, though. I know I'm not the only one who looks back, and thinks, 'How on earth did I *do* that?' And, 'I'm very glad that worked but it seems no help at all in solving this new set of problems.'

Bit like life really, said the author from the middle of her latest dilemma-collection.

* Michael Mangan. *Plays International*, August 1988, p. 51.

A Question of Resistance
Nicki Jackowska

The way I cope is to write a mass of short stories, single pages,
and then weld it all together . . . My novel – its size, scope,
vastness, lives like a backdrop, strong and indistinct in my mind,
and then I dive in and carve a piece, often with quite new
characters (apparently). Only they end up being the same
characters in different aspects. I'm very suspicious of consistency.
One writes about the extraordinary in people, what they are
capable of even if they only do it in the fiction.

Letter from NJ to Philip Gross, 18 February 1988

Let me talk about my last novel, *The Islanders*. I think this book – or
the making of this book – embodies that tension between the 'frame',
or series of frames which are fixed and act as one's chart and series of
reference points, and the improvising of the scene or event within the
frame with the associated need for freedom. I am talking about
structure/skeleton, and invention in the moment.

I held quite rigidly to my Chapters, and I don't believe rigidity is
always a negative. It is necessary, sometimes, to be quite stubborn and
bolshy as a way of resisting the desire to dispense with discipline – just
as at other times one resists the rigidity, lets go. This pendulum swing
isn't easy, and it's not always clear what is necessary. I do know this –
that one can subvert oneself forever by constant change of position (in
the name of freedom) and achieve nothing. It is necessary to decide and
settle for *something*, and then play with one's freedom within that.

The Chapters of *The Islanders* are as follows:

PART I   BEFORE
1. Island
2. Framing
3. Rose

115

4. Bird
5. The Hut
6. Outside
7. Burnell
8. Storm-Trick

PART II   CROSSINGS
1. The Invention of Lucy
2. Dancing with Mister Big
3. Inside
4. Crossing
5. Gino
6. Vigil
7. Aftermath
8. Father Joseph Selby
9. The Retreat
10. R and the Woman's Head

PART III   TELLING
1. Cathedral
2. Out of Egypt
3. Tom's Land
4. Rumours
5. Nancy's Land
6. Those Were Pearls

You see, by creating this chart which is a kind of Odyssey, the theme of departure and return, the theme of witness, I made a string of starting points and holding points, and having committed *that* to the page, was then able to liberate myself from the weight of the whole book. (Not so for *From the Terrace*, which I'll come to in a minute).

The theme of Caroline's story is that all is not as it seems. She rejected the family she thought she was born into and pursued the Burnells as projections of freedom and wildness. Crossing the water is both real and metaphorical. Midway in Part II, Caroline takes the ferry from the Isle of Wight to the mainland. Before and after are a number of crossings (thresholds). I wanted each to have its own particular quality, so modified and manipulated the language to embody each experience. 'Dancing with Mister Big', for example, is an episode where Caroline first experiences the raw intrusion of rock 'n roll, and the equally raw intrusion of deliberately-sought sex under Shanklin pier (1958). I wanted that sequence to have a predatory quality, even if she wasn't 'forced'. Thus in the dance-hall watching Rose, we are prepared for this:

She sees how his face is inches away and how his mouth dives down and back, like pecking her.

Then Rose vanishes and Caroline is drawn out on to the seafront and down below the promenade:

Rose is panting, regular gasps, her white skirt bunched up round her waist. They're below the promenade among the struts and undersides of the pier. His jacket flaps like wings. He dives and pushes . . .

Then later, at the end:

Someone drew back a curtain on the raw edge of joining. He leaves before she knows it. . . . a thin cruel night, after so much penetration.

Cackling on the border, Aunt Doris pouring over Lily Carver, a magpie triumph.

Silence in which only water.

I want to take the character, myself, the reader, to the heart of experience. To do this, I must talk also about, or introduce, the *nature* of experience. And so I use images that are not only the immediate *literal* landscape (pier, stakes, water, fisherman), but also those that conjure the state of mind, the condition of experience. Caroline has previously visited a bird-park and seen an evil-looking bird, and fantasised his pursuit of her. So the bird-images hover. And the family crowd in, intrude, permissive or forbidding. This is a sixteen year old leaving home, enclosure, safety. There is, must always be, more in the moment than immediate events – history, attachments, expectations. Now it isn't possible to create this hinterland for all moments in a novel (it would stretch to infinity!), but it is possible to intensify and extend the climactic ones. The pivotal ones for your character. I am not, in this novel, interested in a detached narration which is merely a description of what is happening.

Not so in *From the Terrace*. In order to explore another mode (for myself), I have swung the new book into another configuration of space and relationship. Here the protagonist, Maggie, is number-one witness to her street and its doings. She uncovers many stories. She is like a detective with a notebook catching this and that fragment, detail. She does not go to the heart of it, but fidgets and lingers on the outside of many lives, haunted within herself by another Terrace in the mountains near Annecy, where men and women resisted invasion.

This book is about resistance. How it must range from a gentle 'no' to the rapid putting-on of armour-plating. (I am thinking of the rigorous resistance we now need, to refuse being *instructed* as to what we are, how we should behave, what kind of society we want, by the Thatcher government.)

Perhaps this will be Maggie's heart-experience, her touching the concentration, the life-and-death struggle of that battle in the mountains. This is growing in a different way, this book. I am in deep collaboration with Maggie over where she should go next. She opens unexpected wounds in others. Shies away from them in herself. The newly written sequence 'Pendulum' is probably the only piece of introspection in the book, and it will probably end it.

Here are some bones from another notebook, which became a thread in the weave of 'Pendulum'.

CONSTELLATION

Lulworth Cove, Aug 7–9, 1987

STAG – Celtic Word – Alford

STAG – outside Cistercian (Trappist) chapel
  French monks 1100's

Chapel-Cottage – blue ceiling – stars – single pointed window.   Wild flowers laid (2)
Six pebbles.

Frescos – pale pink/blue

Baskets – double geranium, large pebble path

Sheltered – vigilante – keeping watch outside the rifle-range (pump, well, sauna)/

Army – ownership of land (within their heads, not ours)

ENCLOSURE

Personal act of preservation 'Lit up'
Fossil Forest
Isle of Wight trees
Fossil-base.   Landslip.
Trees are aiming there.
Keeping watch outside the barbed-wire.
Gerard – what the body contains
Tangled garden outside

Sitting on bench in Chapel
Two sunflowers
The man in deep red shirt.

Christ-Stag

Resistance   To refuse to not-see
Resist blindness
Resist cul-de-sac   Resist *EROSION*

Should I talk about poems? There are so many different ways of crafting. I think a poem has to be worked over many times. First comes the quick and almost furtive gathering of various elements, motifs. Furtive, because something, someone might close down the flow – and this could be a real intrusion or a sudden perverse divergence within myself. So the first draft goes down first – fast and imperfect.

Then I look at it. Extend or cut, working on the level of meaning. How much do I want it to *say*? How overtly? ('A tendency to over-explain.')

All the lines or parts must resonate. Too literal imagery flattens it – too obscure imagery disconnects the reader. I work through for cliché, clumsy connections, over-use of linking words, private (only) references. Then the *sound* of it. Then it undergoes changes as long as I'm sending it out.

My poems are always on the way somewhere. But they also, at some point, become settled, and each word is right and *cannot* be changed. I do not hold off print until this perfection. For who shall determine this? I am interested also in the 'good *enough*' in my own and others' writing.

Let me emphasise what a wide range of completions there are: one poem took three years to gestate; *The Islanders* took three re-writes and was originally *Tom's Land* (about the father). 'Pendulum', a 9,000-word sequence, was written slowly, meticulously over two solid weeks, working every day.

The work, up to a point (being also the condition of one's energy, psyche, love), sets up its own imperatives. These must be met, for they are one's own.

No Discernible Life-model
Sue Roe

I am not sure exactly how I wrote my second novel, *Masquerade*. I have recorded the genesis of it here in this book, in 'Beginning to Write', and I simply recorded scenes one by one, until I had a number of them. All that seemed to link them, at first, was a common atmosphere. They didn't seem to fit together, nor could I see which ones I would keep and which I would discard, until about three or four years into the project.

After a while, you begin to invent. I actually 'hear' dialogue in my head, and need to get to the typewriter to get it down. Usually a moment in which I hear dialogue denotes a turning-point in the project; the introduction of a new theme, angle or aspect. I think it is true to say, looking back, that I needed to re-think myself – what I wanted, the direction I thought I was going in – in order to introduce fully what might be thought of as the sub-text or sub-plot of the novel. I needed to think myself into one of the parts, whereas the others I was able to invent – as it were – from the outside. I wrote the novel in two different locations, and revised it in a third. It sounds absurd, but an actual, geographical move affects the novel's development. I probably could not have finished it if I had moved house at the wrong moment.

I worked very hard, daily, on this novel. I regarded it as my main job, and I worked for a living to support it. I also needed to buy new clothes, listen to new music, drink quite a bit and talk a lot, especially to women friends, about the state of my heart, in order to nurture it along. I can see, in retrospect, how a relatively bohemian existence was important to me in maintaining the seriousness of this project. Because the novel itself – the actual writing – demanded tremendous self-discipline.

I think I began by writing my reflections, recording incidents and conversation, and then, critically, by introducing a completely invented character with no discernible life-model, who turned these reflections and incidents into fiction. The child I invented seemed able to do this. He was always there from the beginning, but how his personality was developed I don't know. I suppose he resembles me as a child, but I had no idea I had remembered so much about myself, and I cannot remember any real-life settings for his insights or for the incidents in which he is depicted. His vision is important, because it adds a dimension to the fiction which he has at least as much to do with as I do. (This will sound entirely obscure to anyone who has never tried to write a novel.) Jacob, the child, is absolutely his own person; I almost feel he helped me to write the novel. Also, I think he kept me company. Writing is almost intolerably lonely.

When I moved house the first time, a change in the novel took place, though not immediately. On my first day in the new house I sat in one of the empty rooms and recorded, quite spontaneously, two incidents from my early childhood. One I discarded; the other appears in the novel in a re-drafted form, and it was a very important turning-point because it introduced another atmosphere and another dimension into the novel. The incident I recorded was that of being taken, as a two-year-old child, to visit my grandmother. Both the child's and the grandmother's views filtered into the novel, and I began to think about history and the family and to realise that in *Masquerade* (it wasn't yet called that, incidentally) I wanted to write about blood-ties and the family, and broken connections, and the family-tree. And passion, and how this has power to break whole structures to pieces. To what extent the family-tree – this strange, arid-looking, untidy document – might constitute a façade, if hidden between the branches – as it were – there were much stronger, much more powerful, if undocumented connections.

At this point in the novel's progress, I also began to have regular meetings with another woman writer – as we got to know each other better, we talked less and less about writing and more and more about the state of our hearts : life, and love, and men. This friendship probably triggered the invention of another character, who resembles her not at all, but I became interested in the whole theme of women's friendship, which also became important to the novel's 'design'.

I am beginning to falter here, because I am conscious that this is beginning to read as though I am recounting that 'first this happened, then that happened', whereas in fact I didn't experience the process in this way at all. The novel was in no sense plotted, but at the same time I knew it was very important for it to have a strong plot, or story-line. The sequence of events would be important this time, because I was writing about history and the disclosing and concealing of stories –

more so than in my first novel, *Estella*, where I was exploring primarily, I think, ways of seeing and feeling. I told someone one day that this time I wanted to create a feeling of suspense. 'Why? What will the reader want to know?' came the response. I kept this in mind, too.

The 'plot' evolved as the narrative developed, but at the same time I had to keep checking that it all still connected. The drafts of the novel were interspersed with notes, which I wrote most days prior to writing the actual novel. I always set up the conditions as though I were about to write; slotted in a new piece of paper, and headed it, *Novel II: Notes.* Then I wrote notes to myself on how what I had just written would connect with what I was about to write, and how those things would connect with the whole, and then I carried on writing until what I was writing ceased to be *Notes* and had filtered into the fiction. I found this a good mechanism which, as far as I can remember, I never used with the first novel. I would just remind myself what I was doing, then, if I went on reminding myself for long enough (usually, for about a page and a half), it would 'magically' turn into what I was actually doing. This sort of thing:

> The point about the woman on the métro, on whom I am basing Lauretta, is that she is so very sealed, so very contained. What interests me about her is the notion that whatever she held in check would be as powerful as the façade she had erected to disguise it. And I could tell that her façade was very strong . . .

> Masquerades. Dumb shows. Am I being over-dramatic? I don't think so, because, interestingly enough, I am beginning to catch this mood of Lauretta's myself. This is what happens when your character begins to take on a life of her own: you begin to catch the mood, exist in the same psychological dimension. Or perhaps it is the other way round: perhaps you lend your character the emotional and psychological resources which are associated for you, the writer, with the circumstances you are inventing . . .

> I am going to try to resist this: this process of bequeathing to my characters – and particularly to Lauretta – the legacy of my own peculiarities. It is important that she should stand on her own two feet, without influence from me, though it does strike me, in passing, that perhaps the pressure of trying to make her exist so independently of me is one of the reasons for my having frozen her as I seem to have. After all, she can't *actually* exist without me . . .

But it is no good, this impossible confusion between myself and my own inventions, my own projections. What are projections; what are they made of, exactly? History and desire, I think: recollection and desire. The imagination fuses recollection and desire. Perhaps it is suggestive of desire in some ingenious disguise, this compulsion to invent, to project. Desire in some clever disguise: a disguise which is so convincing, so successful, that you may be spared the agony, perhaps, of having to come face to face with the real thing. Disguise which has for some reason deviated from its source, staging a reappearance in some other guise . . .

I will need to be extremely careful with her at this point. Her veneer of calm is falling away, but am I pulling it away too rapidly, too drastically? I wonder if I am wise, in having her think back so clearly at this point. Remembering is too dangerous; it is so maddeningly indiscriminating. These are very primal feelings I am giving her . . .

But I will just have to keep going, I think. I have very little choice, now, but to drive this rather odd, certainly very powerful interlude I have staged for her remorselessly through to its conclusion. I will try to avoid making her suffer too much, because she is supposed to be strong, at root. If this becomes unavoidable, I will just have to find a way of pulling her through . . .

It is sometimes difficult, when you are deep in the throes of a project, to distinguish this running narrative from the actual narrative of the novel. Your mind is deeply engaged, deeply involved, it is a profound source of ideas, but you have to find a way of keeping yourself separate, so that you can maintain your position as the controlling force, the controlling voice.

The most exciting moments of writing came when I didn't need to do this, and I think – though I am not sure about this – that the most powerful writing was done in a state of excitement, when I no longer had to ease myself into the writing in this way. In those moments, I 'saw' a scene, heard a dialogue, suddenly experienced, quite sharply and powerfully, the atmosphere of a place; I could see or hear, suddenly, what would happen next. These are moments very like those I have described in 'Beginning to Write', though rather than feeling like moments of instigation, germs of something impossibly large, spanning a large, unknown canvas, they felt distinctly like culminations, they came cohesively and completely. I was about to describe two such moments, and have just realised that they are both centred around the image of a piano. The piano is always recurring as an important image for me, I suppose because I learned to play when I was very young. These are very exhilarating moments – it is a very exciting moment in the development of the novel when you are suddenly able to 'see' a fictitious moment so clearly and in such detail. Suddenly it is as if some missing links are being magically supplied – and these are moments of almost spiritual insight, as if the work is being somehow consecrated.

There is a significant difference between such moments as these, when you suddenly know the novel is 'taking', and a process of reaching into a sort of mental filing cabinet on the novel, and pulling out extra data. For instance, I wanted to depict the child's arrival at school. This is another completely invented scene, but I thought the details out carefully, and put together a sort of invented identikit picture. I did this in a concentrated, measured way. I knew what I wanted to say, and I put together details which I hoped would convey it. This was very different from the experience I have just described, of flying to the typewriter with a completely realised scene already in your head.

There is another way, which I find happens about half-way through, though in the case of *Estella* I think the entire novel was written more or less like this: you find yourself living out your novel. This can begin in quite a detached, bemused sort of way, but it gradually takes you over. After a while, your own vision begins to appropriate you. The practical demands of your actual, day-to-day life become burdensome, then maddening. You are busy. You are inhabiting your novel. Like all aspects of this peculiar process, this is very difficult to describe convincingly, but it happens. Coming out of this is as peculiar as the experience of observing yourself as you enter into it.

The effort to craft or choreograph the novel – the design – becomes more demanding, after a while, than the actual 'writing' – indeed, the writing begins to issue out of this effort to craft the material. There are glimpses of scenes, but they are conceived as separate moments, not with their place in the novel's schema already intact. It is a constant struggle to shape these moments into significance, a ceaselessly demanding effort of precision, and it feels like a skill which is different in kind from the skill it requires to write the scenes. Like the difference, perhaps – I don't know – between writing a play and staging it;

between scripting and directing a film. There is – there must be – as it were 'behind' the novel a continuum of meaning which produces the scenes in the first place, but the effort to establish a cohesive narrative structure which will make a 'story', or make the material accessible to a reader, is taxing: a form of crafting which has to be learned all over again each time, with each new piece of work. I have no idea how it is done; I feel it – painstakingly and gradually and differently each time – into place.

A Realm of Characters
Hélène Cixous

I have two types of writing. I write with two hands. I have one theatrical hand and one fictional hand and they are completely different. They are two completely different processes. The only thing that joins them together is the fact that I am the writer and that, as a writer, I work on language, but everything else, the time-scale, the format, the frame of writing, is completely different. When I write fiction, I let my meaning gather slowly, I give my reader as long as she needs to understand. In the theatre, my writing must be efficient, there must be an immediate explosion of meaning. The spectator has three hours, whereas a reader has the whole of eternity if she wishes. Theatre is the art of urgency. Everything happens in the present. In the ten seconds after the actors are on stage the audience must have understood. In this sense I find writing for the theatre a perpetual apprenticeship. I have a tendency to hang about *en route*, pausing here, stopping to reflect there, and the theatre doesn't allow me to do this.

Theatre is the realm of characters. Perhaps this is why I like writing for the theatre so much. It is difficult, I am forced to renounce many things, but conversely I rejoice because it gives me the world of characters. Until quite recently none of my texts had characters in them. Writing for the theatre, I am haunted by a universe of fictitious but real people. It's the strangest, most magical experience. I live, inhabited by my characters, who give me the same feelings real people give me, except that they live inside me, I am their home. There are those I detest, those I rejoice in, those who make me laugh; some who exasperate me, others I love and admire. They are characters full of colour who tell me their lives. I note down everything they say. I write as quickly as I can, trying to get everything down. I listen for their voices, through their conflicts, their encounters, their struggles. Once I have noted everything down, I begin to work on what they told me.

This second stage, in which I work solely on language, is the same for both theatrical and fictional writing.

If one were able to film the heart of a playwright at the time of writing it would be a most extraordinary sight. For one can give these characters enormous richness, all the richness and potential all of us have but which becomes crushed and thwarted in the onslaught of everyday life. In the theatre, we are no longer in the realm of the banal. I don't believe we can mobilise people in order to recount platitudes. I'm looking to write the essential, and this is what the characters who inhabit me, talk to me, sing to me, help me to achieve.

My last two plays were written in conjunction with the Théâtre du Soleil, and this had a strong determining influence on the writing of the texts. In each case Ariane Mnouchkine (the director of the Théâtre du Soleil) and I lived through a period of latency in which we discussed a number of different possibilities, searching for a theme which would correspond to the needs of the Théâtre du Soleil and provide sufficient energy and inspiration for me. In both cases a number of hypotheses presented themselves and were rejected either by me or Ariane.

Once the general subject-area has been agreed, at this point I set off. I set off in search of my story. For both *Sihanouk** and *Indiade*** I began with long months of historic research. I have always envied Shakespeare who was able to draw on the chronicles of Plutarch and Holinshed for the subject-matter of his historic tragedies, but as far as contemporary history is concerned, these chronicles don't exist. I was first of all obliged to become the chronicler of my story. And this task turned out to be a handicap. I emerged from months of painstaking historic research weighed down with documents and facts, and I then found I had to fight against this great mass of accumulated knowledge in order to be able to write.

Once I start work on the text, I write slowly and at length. For both *Sihanouk* and *Indiade* the troup began rehearsals before I had finished the text. The period of rehearsal at the Théâtre du Soleil is always very long since Ariane gives the actors as much time as they need to work on a play. During rehearsals thousands of things happen which bring about changes in the play. Not in the text, the text stays the same. But in the overall timing and construction of the play. For instance, no writer can say in advance exactly how long a scene will take. A scene

---

* *L'Histoire terrible mais inachevée de Noradom Sihanouk roi du Cambodge*, Théâtre du Soleil, Paris, 1985.
***L'Indiade ou l'Inde de leurs rêves*, Théâtre du Soleil, Paris, 1987.

may be played more or less slowly, and scene-changes can dictate as much as twenty minutes of extra space. So when I write, I write with plenty of breadth. I write without worrying about time, concentrating on the heart of each scene, on giving the scene and the characters everything they need in order to live. Then, as rehearsals get under way, I cut. So there are always several versions of the play. And the original version is always at least one and a half times as long as the version which is published.

Understanding Structure
Emma Tennant

I had many years of stuffing large, unfinished manuscripts under my bed, until finally I met the science-fiction writer Michael Moorcock who told me: 'You don't understand how to structure things. You have 160 pages divided into four parts, labelled "introduction of characters", "development of characters", and so on.' He wrote it all out for me with coloured pens, and I'm eternally grateful, and always try to tell people that you have to become very humble and think: here are my 160 pages, I'm going to split it into parts, and then it's not so frightening. If you tell yourself, 'Here are my first ten pages, and in my first ten pages I must introduce, say, half my characters,' then you've already got something to do, introducing your characters in situations which show what they're like. This will then automatically lead you to think about the development of what's going to happen. Although this sounds so crass and crude, and as if it only belonged to a rather child-like science fiction, it can get a writer going, and away from that inchoate terror of a mountain of white paper. It's a general formula which makes you do it.

I make lots and lots of notes, and do a rough plan of the whole thing before I start. Then, as I go along, my notes become more detailed, and I can tell what the next day's bit and the day after's bit is likely to be. I think it's a mistake to make too detailed a plan before you start, because then you think, 'Oh god, it's changing, and I don't want it to,' I think it's much better to do it as you go along. You have to know the overall length, the sort of tense you're going to use, and the general time-span of your book. You've got to ask yourself, 'Does my book start in June 1988 and finish in July 1989, or does it take place in a weekend?' Of course it's perfectly possible to reply, 'Well, I'll take my characters up to there, and then I'll jump three years, and something will have happened in the meantime,' but you must know at least that much, otherwise you can get very badly trapped in the structure indeed.

Shaping the Intent
Amryl Johnson

(He?)
Leroy/walked ahead
For weeks
I had followed
staring hard at khaki
stretched by fists clenched/tight
A limp noose
of silky stripes
The sun clung to my (own) neck
teeth bit (hard)
relaxing within spasms of seconds
then tightening to bite
Its grip relentless

For weeks
I had followed
A shadow within a shadow
As devoted as my own
more rigid/thinking
moving at an uncertain pace

That was part of the first draft of my poem 'Tracks'. It would first have been written in pencil, on ruled foolscap, on every other line. The shorthand is as follows: / means indecision about a line-break. I could not make up my mind whether or not the word which follows should begin the next line. Anything in brackets, for example (own) and (hard), means I have not decided whether to leave the word in the poem or exclude it all together. (He) Leroy means the finished poem may or may not begin with the name Leroy. If it doesn't begin with 'Leroy' then it will begin with the word 'He'. This shorthand is one I always encourage my students to use. It is very straightforward. Rather than waste time deliberating on the exact word or phrase, put it (or them) in brackets on the line above. Go back to it when you work on your second draft. Too much time wasted in indecision leaves you in danger of the inspiration dissipating altogether. Get it down on paper as quickly as you can. Read through what you have done very carefully before beginning work on the second draft. Better yet, put it away for a few days before working on the second draft. Going back to it with a fresh eye creates good breathing space. There is always a danger of becoming too engrossed in what you are doing and not being able to see the wood for the trees. Going back to it after a few days helps you to look at any creative piece more objectively.

A lot of what I have just said applies to how I approach both prose and poetry. There is, however, one important difference. The concise nature of poetry makes it imperative for me to capture the imagery without too much delay. There is less urgency when writing prose. Consequently, I can take my time and erase as I go along. The flexibility of prose allows me more room in which to manoeuvre.

> Tar spread on pebbles
> rounded by miles of action
> glistened in the afternoon sun
> languid within the confinement of parallel lines
> Steel
>
> I had followed
> For weeks I had followed
> staring hard at khaki stretched taut
> and the limp noose of silky stripes
> lifting with the breeze
>
> I had followed
> A shadow on tracks moving wearily
> towards a conclusion
> Tracks
> Soon, far left behind

This second draft of 'Tracks' found me, despite earlier determinations, opting for a different opening verse. No indecision about line-breaks, deliberations about words which should be omitted or even substituted. I had not, at this stage, given the poem a title. I do not give my poems titles until I have finished the final draft. I am firm about students not wasting time worrying about a title. The final poem may be so very different from the first draft that you will, in any case, want to change the title. Having said that, my recently completed collection of poems began with the title. The title of the collection consists of just one word. The word came to me out of the blue and it is such a *brilliant* word that I simply had to take the idea further. The poems are integral. The title spot-lights the various layers which fit together like pieces of a jigsaw. Each poem in the collection, however, is individually titled and these individual titles were not given until the poem itself was completed. All will be revealed in due course. I am intensely superstitious about revealing too much about any completed piece before publication.

It is possible that even after a poem is completed, you still cannot find a suitable title. This sometimes happens with students. It is important to give your work a title once it is completed, even if it means acknowledging that title as a tentative one. I feel sure that many poets have had to live with a completed piece, albeit on a temporary basis, called 'Untitled'. The problem arises if you find yourself for any length of time with more than one poem called 'Untitled'. Titles are necessary, if anything, as a source of reference. The easiest way to know which poem the other person's talking about. The alternative would be to describe. Less than satisfactory, to say the least. A poem may remain with a reader because of its title. For this reason, I am a great great believer in unusual titles. Wherever possible, try and get away from the mundane. My approach to titles marks yet another dividing-line between the way I approach poetry and the way I write prose.

When writing prose, I prefer to begin with a title. Titles are very inspirational. As with the poetry collection referred to earlier, a word, a phrase, a sentence may well be the first twinkling of light towards a piece of prose. I like to begin any prose piece with a title of some description because doing so gives me a pointer, a leader, a frame in which to hang my creativity. During the course of the various drafts, the title given to the prose may change. I will simply accept this. Titles provide me with an 'eye'. Because I remain with each prose draft for far longer than I work on each poem, it sometimes feels as if I am working in the dark. The title is my walking-stick.

The gap between my poetry and prose has narrowed over the years. I am aware that in many instances my creative writing style is poetic prose. This is because I have become increasingly concerned with what I am saying and the way I am saying it. I have also become even more aware of the pattern of words, the way the sentence is constructed. The incantation of words. By this, I am referring to the way the sentence sounds when it is read aloud.

New poets are sometimes nervous about shaping their work, deciding where one line should end and the next begin. In extreme cases, I encourage any student facing this dilemma to begin by writing the poem as a piece of prose. I suggest they read through it several times before deciding where they think the line-breaks should be. Having decided, they should use '/' before each word which is to begin the next line. They should copy the piece using the line-breaks sign (/) as a guide. It is possible that the shape of the writing on the page may still not satisfy. It is, however, a beginning because it comes closer to the poetic form than anything else they have attempted. They will then work on it and continue working on it until they feel satisfied that they have the makings of a poem. A published poet I know begins her work as prose then translates it to a poetic form, tightening the imagery with each consecutive draft. Once new writers have broken through the inhibition of thinking they cannot write a poem, they are truly on their way. By the same token, if a student is having problems in understanding a published poem, I encourage them to copy it as if it were prose. More often than not, they are able to make sense of it in this new light.

There is a difference between 'poetic prose' and 'prose which reads like poetry'. Poetry, like beauty, is to do with one's individual taste. Nevertheless, I believe that every novice poet eventually learns to tell the difference between the two forms of creative writing. They also need to continue paying close attention to the grouping of words on the page, clearly visualising the inspiration. While one idea may well lead to another, resulting in the finished work being markedly different from the original idea, losing track of what you are doing is not quite the same thing. If you let go of the reins, you need to have another set firmly in view. Otherwise, you will flounder.

As a writer, I believe you have to begin from the standpoint that your work is original. Regardless of whether the theme has been worked by other writers countless times before, you have to believe that your approach is unique. You have to believe that your version is going to be offering a different slant or interpretation from anything proposed before. You need to believe in what you are doing. It goes without saying that when a piece of work which was started with great enthusiasm remains unfinished, it does so because the writer has lost confidence in what she was doing.

I never accept a commission unless I feel confident and enthusiastic about it. If, after due consideration, there is even the slightest doubt in my mind, I will refuse it. I like to feel excited about my work. Enthusiasm is what sees me through. Whether it is face-to-face contact with students or on the page it is usually obvious. On the page, from the moment I roll up my sleeves to begin writing, the adrenalin is pumping. That first sentence is a powerful exclamation mark. An affirmation of everything I want my art to stand for.

Here are the completed first three verses of 'Tracks':

> For weeks I had followed
> staring hard at khaki stretched taut
> and a limp noose of silky stripes
> lifting with the breeze
>
> Tar spread on pebbles
> rounded by miles of action
> glistened in the afternoon sun
> languid within confinement of parallel lines.
> Steel
>
> I had followed
> A shadow on tracks moving wearily
> towards a conclusion
> Tracks
> Soon far left behind

The poem changed direction as my understanding of the incident became clearer. It came as a surprise to see how much closer it resembles the first draft than the second. I believe the very nature of the poem was responsible for this. The poem was my contribution to the publication brought out by a college where I had a Writer in Residence post recently. The theme was 'memories'. The memory I chose to write about took me back to my childhood in Trinidad. As a ten year old, I would walk along the railway lines with an older boy, Leroy, going home from school. Once, a train came hurtling towards us. It was the last time I walked home along the railway lines. I only just managed to leap out of the way in time. That would have been one of the last trains to use that line. By the end of that year, the railways on the island were defunct. Not long after the lines were closed, I left Trinidad to join my parents in this country. So much of the poem was to do with finalities. Things were coming to an end. Cessation. I felt unbelievably sad writing it and found myself going back over those early years, recalling things I had done and the people I knew then. It was like wheels within wheels, the constant churning of emotions. It is the first time it has happened but under the circumstances it really isn't too surprising. That first draft is the one born of original inspiration before you begin working, crafting it. So, no, in the final analysis I could understand why I should have remained faithful to the original draft.

The most crippling experience for any writer must surely be to feel that she ends up saying the same things as when she first started out. And saying them at the same pitch of awareness. While acknowledging that the one theme can, to some extent, be worked over and over again we have to remain constantly aware of incorporating an unusual enough slant. My next few books are all going to be set in the Caribbean but they are all going to be different one from each other. That is a promise!

Some Untidy Spot
Sylvia Kantaris*

Most poets know what it is like to sweat through draft after draft of a particularly stubborn poem, only to see it gradually dissolve in the working. Often, it is because we simply can't grasp where the poem is leading – perhaps because we are not yet ready to grasp. I find that I get sidetracked into cul-de-sac after cul-de-sac instead of keeping in the mainstream – or else I never quite manage to enter the mainstream in the first place. The times when I actually bring off a poem to my own satisfaction are very rare, and in those moments I feel I've received a gift. Occasionally, I end up faced with several apparently finished versions and don't know which, if any, is the 'right' one. Probably they are all faulty. You fall back on the old adage that it is better to travel than to arrive, and hope that you've at least learnt something from the journey.

I want to tell you about one of my journeys which lasted nearly two years, at the end of which I was left with several versions of what should have been one poem. Two versions have been published, but I don't think that is the end of the matter. If certain editors had a preference for this or that version, I don't think their preference necessarily invalidates the rest. Maybe they all need to be published together as variations on a theme?

The story of the poem (or poems) began in 1983 after a tragic accident in which the small son of a close friend was drowned. I was so shocked and moved that I wanted to write something, anything, that might seem worth saying to the parents of the child. I couldn't, of course, and had to resort to the usual letter of sympathy. It didn't stop there, though. After months of struggling to say something a bit less bland than that I merely sympathised, I surfaced with the following:

*Adapted from an article first published in *Prospice* 22, 1987.

SOME UNTIDY SPOT

(In memory of Meryon)

Tragedies happen anyhow, in corners, when other people
are working or just walking dully along,
As Auden said, thinking of Brueghel's Icarus
who fell into the water in the space between
two glances, and then into the painting, then the poem,
as if the whole Aegean was not wide enough
to hold the impact of the moment of his death.
But this poem is about your son
who was too young to fly like Icarus
and simply walked behind you on an ordinary path
along an ordinary river's edge
then wasn't on the path when you looked back.
So all the lives he might have lived slipped out of him
in ripples and were gone, to all appearances,
yet grow in circles which are not contained
by any accidental river-bank, or even
by the confines of your heart which held him
firmly, safe behind great dykes of love,
but couldn't ring the moment or the one untidy spot.

This was already about my fortieth draft, but my first *real* one. You
will see that the only way I could find to approach the tragedy was
obliquely, via reflecting mirrors. In order to avoid appearing to
appropriate a particular death for the purpose of a poem – the last
thing I wanted – I chose to reflect on Auden's 'Musée des Beaux Arts'
in which *he* reflects on Brueghel's painting, 'The Fall of Icarus'.

Early in 1984, I felt the poem might be ready for publication. The
editor I sent it to said he liked it but felt it was flawed, that it 'peters out
in poetic gestures after the words "you looked back". I thought you
should end it there,' he wrote, adding, 'but this would/might mean
changing the line "But this poem is about..." which I wasn't too keen
on either. Why not go "moment of his death. Your son" etc. and end at
"back"?' Poets get precious little feedback, so I was very grateful for
such detailed comment from an editor whose own poetry I like very
much, on the whole. I felt he was probably right. After a lot of finicking
with words, I made a two-verse poem out of the original, the first
stanza ending with 'death' and the second starting 'But this poem is
about your son ...' and ending with 'when you looked back'. I sent it

back to the editor in this new, abbreviated version, saying, 'I think it still isn't right.'

The editor replied quickly: 'Your compliance has made me greedy or cruel. You are right, the poem still isn't right. I think the reason is that if the second verse were filled out with a proper conclusion, it would be something about the nature of poetry rather than the death of a person, so that a slightly egotistical feeling would result. This is held back from, but perceptible. But supposing we trimmed it some more, back to "death"? How would that do? Probably not . . .' At this point he was foxed and thought perhaps I should just give it up as a poem that didn't quite work, but I persisted. I got deeply involved again and sent him a version in which the first stanza still ends at 'death', but the second is as follows:

> What circles of mythology contract
> on nowhere noticeable, some blank spot
> recorded on the retina. The sun still shone.
> Your child had not yet heard of Icarus,
> and simply walked behind you on an ordinary path
> along an ordinary river's edge
> then wasn't on the path when you looked back.

After a bit of doubt with regard to where this second verse could be cut, the editor eventually crossed it out completely, thereby sticking to his earlier notion that the poem should end on 'death' – substituting 'your death' for 'his death'. 'You'll sigh in exasperation,' he wrote, 'but I feel sometimes your poems need contracting, like an accordion with a picture painted on the side. No, that would need expanding, wouldn't it? (Unless the picture wasn't much good.) Please keep in touch over these.' ('These', by this stage, included a short poem called 'As Grass', which he liked almost entire.)

I finally agreed to end the poem at 'death' and have it closely followed by the other poem, 'As Grass', which, as he said, made exactly the right kind of follow-up to the curtailed version of 'Some Untidy Spot'. Reduced to its first seven lines, and with 'your death' instead of 'his death', it was published on the anniversary of Meryon's death. However, I did not feel I had yet done with the poem. It nagged me. I kept on staring at a print of Brueghel's painting and re-reading Auden's poem. At one stage I came up with the following:

Tragedies happen anyhow, in corners, when other people
are working or just walking dully along, as Auden said.
Some child is always skating on a pond
or dawdling on an ordinary path
along an ordinary river's edge. He understood
the blankness at the centre of Brueghel's *Icarus*,
the way the eyes sheer off and tack but will not fix on
one boy in a corner who is always going
down under the surface in the space between
two glances, and falling through the painting, and the poem.
The sun still shone.
Your child had not yet heard of Icarus.

I realised that, by now, I was writing a poem about not being able to
grasp its subject ('the blankness at the centre' – death) and had sheered
away completely from a particular death ('the eyes sheer off and tack
but will not fix . . .'). Having understood that I was now trying to write
a poem about being unable to write a poem, it then occurred to me that
I might focus on *that*, gather my bits and pieces together and rearrange
them into a long poem about how time erodes the original feelings. I
am sure it was largely about the erosion of my own first draft, but no
one has ever come up with a fully satisfactory explanation of the
dividing-line between art and life (embracing death), and the heart of
the matter did not seem to me to be cancelled by the apparently
heartless examination of what I might be really on about by this stage.
This is my longest version:

SOME UNTIDY SPOT

(In memory of Meryon)

1 month
Tragedies happen anyhow, in corners, when other people
are working or just walking dully along
as Auden said, thinking of Brueghel's Icarus
who fell into the water in the space between
two glances, and then into the painting, then the poem,
as if the whole Aegean was not wide enough
to hold the impact of the moment of his death.

But this poem is about your son
who was too young to fly like Icarus
and simply walked behind you on an ordinary path
along an ordinary river's edge

then wasn't on the path when you looked back.
So all the lives he might have lived slipped out of him
in ripples and were gone, to all appearances,
yet grow in circles which are not contained
by any accidental river-bank, or even
by the confines of your heart which held him
firmly, safe, behind great dykes of love,
but couldn't ring the moment or the one untidy spot.

6 months
What circles of mythology contract
on nowhere noticeable, some blank spot
recorded on the retina. The sun still shone.
Your child had not yet heard of Icarus
and simply walked behind you on an ordinary path
along an ordinary river's edge
then wasn't on the path when you looked back.

1 year
There is a blankness at the centre of *Icarus*.
The eyes sheer off and tack and will not fix on
one boy in a corner who is always going
down under the surface in the space between
two glances, and falling through the painting, and the poem.

2 years
Tragedies happen anyhow, in corners, when other people
are working or just walking dully along,as Auden said,
noticing precisely how the eyes shift.

It is a very rare thing for me to tote my poems around, asking other
people's opinions, but this one seemed to be a special case since it had
obviously become obsessive and I could no longer see the wood for the
trees. So I sent the long version to my friend and fellow-poet, Anne
Stevenson, seeking her comments, knowing she would tell me straight.
She was more enthusiastic than I had expected and told me she felt the
longest version to be easily the best. She said she liked the way the
poem becomes shorter and shorter as time passes and the experience
becomes *only* the 'fiction' of the poem, as pain does. She also liked the
'calculated repetition', thought I should emphasise rather than
suppress the circles – expanding/contracting. She did not like the last
line and thought I should definitely omit it. Anne questioned a few of

the words – e.g. 'impact', 'moment', 'confines', 'ripples' (all of which I felt I needed to keep by this time) but assured me: 'The poem is very impressive and needs *all* its parts. The first stanza won't do alone.'

I wrote one last 'arrangement', concocted out of insistent bits of earlier versions, with the addition of two lines at the end which seemed to be saying that I had gone far enough, and maybe too far. It was a poem consisting of three stanzas of seven lines each. The first is unchanged, starting 'Tragedies happen anyhow, in corners . . .' and ending with 'his death'; the second is a repeat of the '6 months' stanza, starting: 'What circles of mythology contract . . .', and the third is:

> There is a blankness at the centre of Brueghel's *Icarus*.
> The eyes sheer off the tack and will not fix on
> one boy in a corner who is always going
> down under the surface in the space between
> two glances, and falling through the painting, and the poem.
> The sun still shone on nothing much, mere
> rings of water breaking at the water's edge.

I sent this final version together with the first one to my editor, asking him to choose one version, on my behalf, for inclusion in my collection *The Sea at the Door* (Secker & Warburg, 1985), or to reject both. He had no doubts. He simply wanted my very first version, complete – and so it went into the book, which appeared on the second anniversary of Meryon's death. I still don't know which of my versions was really 'best'. I suspect they were all faulty and all somehow necessary. Evidently, on one level I was genuinely attempting to empathise with Meryon's parents. On another level I was in the process of discovering that elegies are so problematic because the person just is *not there*, and can only ring an absence. All the poems are about the absence of the child and the impossibility of envisaging absence except in terms of things (or words) which encircle the gap as *if* to define it, even though they never can, of course. In the end, my poems seemed to be nothing more nor less than a wreath, and it would have been a lot easier just to buy a real one from a shop than to try weaving one out of words. It took two years to learn that I was striving for the impossible and that I had already said all that could be said in my first draft. Whatever my obsessive reworkings amounted to, it seemed that I really had no choice but to go along with them, until they petered out into 'nothing much'.

'If poetry come not as naturally as the leaves to a tree . . .'
Medbh McGuckian

I persist in the stubborn practice of writing by hand, without recourse to a typewriter, let alone a word-processor. Some purists find poets ridiculous if they employ a biro, but if I used machines I would feel myself becoming mechanical. The poet is her own word-processor. The pleasure of writing is partly the direct traditional cooperation between paper, ink, brain and fingers, the flow of blood and chemicals. Even a biro misses out on something more liquid and free.

I don't make all that many alterations or drafts. My best poems emerge all at once like a full-term child, poems I labour over and doctor up remain at the handicapped stage, like a person not fully equipped for life, missing a gene. If the sequence of the lines does not have its own inbuilt momentum, volition or force, there's little I can do except put down my pen and wait. I rarely have an overall envisaged structure, like an architect's plan, so if the poem changes direction it does so of its own accord. Although consciously I might believe I have total or some control over the management and meaning of the words, my subconscious is, or ought to be, doing all or most of the driving. The process of composing is akin to that of sleep or dream, the gathering and disposal of fluids through the system, the ticking of pulse or heart. It becomes an art you can be trained into, like walking, swimming, cycling, which is at first awkward and needs to be learned, but ends up as if you could always do it. Presumably it can also be forgotten as easily as any of those physical skills, through illness or accident or lack of exercise. The game of poetry is a function as much of experience as technique, depending on having something interesting to say and the tools to achieve a vehicle or form in which to say it. It took a long time for me to evolve a personal style that would be my own authentic voice and no one else's. Even then I must always grow and develop, if I'm not to repeat myself or degenerate into self-parody, pastiche or trademarks. At present, I'm at a stagnant if not regressive point in my work, because my life is somehow arrested at a crossroads and indefinite. I try not to worry too much since things eventually thaw or move or ripen, hopefully.

When a poem begins, I sense at least it will be short or long, a busy intense moment of crystallisation, or an extended meditation. Because I've not had a full-time job lately, my poems have been dense as forests, with small vignettes appearing as clearings.

'Petite Maison' is an example of the latter, a thought or sad perception. Even though it is negative there is a concealed bounce. The conflict of the poem is left open, as if the people stopped in the middle of an argument. I have tightened the form into three paragraphs or stages which seem to set out alternatives though there is no real choice. A good poem should have a mystery, setting up and toppling the words like steeplechasers or the water-jumps in horse-riding tournaments. There is the same kind of time-limit as in a race. The rule is to maintain a logical thought-pattern in a grammatical sentence, but pad or fill it with the extraordinary or what you would least expect or even want, to stimulate the mind's muscles into aerobics that resemble an enjoyable dance, not the effort of work. My short poems sound clever and prim because they think they are so smart and all they are is a breathing-space. This in particular is a very frustrating piece, but that may be because it's about frustration.

PETITE MAISON

When someone breaks the rules of colour,
No one is born.
Your name becomes a vessel to receive
The long out of fashion emotions
Of my brown checked skirt.

Perfume buries perfume asking
Whether you would rather die on horseback
Or reaching for an apricot.
Shape embarasses shape saying
Where did the air come from
(Because there was some).

And spring is the explanation of the flower
When two interrogations end
The blue which is the suspense before gold
With – 'To be continued'.

The lengthy, almost unwieldy poem 'No Streets, No Numbers' deals with a much more complex network of emotions, which could not have been treated otherwise. It was built up from four segments, written over several nights. I ought to be more careful about dating poems, but the poem itself tells us it was just after Christmas, and anyway I like the mystery of the vagueness.

NO STREETS, NO NUMBERS

The wind bruises the curtains' jay-blue stripes
Like an unsold fruit or a child who writes
Its first word. The rain tonight in my hair
Runs a firm unmuscular hand over something
Sand-ribbed and troubled, a desolation
That could erase all memory of warmth
From the patch of vegetation where torchlight
Has fallen. The thought that I might miss
Even a second of real rain is like the simple
Double knock of the stains of birth and death,
Two men back to back carrying furniture
From a room one side of the street
To the room on the other. And the weather

Is a girl with woman's eyes like a knife-wound
In her head. Such is a woman's very deep
Violation as a woman, not like talk,
Not like footsteps, already a life crystallises
Round it, and time that is so often only a word,
'Later, later', spills year into year like three days'
Post, or the drawing-room with the wall
Pulled down.

I look into the endless settees
Of the talk-dried drawing-room where all
The colours are wrong. Is that because
I unshaded all the lamps so their sunny
Unhurt movements would be the colour
Of emotions which have no adventures?
But I'm afraid of the morning most,
Which stands like a chance of life
On a shelf, or a ruby velvet dress
Cut to the middle of the back
That can be held on the shoulder by a diamond lizard.

A stone is nearly a perfect secret, always
By itself though it touches so much, shielding
Its heart beyond its strong curtain of ribs
With its arm. Not that I want you
To tell me what you have not told anyone:
How your narrow house propped up window
After window while the light sank and sank.
Why your edges though they shine
No longer grip precisely like other people.
How sometimes the house won and sometimes
The sea-coloured sea-clear dress,
Made new from one over a hundred years old,
That foamed away the true break
In the year, leaving the house
Masterless and flagless. That dream
Of a too early body undamaged
And beautiful, head smashed to pulp,
Still grows in my breakfast cup;
It used up the sore red of the applebox,
It nibbled at the fortnight of our violent
Christmas like a centenarian fir-tree.

I talk as if the evenings had been fine,
The roof of my shelves not broken
Like an oath on crossed rods,
Or I had not glimpsed myself
As the Ides of September white
At the telephone. Two sounds
Spin together and fight for sleep
Between the bed and the floor,
An uneasy clicking-to of unsorted
Dawn-blue plates, the friction
Of a skirt of hands refusing to let go.
And how am I to break into
This other life, this small eyebrow,
Six inches off mine, which has been
Blown from my life like the most aerial
Of birds? If the summer that never burnt
And began two days ago is ashes now,
Autumn's backbone will have the pallor
Of the snowdrop, the shape of the stone
Showing in the wall. Our first summer-time
Night we will sit out drinking
On the pavement of Bird Street
Where we kissed in the snow, as the day
After a dream in which one really was
In love teases out the voice reserved for children.

Things have been left in and bits shuffled here and there like a pack of cards into the most coherent order. The poem means a lot to me because it 'delivered' me from a deeply entrenched and ambivalent longing for another child. It mourns as well as celebrates the non-conception of this child by identifying practically with a friend's actual loss of an actual child, describing this to me while in the early hopeful stages of a new expectation. I had to make the title dark because the more important or fundamental acceptance was of my own childless-ness, or not being fertilised at that time while being fertile – there seems to be no easy way to say in English, to have children, but not to be with child. Also to join in my friend's clear grief and desperation at what had happened to her, which was like Hitler's eyes. Part of the theme is my own guilt at my greed for life, when she had been through so much and had still no guarantee of being a mother. Here survival, courage and determination to have another go were inspiring, and what inspired the poem. The end of the poem attempts a kind of apotheosis, where I wanted to be generous enough not to behave like Solomon's women but to transfer the painful violence of my own fantasy into a caring and naming of *her* street, *her* dwelling, her as a dwelling. A full discussion of the imagery or what was discarded might not make anything clearer. I can explain it as usual autobiographically in that after it I was relieved, exhausted, released from my obsession and jealousy. The story might be of little interest, but it might be valuable for any woman who has passionately deceived herself in this common enough way, or any man or woman who has undergone their child's death, which is a suffering hardly to be imagined. I am mortally confused, like everyone else, by the end being in the beginning, the similarity between birth and death, our ignorance of both, since one is forever caught up in an induced distraction. The poem avoids directly confronting these issues, but at its centre is the brutally shocking image and fact, just touched on, of a child born not merely dead but murdered, and not merely murdered, but by its own father, which jars against Christian doctrine of paternalism and death as a charitable rebirth. Perhaps because of where I live – Belfast, where such dreadful deeds happen daily – I am drawn to surround the most cruel crimes with these tentative questions, these light flags and streamers. Perhaps I identified with the sick and disturbed parent-figure, in the sense that I might have refused someone selfishly their opportunity to live. There are situations women especially find too intricate to articulate – have I fully explored my nexus of symptoms here? I doubt it, for I cling too easily to the safely plotted districts of Austen, Eliot and Woolf, 'I'm afraid of the morning most'.

'Moment of Faith': Worksheets
Carol Rumens

I was asked by Birthright, a charity researching into safer childbirth, to write a poem for an exhibition on the theme of Mother and Child. I decided to interpret the theme literally, because I have long felt I wanted to write more about the birth of my first child, and particularly the moment of 'bonding' which I remember extremely well. She had been washed and wrapped and put in my arms; she was crying lustily and one of her little hands stuck out of the shawl. I stroked the palm with my own finger and this tiny hand shut round it and the crying stopped! It was the most magical thing that had ever happened to me. I'd hardly ever *seen* a baby before, and didn't have a clue how to look after one. But at that moment I felt I was a mother.

I realised this would be a risky thing to write about, so never did. (My early birth-poems are dreadful, Plath-derivative, blood-and-guts stuff.) Having the commission decided me: I'd write that poem which has been waiting for twenty-one years! The first four drafts show its gestation from the time of the commission to the publication – about three months. I should add that, eventually, a sequence of ten birth poems sprang up around it. Some of these are still work-in-progress.

First draft (longhand):

> It was the crying hand
> that stuck out tense, fully opened
> like the sudden appearance of a star
>
> it was the way the palm
> and each of the little jointed wands
> was waxed for its own protection
>
> that made her think
> that this had somehow all been planned
> and when she touched it

it was the way the hand folded
shut round her stroking finger
and the crying died away

that made her begin to dream
that somehow it had all been planned
and the plan was matchless.

When I got to the last stanza, I realised that this was where the
material originally put in the third stanza should go, so my next step
was to erase stanza three.

The next draft was typed:

It was the crying hand
Thrust from the shawl, wide-opened:
a celandine in cold March grass

It was the way the palm
And each little jointed wand
had been carefully waxed like a swimmer

It was the way it clammed
Tight round her probing finger
And the crying shivered into stillness

That made her begin to imagine
This had somehow all been planned
and the plan was matchless.

It will be obvious what seemed to me okay from the first draft and
what did not. The basic structure seemed right: the first and last lines
seemed right. I was specially pleased with 'matchless' because it echoes
that mediaeval carol, 'I sing of a mayden who is makeles.' I had not
heard it for a long time but I'm sure it was a shaping force behind the
poem. At school I learned the Britten setting, and I can still sing it. I
like vigorous, colloquial language, but 'stuck out' seemed clumsy, so I
substituted 'thrust'. The main problem was describing the hand and
what happened when I touched it. Should I talk about the hand or the
fingers? I couldn't talk directly about the baby's fingers, because then
I'd have a repetition when I spoke about 'her' finger. 'Wands' is a
pretty feeble metaphor. I feel I want to do something more with the
idea of the swimmers. Supposing I make each finger a swimmer? Is it
too 'Martian'? I have always thought of fingers as miniature people, so
I'm not simply copying a manner. Let's try . . .

It was the crying hand
Thrust from the shawl, a sharp-petalled
Celandine in cold March grass:

It was the five little swimmers,
Sea-wearied, bent at the waist,
Waxed still in each hair-fine crease:

It was the sealed fortress
They built round her terrified finger
As the crying shivered into stillness

That made her think that the seeming
Shambles of it all was planned
And that the plan was matchless.

As usual, I made changes as I typed: 'fully-opened' became 'sharp-petalled', and I added some descriptive detail about the finger-swimmers. A new idea came into the third stanza – that of the child somehow comforting and protecting the mother. I finally lost that: a pity, but in such a short, lyric form there is only room for so many ideas. I tried 'wall' instead of 'sealed fortress', then pencilled in 'strong-hold' but crossed it out.

MOMENT OF FAITH

It was the crying hand
Thrust from the shawl, a sharp-petalled
Celandine in cold March grass:

It was the five little swimmers,
Sea-wearied, bent at the waist,
Still waxed in each wrinkle and seam:

It was the stronghold they closed
Round her probing finger, the way
The crying shivered into stillness,

That made her think that the teeming
Shambles of it all was planned,
And the plan was matchless.

This was the version I considered finished enough to submit: it is the version framed and printed in the Birthright Exhibition catalogue. As soon as I saw it in print my eye flew to the repetition of 'Still' (1.6) and 'stillness' (1.9). Damn and blast! The more I look at it and say it to myself the uglier it becomes. I can't just get rid of that first 'still', not only because it fixes the swimmers in time, i.e. they've now finished swimming but only just, but because if I do I've got a horrid repetition of Ws ('waist' and 'waxed'). The other obvious device, to change 'stillness' to 'silence', also offends my ear: anyway, 'stillness' in the context has a much richer meaning than 'silence'. At the moment the problem seems insurmountable and it might even be better to leave it unsolved.

There are other worries. If the celandine is taken literally as a metaphor for the baby's hand it's clearly not right. What I meant to convey was suddenness: the celandine is always the first flower I see after winter, and the sight of it, so clean and bright on some ghastly grey March day, always moves me. I can't help if this sounds pseudo-Wordsworth. It's what I genuinely feel. I wonder if I should change 'sharp-petalled' to 'astonishing' or even 'sudden'. 'As sudden/as a celandine in cold March grass?' 'Abrupt' is better. But it doesn't convey the thrill, or the 'thereness' of the flower. I want to see the flower as well as the hand, but separate. I want the feel of utter newness, that is what they have in common.

The 'Martian' flavour of the 'swimmers' stanza still worries me, but I refuse to be intimidated by categories. I shall let it stand.

On the whole I like the poem. I like its sound, and the faint bits of rhyme ('hand' and 'planned', for example. Those words are far apart but I still think the echo can be heard. 'Distant rhyming' is something I'd like to explore further). I feel a strong emotion in the poem, I am moved by it. I think I've avoided sentimentality. I've certainly managed to avoid rhetoric, something I find very difficult when strong feelings are involved. My most deeply-felt poems always sound my most fake. I feel it's a very English poem. I just hope the scepticism comes through sufficiently. (A very English wish, that!)

MOMENT OF FAITH

It was the crying hand
Thrust from the shawl, unannounced
Celandine in cold March grass:

It was the five little swimmers,
Waxed in each wrinkle and seam,
Bent at waist, sea-wearied.

> It was the stronghold they closed
> Round her probing finger, the way
> The crying shivered into stillness,
>
> That made her think that the teeming
> Shambles of it all was planned,
> And the plan was matchless.

'Unannounced' now worries me because although it's true – or seems true – of the flower, it's not really true of the baby, which has been announcing its advent for the last nine months. I'm reasonably pleased with stanza two now, having got rid of the 'still' and indicating the time-factor by making the line-order more logical as narrative.

On reappraisal, 'unannounced' seems okay: after all, it's the baby's hand I'm referring to, not the whole baby! I miss the 'still' (still), and prefer the previous arrangement of stanza two after all, but I shan't change back, as the repetition ('still' and 'stillness') seems to me the greater of two evils.

I *still* feel I may re-work it! I went on being dis-satisfied with version 5, and feeling that 4 was better, provided I got rid of 'sharp-petalled' and the 'still/stillness' repeats. I decided to try it with a simile instead of a full metaphor in the first verse and deleting 'stillness'.

> It was the crying hand
> Thrust from the shawl, unannounced
> As celandines in March grass.
>
> It was the five little swimmers,
> Sea-wearied, bent at the waist,
> Still waxed in each wrinkle and seam.
>
> It was the stronghold they closed
> Round her probing finger, the way
> The crying shivered, and ceased,
>
> That made her think that the teeming
> Shambles of it all was planned,
> And the plan was matchless.

Is that it? God, I hope so!

• Endings

Anyhow, it is done; and I have been sitting these 15 minutes in a state of glory, and calm, and some tears.
Virginia Woolf

Trying to Get Rid of It
Sue Roe

I think the ending of a novel should be a culmination of all that has gone before. If possible, the ending should surprise. In the best short stories, all the reader's expectations are set up to predict a certain outcome, then the opposite – or something at an obscure or oblique angle – turns out to be the case. Something that feels like a reversal but is actually absolutely true to the central dynamics and direction of the narrative. The ending should answer a question the reader has been asking all along, without even realising it. This is my idea of a perfect ending.

In both of my own novels, the endings were written last – when I knew I had all but finished the book, and there was only the ending to go. It is possibly the only part of the process which happens more or less as you might imagine it would. In *Estella* I show the character changing tack and beginning again; in *Masquerade* I create an opportunity for one of the characters to make a little speech, in which she tells her son, and the reader, what I take to be the 'story' of *Masquerade*. There is also a surprise at the end; something in the form of a revelation. Both endings were written like the scenes which initiated the novels, seemingly out of nowhere, spontaneously, coming very suddenly (though after months of fruitless speculation on the problem of drawing all the threads together), complete with dialogue and setting.

When the ending is written and I am satisfied that the crafting of the novel is complete, then there is a period of black despair. I don't really know what I am doing. Nothing means anything. Nothing has come together. There is no future. You are absolutely reeling with exhaustion. You feel as though you have finally heaved something enormous – a huge, great weight of a thing – out of the place where it had been lodged, at about the level of your ribcage, and now it is sitting impotently on the floor in front of you. It hovers there, in front of you, wherever you go. You keep falling over it. It won't go away, just when you thought you had got rid of it. WELL MOVE, THEN, you feel like telling it. It is an extraordinary thing, this thing you have just expelled. It is a great unexploded bomb, it is a fireball of energy, it could ignite a building. But there it is – just a used-looking pile of paper covered with your typing. As you pass it, you catch a glimpse of the odd word, the odd sentence, and it makes you squirm. You think you ought to cut it; you have not said enough. Perhaps the ending is not quite right after all. Perhaps the whole thing is completely unintelligible, except to you. What have you said in it, anyway? (Suddenly you cannot remember anything at all about it.) And, who are you, now? (For years, as far as you are concerned, your entire identity has been bound up with the writing of this book.)

For me, the placing of the book, its publication and even reception, together constitute an entirely separate process. Things like timing and chance now come into play; and other people's judgement, which, by this stage, is a relief. After I am satisfied that I have finished the writing, I still go on having misgivings: I am never entirely sure that it is finished; that I have done absolutely everything in my power to make it as complete, and as good, as I can.

I still don't know quite how I got over the writing of *Masquerade*, in rather the same way as it is never quite clear how people recover from illness. But thinking about it to write the *Notebook* brought it all vividly to life again, as though during that period of my life something quite momentous happened. I feel that I have somehow put something extremely demanding, extremely arduous and exhausting and exhilarating and enormous, behind me. And that I want to go on, now: I can't 'see' it yet, but there must be a way of making something different now, something new . . .

'I've boarded the train, there's no getting off . . .'
Medbh McGuckian

The poem stops when the desire to speak is exhausted, sometimes in a pat summarising conclusion, with a clinching rhyme, sometimes left very open and questioning, so one poem runs into the next. Organising poems into sequences and books can be difficult, can end up like an omelette presented in a French sauce. There is a good feeling of triumph and peace after finishing a good poem, you can say most of it over to yourself and its meaning will grow. Others are easily forgotten. Reviews are always interesting, hostile ones tend to have examined the poems more closely. The demand for public readings – whether on radio, television, at academic conferences, clubs or theatres – creates other dilemmas. It is healthy to mix with other poets, perhaps even to compete, travel can be inspirational also, but the ego is highly vulnerable to 'media' and the artist must always protect her integrity. Reading a poem can encourage the dramatic pose or make the poet push her personality ahead of the work's merit. And it is useful to write something like this once in a while; but as I have written also in a poem, 'Looking at what's most important leaves me blind.'

The Black Woman Writer
*Alice Walker**

There are two reasons why the black woman writer is not taken as
seriously as the black male writer. One is that she's a woman. Critics
seem unusually ill-equipped to discuss and analyse the works of black
women intelligently. Generally, they do not even make the attempt;
they prefer, rather, to talk about the lives of black women writers, not
about what they write. And, since black women writers are not, it
would seem, very likeable – until recently they were the least willing
worshipers of male supremacy – comments about them tend to be
cruel.

*From 'From an Interview', in *In Search Of Our Mothers' Gardens*, The Women's Press,
London, 1984, pp. 244–72.

The Bottom Line
Amryl Johnson

I am going downhill at a speed which is proving impossible to judge. All I know for certain is that I have come over the crest of the hill and am now angling my way downwards. I cannot see the bottom. I cannot see where my journey is going to end. I am confident, however, that I am now well and truly on the way.

Time and time again, I tell my students, 'Do not overwork an ending.' Don't overplay. Be sensitive to the mood. Be faithful to it. Learn to draw the line between moody, magnificent and overgenerous, gushy. Don't spoil it for the reader by overstating. Don't bombard them with the obvious. If anything, leave them fractionally in the dark, teetering on the brink. Leave them salivating. A good piece of creative writing will remain with the reader for some time after they have closed the pages.

The beginning is what attracts a reader. That first paragraph is what will make them want to read on. As much attention has to be paid to that final paragraph, that final line, as to the first. For this reason, I am a great believer in the meticulous shaping of these two sections.

Picking up her needle, I had already started to sew.

My travel-biography *Sequins for a Ragged Hem* (Virago Press, 1988) ends with that line. I had already decided that was how I would end the book, long before I committed the line to paper. I had already penned it, in my head, before I was no more than half-way through the book. The same applies to the novel I am working on now. The first paragraph and the final paragraph are already worked out – in my head. There is some distance between deciding how you are going to end and the actual words which will seal it. The very final line of the novel is branded in my subconscious. Consequently, I am writing within a framework. It is not, however, a very rigid one. My temperament belies anything which curves towards stringency. As a

159

writer, it is necessary to work within some sort of framework. This isn't necessarily anything to do with ideas which dissipate. This is everything to do with being able to control the story-line.

I get really excited when I know I am getting close to finishing. Not relieved that it is coming to an end. I really do mean excited. It is the culmination of the project. The sum, the summary. What happens then? What happens after the excitement has died down? On a full-length piece, the withdrawal symptoms. The symptoms are plainly visible to anyone around me. I am never tempted to write 'the end', not even as a gesture of finality, but the end it most certainly is. When I finished *Sequins for a Ragged Hem*, my first full-length piece, I felt lost. I mooned around the house in a trance, for days. I just didn't know what to do with myself. I was lost. I could have launched myself straight into the next piece. There is always a next. The poem, short story or article which would have followed, would have done so on the rebound. The circumstances demanded some respite. A period of mourning. *Sequins for a Ragged Hem* recalls the six months I spent in the Caribbean from January to June 1983. I brought to life, tried to immortalise those wonderful people I met during my stay. It came as quite a shock to find a period of blackness lay beyond the initial feeling of exhilaration at having completed the book. I had lost the characters. The white handkerchief had been disappearing further and further into the distance. I had said goodbye. And, in short, I missed them. I strongly suspect that I will react in exactly the same way having completed subsequent full-length pieces.

Could this be the reason why writers are sometimes tempted to write sequels?

'No, no. My characters are not dead. Merely sleeping.'

Sequins for a Ragged Hem was based on facts. What will it be like with my novel? Infinitely worse, I would imagine. This is where creation, in its true sense, becomes a liability. The analogies are the same.

'Delivering' my manuscript may well be the closest I will come to giving birth. I 'conceived' the idea. I 'nurtured' it. Those withdrawal symptoms must surely be post-natal. The emptiness. Depression. I was not able to keep the child. Curious situation.

I am extremely superstitious about discussing any work prior to publication. Having experienced a mental-block, once, I have this horror of it happening again. Abusing the Muse's generosity may put me in danger. It is she who dictates that I maintain a closed mouth. Going back to keeping a diary smacks a little too much of compromise and there is no guarantee that it will work a second time. Consequently, details of my collection of poems recently completed can only be hinted at. Five characters dominate. I became particularly fond of one of them. And although the sense of loss felt at the finish of *Sequins for a Ragged Hem* cannot truly compare with the one I felt for my poems, I certainly pined for them – especially the one character.

What is the end? Okay, it is partly to do with some decision on the part of the creator that the time is right to bring the curtain down. The reader may or may not agree with the decision (abrupt endings, I think they call it). Readers have argued that the impression gained was that the writer became bored with the characters. Do writers sometimes end up loathing their characters? Even the unsavoury ones have a place in my heart. But I dare say it is possible to detest something of your own creation. Regardless of the circumstances under which the piece is terminated, this marks the end of the writing. The genuine end must surely be the urgency with which you have to despatch the 'baby'. However, unless you write specifically for yourself, it wasn't yours in the first place. It is the community's. If you write to be published then this has to be the case. The satisfaction has to be in the creation. Once the editors get their hands on it and, later, the critics, then heaven help you! For as long as the creativity lasts, your life becomes a process of conception, nurturing and delivery. Abortions are, entirely, by the way. They get filed in waste-paper baskets or, constructively, for any subsequent attempts.

Perhaps it is best not to think too deeply into analogies, in this instance; precisely where the 'merchant of words' fits into the vast spectrum of creativity becomes a very tenuous one. You know there is infinitely more to it than sitting at your typewriter to sift words poetically on to the page. More and more I find myself questioning that hollowness and emptiness felt after delivery. It leaves some sense of being orphaned myself. This is a strange but very precise haunting:

ENDINGS:

My own!

Knowing When to Stop
Sue Stewart

The end of a poem usually finds itself quite naturally. It shouldn't jar, but should have an inevitability to it, as if it couldn't have ended any other way. Some poems need a falling-off ending, others a thumping resolution; some signal the approaching finale in the last few lines, others finish with little warning. A too-conclusive ending can irritate, seem too neat; a sloppy, uncertain ending leaves the reader hanging in the air. There are, thankfully, as many ways of ending a poem as of starting one. One time I got a bee in my bonnet about ending a poem with a hyphen. Could it be done, would it work? I let the idea settle for a while then woke up to it half-way through writing a poem about bread-making, called 'Too Many Cooks'. In the poem the diverse ingredients that make up the dough – yeast, sugar, water, flour, salt, egg, poppy seeds – conspire to confound the hapless baker by their very aliveness. Even as the loaf enters the oven and is 'set' in, as it were, the gesture of the moment, it's as puffed up and airy as ever. This reminded me of the eerie photos I'd seen of the people of Vesuvius mummified in volcanic lava. My hyphen had found its home:

> Our dough grows outlandish,
> meets the oven's burnt truth
> and comes out terracotta –
> Vesuvian, fixed in mid-

But how to know when you've finished – or finished with – a poem? I don't know the answer to that; perhaps you're never finished with it. I know I've gone back to poems after they've appeared in magazines or books, still fretting and fiddling with them. I think in that respect I've had to learn when to leave well alone. Other times, I know the poem is complete and am happy with it. I find it's easier to let a poem go when it's in a traditional verse form. The form offers a solid framework to build on, so there's less anxiety about structure. This is too easy a let-out though. Free verse can be far more rewarding, mainly because it's more difficult to get right and so more of a challenge.

I find it useful to tape a poem once it's finished. On playback I can hear all sorts of discordances I might not otherwise have picked up on. I can also hear if I'm slurring over a word and giving the line an altogether different, usually unwelcome, meaning.

Once a poem is well and truly finished, I tend to go through three stages which I suspect are fairly typical. The first is one of satisfaction, a feeling of having achieved something. This lasts an hour or two, then peters out. The second stage, which sneaks up on me like a yawning doubt, is one of disenchantment. I wonder how I could ever have written it; it has nothing whatsoever to recommend it; I just wish I hadn't sent it to such-and-such magazine; it's not tight enough/loose enough/true enough, it's too personal/surreal/clichéd. And so on. The third stage is when I approach relative objectivity. Then I'll read it with a cool appraisal and, if I'm lucky, will still be glad I've written it. I try now to wait until I've reached this third stage before sending work out to magazines.

Editors are as idiosyncratic as people generally are, and each has her/his own taste. I don't think one can expect confirmation of one's innate genius from them, or be too much of a sensitive flower. They will accept or reject work on grounds of its quality and their opinion. Sometimes, too, an editor might well be looking for poems that will be compatible in a sort of pot-pourri within the one issue. (Some editors keep work for longer than others. If it's a quarterly magazine, it's reasonable to wait up to three months for a reply. Double that for magazines with editorial boards, the editors have to shunt the poems back and forth between them.)

The same goes for reviews. It would be an unusual person who didn't get upset by hostility or indifference, but I do think the reviewer's own work has to be taken into account. If I had a bad review from a good poet (or an exceptional critic) I'd be pretty upset, but the odds are that criticism from such a source would be constructive; the reviewer would want to improve the work, not crush the spirit. Others might be more concerned with writing an entertaining review, and there's room enough for this in the sometimes dry world of academic criticism. Some make their names by hostile reviewing, but the best of these use wit to get the point across. I have to admit that I've read some very entertaining reviews in some of the poetry magazines, but the targets have been easy ones, and hardly defenceless. This sometimes leads to counter-attack, and develops into an art form all its own.

Cutting Loose
Rosalind Brackenbury

What is an ending? The point at which I decide to stop. The image I have had in my head for the whole of the writing of the book, towards which I have been moving. The moment where I hand over to the reader: now it is up to you. It is as far as I have got. This far the maps go, and no further. Beyond is uncharted, is open; but here is my last sign-post. Sometimes, a return to the beginning, but differently, spiralling past the place again, singing the same note in a different key. Sometimes a place to rest, to let go; dense with the import of another story, which may take ten years to unfold. Endings have been all of these things. I have difficulty with them, because life never shows you endings, and they have to be made artificially. Beginnings do, too, but you can leave them quickly behind you, in the impetus of moving forward. An ending is, transparently, where you have got to; it can show you standing nonplussed, mouth agape, or it can give a falsely sure statement of where you think you are. I, I mean. Where I, as the writer, think I am.

I have faked endings, laid traps for the reader, hidden clues in endings so thoroughly that nobody but I can know where they are buried. This is a failure; there is no point in burying the vital clue so thoroughly – as I think I did in *A Superstitious Age* – that nobody can find it, and only the writer knows it is buried there. And in giving a choice, a multiplicity of endings, as I have also done, you have to know the implications of each one, and which one bears for you most weight.

The final image of the books is what counts for me, not the outcome or explanation. A swing, a door opening, somebody plunging into water, the owl which lays its ball of digested food upon the threshold. I work, tunnelling or swimming, either of these analogies will do, somewhat submerged, towards the final image. I think that where I have really followed this through and not got stuck in some intellectual impasse, the ending works. There – without quite knowing how, I have got to it, the point where the image presents itself again, unstrained and coherent with the rest. It is a matter of finding out what you are moving towards and doing it, all in one movement.

Then rolling the page out of the typewriter and knowing, that is it. Finished. But only finished in a certain sense, for the whole point of writing the novel in the first place was to find out where it was going, and now that I, or it, has got there, I have to look again at all the rest in the light of what I have just discovered. Some of it will be extraneous, irrelevant, to be cut out, and other parts will need bridges built, things made more evident, sections added. So I often re-write once I have discovered the ending, in order to pull the whole thing into shape. The ending shows me what all the rest means; throws light upon the beginning, often means a different beginning is needed, in place of the one which was simply a way of sliding into the narrative, an easy way in.

And once I consider it really ended, what follows: elation, panic, confusion, all these things. I want someone to read it, I want it published. I also feel I want to hide it, to protect myself, to forget about it. I think the feelings of fear which I still associate with being published are old feelings, to do with being visible, being judged, being a child who might get punished for what she has done. The more the piece of work really breaks new ground for me, the more persistant these feelings are. But if even one person reads it, responds to it, loves it, understands it, the feelings drain away; it simply matters that it has an understanding audience of one. So I choose (quite carefully) the first person to read what I have written.

When a novel is published, I often feel as if something should have happened in the world that has not. There should be some visible sign of its appearance. It's a bit like it being your birthday, and nobody knowing. But when it's reviewed, you have to realise that people are reading it, that it is visible. My own experience of reading reviews is still linked to my experience of reading school reports, and they scare me. I can't believe they are going to be positive. When I have written about all these things on which we are supposed to keep silent, when I have said all this, is somebody actually approving of me? And yet at the same time, once a book is published it is independent of me, it is not me any more or even mine; it is out on its own now, become something solid that can go anywhere in the world without my knowing, and I am free of it.

Coming to the end of a novel is not like anything else in my experience, not like ending a relationship, or moving house, or having your children grow up, or ending a practical activity. It is calling an artificial end to a process in life, saying, 'That's it for now, I'm there,' but knowing too that the seeds of the next novel are somewhere there, and that although you may take a holiday or do something else for a few months it will reach out and claim you. The process of writing novels, following a curious need to create something which runs close to, parallel with and different from, the processes of one's own life, is not the same as writing poetry. I rarely have the sense of having 'finished' a poem, but may come home from a reading one day realising that this one or that one has more or less jelled into its final shape; otherwise they may go on changing for years, or until I see them published, set firm upon the page. With a novel, you have to cut it loose, say goodbye to it, cut its cord, if you like; it is bad to have it lying around the house, preventing the next one from getting moving. I have a chest with dead novels in it, and one day will get around to throwing them out; they weigh me down, the ones which never saw the light of day, which had not enough guts in them to get going.

Stations
Nicki Jackowska

If we take for granted that ending a poem or story is a relative condition, nevertheless that 'ending' always has a sense, not of loss exactly – since one has created a journey and opened a reality which belongs both to the writer-reader and the page – but of something completed and thus, for the moment, partial separation. I can't say total separation, since the work lives on in its internal and external form.

My poems and stories run out of steam. They have their own energy-span and I can feel it coming to a close, I always follow that, rarely act against that gradual slowing, or the sight of the terminus up ahead. If the vigilance is there, the antennae out, this ending is easy, is visible and known.

I always think I'll never write again. Can never understand how I've done it. It is both something given and mysterious, but also known and recognised – that event, encounter that now lies behind me.

The work is a meeting and shaping of myself as well as the page. As now, I can feel that shape (with all its ambiguities and contradictions) satisfactorily moulded, and so will come to a close. For now. It is always a temporary step. Tomorrow the same story continues perhaps. Thank Heaven for the pull of publication. It's a way of insisting that this will do for now. I carry my assessments forward, not back. That endless picking over what one's done is no use – the work had its own drive, its own dynamic.

So when the rejections come, I read seriously what contempt or empathy may be contained there (it's that wide a margin), and take it with a pinch of salt. And a double g. & t.

I am a Self-contained Collective, or Mountain Woman Waves Goodbye
Marcella Evaristi

This is the last piece of writing before the babies are born. If it's to have a chance of being published I must send it off now. It was mostly hell to write but, as always, I eventually enjoyed myself and now, having yearned to finish, I just wonder why I made such a song and dance about it. Still, I don't have a sense of anti-climax when I've finished writing as some people do. I do have a back-ache though. I shall now submit to the demands of my next production. Forgive the disjointed nature of this poor coda. (Feels like the end of Orwell's *1984* as my face takes on a gormless expression and I realise that, after all, I love Big Belly.)

What a mysterious business, then, this creativity!

What a PUZZLE

Though it carries two babies
Its arms dangle free
Boy baby girl baby
Now we are three.

Question: What is it?

I'm about one in eighty
My sex is not man
Seems the odds would be less
If I lived in Japan.

Question: What is she?

She lumbers at night
Her body's a shelf
She counts the late cars
And outnumbers herself.

Question: Is she twinned?

Answer:
Close, but no, sorry,
You're warm, but you're wrong.
'Twinned' is for babies
Curled up like two prawns.

'Twinned' is for cities,
Mad-matched in their pairs,
Little Belgrade and Little Coventry,
Please try not to stare . . .

So Mother's *not* twinned,
Mother's *got* twins,
Mother jokes she came twice

Now she's split. Was that funny?
Or not very nice?

• *Women and Writing*

I'll walk where my own nature would be leading.
Emily Brontë

On the Margins
Rosalind Brackenbury

I inherited the English language, with all its richness and complexity, and its lack of masculine and feminine nouns, and have not felt ill at ease in it, or that there are things it will not allow me to say. It is not a language that insists upon gender, as French does, or German. But it is the language of my upbringing, and it carries also the taboos of childhood, the restrictions of education and manners. In writing in my own language, I enjoy all the freedoms which other writers have found in it, and use the ways they have paved for me; I have also had to struggle with its maternal nature, the fact that it is the language I grew up in, and all the attendant struggles of that process still have their effect. In my childhood, there were things that were not mentioned, not named – my own sexuality, for a start – and which therefore might either not exist or be so dangerous as to be nameless. I grew up with a sense of what existed outside the named, established order: for instance, when I thought of colour, and the colours of the rainbow, I imagined that there were other colours, not yet named, not in the spectrum. Similarly, with the alphabet: that there were all the letters in the alphabet, and then the ones outside. So, with every sort of classification. I believed that after learning the names of the colours, or the letters of the alphabet, or the countries in the world, we would get on to the others, the ones not yet named. In some way, this belief informed my use of language; I was always waiting for the languages nobody had yet told me about.

I think that this sense of there being another way to say things informed and encouraged my own writing; but at the same time, I loved passionately all the writers who showed me how far they had come, and encouraged me to go further. I particularly loved the things I did not quite understand, and did not want them explained to me, but rather wanted to live with them until they gradually became clear. For this reason, I am glad not to have studied English literature formally,

173

and to have stumbled my way into various French writers, following nothing but my own curiosity. And when I came to write about my own experience of the French language, in my novel *Crossing the Water*, I made it analogous to some of my experience as a woman writing; that there are ways of being and thinking that we grow into, and others that we have to leave behind. A new language is a chance to be a new self.

We would drive on, up the harsher roads of northern France, heading for Boulogne and the channel port, and everything that had loosened in us would be braced, everything that had flowed, tighten, as we came home. Our own language would enfold us again, with its impassive parental assumptions that nothing had changed. No longer would we stammer and feel our way through what we said, trying out new forms, matching a rawness of experience with a newness of language, fitting experimentally the words, the phrases, to what was new in us; we would be back in English, that fitted us exactly as a well-made winter shoe, allowing no room for growth. I was dismayed, to lose the fragility of this tender new growth. What could I say now of all the unnamed, unclassified rambling tendrils of life, the experiences that had no name, or for which the name existed like buried treasure, in the earth of a language that was new to me? My life had grown out of me like green shoots through concrete. My feet felt the ground through the thin soles of floppy espadrilles. Whichever way I looked at it, whichever metaphor I chose (and they all seemed equally tired) for what I had to say, my own language would no longer do. And in your language, which I have borrowed, which I wear loosely, an ill-fitting comfortable garment that allows my body to breathe, in among your words and grammar and subjunctives I can exist, but am childish, entirely vulnerable, subtle and unsubtle with no control over which I am, wandering from tense to tense, making what is masculine, feminine, and vice versa, overturning all the rules, allowing myself to be obscure, violent, vulgar, imprecise; breaking open the confines, because they are not mine, not inherited, not imposed, and therefore not quite real. Because I am a foreigner, an outsider, a vagrant, an illiterate; picking up and using language to suit myself, making poems, spells, nonsense, leaving myself wide open. To English, then, I would return: as to shoes, clothes, doors closed, houses known and recognised. I would be

well turned out again, and know where I belonged. But how, in
the language of my mother and father, of school, of instruction,
of taboos, of this inhibiting clarity, would I write of what
concerned me, what came close?

Finding the exact language for what we have to say is not only a
woman's problem; it is the one all writers wrestle with all the time. But
I think there is some particular way in which I, as a woman writer,
came to the search. It is to do with not agreeing that there is a right way
to say things, not accepting the monolithic shape of the prevailing
culture, but seeing that there are many ways, a wide variety, as wide as
people's experience, and that in among them, there is mine. It's a
subtly different approach, a relaxation, an inquiry. It allows us to
break new ground.

For me, it connects with what I have written in the 'Crafting'
section, about writing in the margin, being interested in the sub-text,
the story beside the story. So often, in women's experience, what seems
to be going on is not what is going on. We have perfected a way of
abstracting ourselves, of being 'elsewhere', our thoughts and desires
being somehow sealed away, beneath the surface of what we are doing.
I think that conversations between women – in which links and
assumptions exist, that do not have to be explained – often show this.
Women's humour shows it. It is very rapid and intuitive and often
quite off-beat. Now, all the theorising about sub-texts and so on may
sound very 1970s fashionable and jargon-ish; but at the time I was
seized by the possibilities that this way of thinking and writing
presented. It was at last possible to make central what I had been
brought up to think of as marginal; or to assert that the marginal can
be central. It represents a whole shift in experience. It also allowed me
to put myself somewhere directly in the narrative, and to move quite
freely in and out of the 'I' character, where things are told in the first
person. In *The Woman in the Tower* I think I grasped this for the first
time; it is why it is an important book for me. The tension, or where the
accuracy needs to be, is in the connection between the story that is told,
and the comment on the story – or what is felt and experienced from
the sidelines, so to speak. This may have its roots very early in my life,
in the experience of having stories told to me: there was the story-teller,
a certain cousin, and there was the story, but there was also the story of
what was going on for me, the listener, and how I was making the story
my own. My own comments, my own desires, mattered; and the story
could be shaped by them. I think that this counts. The story, thus

experienced, becomes the listener's own story, and she becomes the story-teller. The process of gradually daring more and more to believe in the truthfulness of this way of working has been important, to me. The small girl becomes the person telling the story – but the story, which is history, which happened, also exists in its own right. Language is therefore intimately connected not only with expressing what is happening in the margins, but in its connection with the 'official' version. And I think that for many women, the official version is not our own, however well we train ourselves to make use of it. This is how I see the flexibility of the novel – as a way of continually finding new ways of using language, to match the quality of lived experience to show the tension between it and what has gone before.

'There is no feminine in eternity . . .'
Medbh McGuckian

Poetry concerns taboos. Poetry is what we are not allowed to talk about. A poem boils out of a specific occasion, a state of mind, a poem is an occasion of sin. When I look at the trickle of women's poetry, I am drowned in the immensity and grandeur of male surnames. I prefer to hold on to Virginia setting *The Waste Land* in type, absorbing and disgorging Joyce. That is more satisfying than deifying Plath and Dickinson, it's like Alice James choosing to die in England. I touch the foetal body of women's poetry like a tear in the human ocean. Did any of them in their time sufficiently surmount their gender to make a single universal poetic statement? Whereas when Eliot said, 'We are the hollow men', women were automatically included, or when Yeats said, 'A man must choose /Perfection of the life or of the work', women were automatically excluded. I have to live under this mountain and try to belong to it without becoming narrow or jealous, to be eternally grateful to Milton without being deluged into silence, to continue what women have begun without succumbing to the inevitable real or ritual self-immolation. Far from being comfortable, it is hazardous, the woman artist because of her ambition, treads a lonely and treacherous path. I have only to quote Isadora Duncan, in her autobiography:

> My life has known but two motives – Love and Art – often Love destroyed Art, and often the imperious call of Art put a tragic end to Love. For those two have no accord but only constant battle.

That prospect seems gloomy enough, but she adds, bereft of her children:

> I remained calmly in the garden by the blue sea, pondering on the strange difference which divides life from Art, and often wondering if a woman can really be an artist, since Art is a hard

taskmaster who demands everything. Whereas a woman who loves gives up everything to life. At any rate . . . I was for the second time, completely separated and immobilised from my Art.

Certainly, this seems to have been the case in the first half of this century – witness also the miserable fate of the painter Gwen John. It is easier in this age for many reasons, and I take support wherever I find it, in the young, in children, in other women who do not have children but write, in other men who write and other men who have children. Motherhood, as it has become less of a risk in general, seems to me not only not incompatible with poetry, but the necessary prelude to it. The nineteenth-century stereotype of the blue-stockinged virgin poet has almost entirely given way to an almost exact twentieth-century equivalent, that of the free-living feminist or lesbian, from Miss to Ms. I have a great affection for the picture of Emily Brontë's loaves rising, but am fonder of Tsvetaeva, one daughter living, one daughter dead, clearing a defiant space on the kitchen table. To be torn apart by births or revolutions or both, and survive at least for a time, is a prerequisite for the fullest genuine genius to flower. But everyone lives their life.

My own language and grammar is so doubly foreign it is practically an advantage; my fellow Irishmen are so busy reclaiming the myths and genres, I don't have that to do, the spade-work has been done. They are enmeshed in political dilemmas which distress me less radically than my geological dissociations. Whether Ireland is sewn up or not it is still my Genesis, my wilderness. I feel closer to Anna Akhmatova or Alice James than to the women of Cork or Galway, because my experience is the inheritance of amputation and volcanic bloodshed. These multiple conflicts fragment me every time I stop thinking and begin to write.

I was reading a war diary the other day by an Englishwoman, Mrs Milburn, whose fears and nerves were so well disciplined by her imperial culture that they only leaked into anxieties over a new hat or the dwindling of the joint. My identity as a person, plus my validity as a woman, are in turmoil day and night, and any attempt to stabilise me by dredging up a bevy of Anglo-Irish poetesses is as futile as reading 'Aurora Leigh'. We go on from here, we take our past with us, we bury our genes.

Among my own poems, I have none that say instantly 'mistresspiece' to me or capture the vital esence of womanhood, her childhood, her growing up, her constantly re-evalued relationships. Men also are finding the pose of poet embarrassing after Passchendaele and

Auschwitz. We share their diffidence now like the landgirls and civilians, it makes an important bond because it is a defect. Not even Wordsworth could smoke a blithe pipe on Westminster Bridge if his spirit happened to pass that way. It's up to us as women to subsume our particular and well-earned neurosis as sexual misfits into the general sense of millenial crisis, which is far more nourishingly unhealthy. If men have to learn how to be men again, women have to learn with them for the first time what it is to be women.

I'd like to see honest, genuine, moving, memorable, quotable, accurate poems in English about women's pleasure and pain. There may be some in other languages, but searching for *the* poem on birth I find a euphorically sentimental journey by Molly Holden, elsewhere so worthwhile: 'I assure you that it's never blood'. How many would assure her that in their experience it's never anything else? Women seem so eager to be corporate they will not be individuals, they generalise their experience instead of stressing the uniqueness of each woman's separateness. There's a forgetful and regressive clash between the will of nature and the will of the mind over the body, so we fail to paint poetically the ultimate stretchings. Something pulls the edges together quickly again. Because the pain is so often so close to the pleasure – as, for example, in breast-feeding – we express ourselves coyly. Poetry shouldn't be a surgical bandage over miscarriages and mutilations. Perhaps our lives are too gory for fiction, as Wordsworth may have meant, too deep for tears, though I think Fleur Adcock's 'Blue Glass' the most delicately inoffensive evocation of female autoeroticism.

The subtlety of not offending with details that can so easily slip into the squalid and the entrailly. It's simplistic to say, men's perceptions of themselves are more immediate, when the 'Ode to a Nightingale' was a direct sublimation of a sore throat and haemorrhage. I think Keats and blood-covered Owen must have known more about women than Yeats parading in his fur coat. Clare and Edward Thomas were closer to us in their depressions than Coleridge on his highs.

It seems to me the poor were all women, and death has been such a leveller, had such dominion in this age that no one feels masculine any more. Douglas Dunn suggests that Michael Longley is 'one of the few poets writing who has had the candour to draw extensively from the anima of his personality.' I like that idea, the spectrum of animus-anima being common to *all* poets.

'I am a feminist, and . . .'
Marcella Evaristi

It's very hard to know where to begin with this section. My sense of being a woman; my writing; my feminism – they are all so bound up together. I think it's a pity when women writers disavow their feminism, as if it suggested they were members of some restrictive partisan cadre. I'm a feminist writer. I'm also a writer whose sympathies are socialist. I've never understood why being personally apolitical suggested a sort of literary purity. I think it would be very odd if I wasn't a feminist, I don't know many black people who are take-it-or-leave-it on apartheid.

So much of writing involves bearing witness bravely and it's hard sustaining the confidence to do that. The kind of humour which operates in my plays does so by eliciting a response of wincing recognition. And that *recognising* is what happens, at the simplest level, when women confide, admit, anguish together. The feeling of, 'Yes, it is so.' The relief of, 'God, I'd never have thought it. *You* too?'

Whenever I have been completely won over by a piece of writing, whenever a literary work has totally excited and impressed me, I've always been aware of something that we should all as shakily confident writers keep in mind. It's that the response is rarely, 'Well, goodness me, I never knew that about Papua New Guinea, if only I *had*, I could have written a terrific novel,' but rather a sense of, 'Yes, I have always known that in my bones.' This sounds as if I'm saying that good literature just feeds our prejudice, flatters our ignorance. I'm not. It's not a literal thing about *information*. But about recognising; about valuing our perceptions. Good art gives people back their dignity. Which is exactly what our politics should look to.

Holding the World Open
Nicki Jackowska

We romanticise the front-line that lies elsewhere: Nicaragua, Chile, South Africa . . . *Our* front-line is tricky, and demands all our attention and commitment; *there is a war on, a war on consciousness and thus on reality* . . . the tools we use to see and understand each other are as much under attack by the state apparatus as are our health, education and social services.

> *N J, from a letter published in* Granta *magazine*

We are witnessing an attempt to re-educate the entire British population at the most fundamental level. We are being educated as to what attitude we should take to our fellow human beings, what our 'enterprise' in life should be, and even as to what we are.

An example of the highest mode of citizenship is now a man who got hold of a large quantity of leather and made clothes out of it to sell in one of the smart new shops in Sheffield.* This man answers the ministerial instruction to 'find something people want, make it and sell it.'

We are all now valued only in terms of what we can earn. How long will it be before 'rationalisation' and 'balancing the books' can find no place for imaginative language? How long before language itself must be rationalised to meet the dominant market-oriented reality? What then of the delicate and subtle 'thing' that is a person's writing – not an object (except in book-form) but an entire world?

At such a time, I find it difficult to perceive a theft and appropriation of language by men to the deprivation of women. It seems to me that what we are witnessing is the theft of the language which represents or

---

*Featured on Panorama's investigation into the New Social Security Act, BBC 1, 14 March 1988.

embodies a certain level or dimension of experience, to the potential deprivation of all human beings. We are being asked to take a stand towards our fellow human beings which is composed of fear, suspicion, contempt – and even disassociation as members of the same community. How far from this to the view of Jews, blacks, homosexuals, the disabled, as sub-human?

People are dying from lack of resources. But there is another death – of ourselves as alive and realising our full potential, in touch with a spectrum of subtle and enriching experience, which alone can give meaning to what we normally term 'reality'. I do not consider the current British government fully human in implementing these divisions. The only rational response is refusal to comply.

I refuse, therefore, to write of male and female language. I will speak of a language which is concerned with experience and embodies or enshrines an attitude. Language is a carrier of values, attitudes, relationships – whatever the overt subject-matter. This is not a question of vague and amorphous directives to 'love the world and all that is in it'. It is more rational than that. Language – with its images, associations, resonances, metaphors and comparisons – is in the business of a subtle and complex process of education and persuasion. If this government is closing down *options* – and I mean options for extending our experience as well as our choice of food – then my writing must, *of necessity*, act against that in its *holding the world open* and continuing to expand the consciousness of myself and male and female readers together.

Both men *and* women are presented with choices of what to uphold, what to represent. There is male and female writing which embodies a cynical, cheap and alienated view of reality and people, just as by contrast both men and women contribute to a sentimental and nostalgic literature which shrouds and distorts what is really happening.

I have always been suspicious of archetypes. I do not experience a male entity or 'soul' (in the Jungian sense) within myself as my muse or anything else. What I do experience, and believe, is that each human being has the capacity to utilise an infinite range of qualities and behaviour. At any given time, under certain specific conditions and influences, a certain quality might dominate. A combination of history, education, material conditions, relationships (inner and outer forces), will all exert force and produce a state of mind, an act.

We cannot entirely unravel each moment's truth. But what else is literature but the tool or container for reaching towards it, and what else is fiction but the capacity to enter an experience that is not *entirely* one's own? I'm thinking of the Brighton vicar who wrote from the point of view of a twelve-year-old Muslim girl. Or my own sense of identification with the Vietnam veterans who now live in the woods, unable to cope with society and its mores. Isn't this what unites us, this bridge the imagination builds to step into another world? Aren't we all juggling with questions of rapport/identification, and disassociation/disconnection, all the time?

I have found my books understood and entered into by men as well as by women. As though women *and* men are struggling to break out of the limited experience expected of them by society, and thus imposed on them by each other. For me the 'work' of literature is to open up these dimensions – for myself and for anyone who cares to read me. How else can we know anything, or how continue, if we are not *more* than our own self-definition? And how else can we deal with the smile on the face of a politician who dares to tell us what we are. For this, we need a language which will both resist, redeem and celebrate.

> Tenderness is political dynamite because of the way it equalises subject and object . . . Power relations, by contrast, depend upon inequality and imbalance, an oppressed and an oppressor.
>
> *From a review of 'Kiss of the Spiderwoman'*

If I can't dance, I don't want to be part of your revolution
Emma Goldman

Writing (Capital W)
Valerie Hannagan

As a child, I enjoyed writing. However, it was an uncomplicated relationship: no agonising over the right word, no deep love; not yet. I mainly wrote what I was told to write – essays, thank-you letters – and took absolutely for granted the quiet pleasure I felt. I also kept a diary, of course, and wrote long letters to my best friend; but there again, I told myself that such activities were commonplace: I wrote like all the girls of my age.

Something happened when I was in my late teens. I don't know what exactly. Perhaps a feeling of insecurity and panic, of 'I'll never make it'. Anyway, the quiet pleasure of writing disappeared overnight: one day I picked up my pen, as they say, and nothing. That's when I realised how much writing had mattered to me, how formative it had been and how I would miss the tender excitement I used to feel each time I locked myself in the shelter of my bedroom, to cover sweet-smelling paper in blue or purple signs. Of course, I tried to bring it back to life: I searched through memories, dug out old school notebooks; but I found nothing there but sadness and nostalgia. The thread was cut and there was no turning back. It was time to put aside childish things – including the joy of writing.

This state of mind lasted a long time. I went to university in Paris; I must have written dozens of essays: I don't remember a single one. After my *licence* I left France, full of hopes. At last I was going to earn a living, make a mark on the real world. I first tried my luck as a bank clerk – a total failure, I've no head for figures – before opting for teaching, which suited me much better. I liked my pupils; the school was in a working-class district, the teaching staff fairly militant. I joined groups, went on marches, discovered the exhilaration of political action. Writing (capital W) was a thing of the past; I didn't miss it at all – or so I thought. Of course, I wrote various things – worksheets, minutes, pamphlets against racism – but the aim was to translate as clearly as possible the ideas of the group to which I belonged. I liked this anonymity, or rather my new collective identity.

A few years went by. I moved to another school and was given sixth-form groups, to whom I was to teach A-level French. How amazing to come upon my childhood friends: Rimbaud, Baudelaire, Queneau, Camus, Zola . . . and to realise that I had aged, and they hadn't. For my students, it was a first encounter. Excited, brimming over with questions, they interrupted each other, frowned, laughed. And although I had through my teaching made such a meeting possible, I suffered pangs of sadness. I envied them, I would have liked to be their age. I felt excluded from their group by the role of teacher I took so seriously. I didn't yet know that this vague sense of exile and loss was in fact Writing getting in touch at last, after years of separation and silence.

Patiently, it tried to seek me out. A difficult task: I was determined not to respond. What did I have to say, after all? Everything had already been written, libraries overflowed with books . . . I had nothing to add. Sometimes Writing hid in a Brahms symphony, in Debussy's *Estampes*; it pestered me, brought tears to my eyes: 'There!' it would say, 'they've managed to find a way of expressing their inner vision; you could do the same, if only you listened to me, if only you *wanted* me'. I would shrug my shoulders, slip away quietly, and the chase would start all over again. It was a little like a game of Blind Man's Buff; Writing kept inching towards me and I kept saying, 'You can't catch me.' I jeered at it, believing I was free.

One day, however, it got the better of me. I was teaching a third-year group and it was the blessed moment where, after oral work and reading, a written task is given out. If all is well, the pupils have understood enough to manage more or less by themselves. A pleasant silence spreads over the class and the teacher takes a break. You can daydream while pretending to catch up on paperwork, or wander about the room, stopping now and then to look over an absorbed pupil's shoulder.

I suddenly felt very happy. It wasn't because I particularly liked that group; rather, it had something to do with the quality of silence, with the way it was filled with all the little sounds of writing at work. Hands whispered over the pages; titles were underlined with brief, neat strokes; full stops and commas fell like muffled hail. I looked at my pupils. One of them was staring out of the window, seeking her inspiration in the trees, the sky, the modest horizon of institutional buildings; the hand holding the pen was poised in mid-sentence and waited, trembling slightly. Another was writing non-stop, sheltering her book with her right arm (she was left-handed), keeping her work jealously to herself, while her neighbour noisily threw down her pen, gave a half-exasperated, half-satisfied sigh, yawned and stretched noisily. 'Finished, Miss.' She gave me her book. The paper smelt good, the pages crackled under the force of hastily framed words; and that's when I became two people. The teacher in me patiently explained that in order to master French grammar one had to slow down a little, take time to read through one's work, to correct any mistakes. But my other voice – the writer's – delighted in her enthusiasm, in the potent miracle of creativity. She heard both my messages and when I looked into her radiant face, I realised with infinite relief that she saw no contradiction between them. Writing stood on the threshold, bearing gifts; and this time, I opened the door.

My problems weren't over, alas. For a long time it remained coiled up inside me, rather lazily I must say. I tried to write poetry, short stories; Writing slept on, or else pulled a face at my offerings.

I decided to consult the experts. What was needed was a thorough study of Literary Theory. Surely that would bring on labour. So I went back to University, in London this time, and launched into my M A with great determination. How hard it was to be on the other side of the fence! I pored over huge books, agonised over the meaning of it all and went through hell with each essay: hardly a flicker from Writing. The study of the *Nouveau Roman* did create a minor stir, however: the importance of language . . . of dreams . . . of the unconscious . . . of puns . . . Like a cartoon character, Writing opened one eye, cocked an ear towards these interesting sounds; but when it saw I didn't really understand them, it sank back into its torpor. And I looked on as Robbe-Grillet, Sarraute and Butor frolicked in green pastures from which I felt utterly excluded. I was nothing but a tiny eavesdropping child; they were grown-ups in the Land of the Great.

Then something extraordinary happened. I made new friends. Which doesn't mean I abandoned old ones. It wasn't a matter of rejecting Zola, Camus, Barthes and company, not at all. Rather, I discovered that others had been eavesdropping by my side, and one day all of us tinies got together and realised that, well, the grass on which we stood was green. Not greener; no comparison with the Land of the Great was necessary any longer, since lo! it had vanished out of sight. And we grew big and strong on our own terms, and Writing quickened under the watchful eye of my midwives: Annie Leclerc, Emma Santos, Luce Irigaray, Hélène Cixous, Chantal Chawaf, and

Monique Wittig; and also Adrienne Rich, Sylvia Plath, Jean Rhys, Alice Walker, Michèle Roberts, Sara Maitland . . . Such a vast crowd of them, of us; and getting larger all the time.

And then it was born, at last. A harrowing process: Writing had set its conditions – the rigours of passion, a broken heart. (Nothing soft or gentle about women's writing, or women's love for that matter.) I had just turned thirty: I honestly thought that my life was over, that nothing more could happen to me. One should never think such things. The superstitious say, 'The devil will hear you,' and that is exactly what happened. Looking back, I can laugh at the memory of sleepless nights and mad desires. At the time it wasn't so funny: love made me ill, I lost weight, did all sorts of foolish things. But what a wonderful illness! This was Life: it wasn't over, it would never end; I was immortal. And Writing decided that its time had come, and filled the air with its cries.

My very first text came into the world on a stormy, sorrowful night. Hurt by the one I loved, I yelled, shook, thrashed around; I wanted to smash everything. And a little wild child came out of the darkness, running. She was running through the city, a city devastated by some apocalyptic event. She was running to conquer fear; she was running so fast it was like flying. And with each step she gave a new name to what surrounded her. She had a body: she was there, all of her, in her movement. She was the exiled child I had missed so much.

Newborn, Writing wasn't easy. Her screams pulled me out of bed in the middle of the night. Horrified, I wondered how to make them cease, how to soothe her. Madness lurked. I soon realised that to remain sane, I had to take care of myself. I would make some herb tea, wrap myself in the blue woollen blanket my father had given me for my twentieth birthday, place a hot-water bottle under my frozen feet and light an incense-stick. It was only when this little ritual had been observed that I could understand what Writing wanted, why she had woken me up. I would then open my notebook, write the date (like my pupils!) and begin.

These first texts, as you will no doubt have guessed, were rather tormented, not to say hysterical. I wrote them for myself, or rather for her, Writing. There was no other reader. At the thought of being read I would shake my head: 'They'll never understand.' I was all alone with my autistic child.

Fortunately, things gradually got better. I at last agreed to talk to other mothers, so to speak. I was lucky enough to meet writers who had gone through that terrible time and had not only survived, but gone on to produce texts all the more beautiful for being written in hope and joy, rather than just in anguish. We could love our readers; we could love writing; we could love ourselves. Creativity was no longer a crime.

In August 1985, I had a short story called 'Una' published in *Spare Rib* under the pen-name of Vanessa Grey.

'Una'. I look at you now, a few years on. You have many faults but you've aged well, and I still love you as much as the day I wrote you, or rather as the day you wrote yourself. Do you remember how you made me stay away from school to finish you? And how I kept reading you, over and over again, until I knew you by heart, down to the last dot and dash and comma? Clever, subtle child: there isn't a single masculine pronoun about you, but it doesn't show; no rules broken: you look perfectly normal.

I promise to give you lots of sisters, to keep learning from other women and to sign my own name with pride: no more pseudonyms.

The time has come to celebrate.

Writing has come of age.

A Pandora's Box for Writing
Emma Tennant

The fact that I am a woman is a very important element in my work. My books have run alongside the women's movement, so that if there hadn't been a women's movement (which now seems impossible to imagine), I don't know what kind of books – if any – I would have written. Whoever said that the women's revolution would be the greatest revolution of the twentieth century was right: the women's movement is the most interesting and extraordinary movement of this century, and all its new ways of looking at the world have produced a rush of new talent, together with the vital rediscovery of women writers of the past. I don't think it's so much the case that women generically see things in a different way, as that years and years of being downtrodden has given women another eye: often, women see things in more detail, with more colour, and observe psychic states more closely, than the equivalent 'male' eye. The women's movement has opened a Pandora's Box as far as writing is concerned. All the novels of madness are hardly surprising when you think that, in the fifties, women were actually being subjected to electric shock-treatment, tied down with E C T clamps wired to their lips, in an attempt to shake them out of what was often simply their refusal to belong to a society which pigeon-holed them housewife/mother/cook. Whole states of mind formerly laughed at by male critics have flooded out, and I think there is now a return to a *Golden Notebook* realism, a clearer look at women's situation and what can be done. Personally, I wouldn't have embarked on the *Jekyll and Hyde* project if I weren't hoping that as a fable of women's position and the ludicrous inequality that still exists it might be of interest or use to someone.

I don't think there is such a thing as a 'woman's sentence' as opposed to a man's sentence. I think a woman's eye will often see things that a man will not see, or hear things a man will not hear, but I think this is to do with upbringing and environment rather than with generic differences. This other ear and eye will produce a different kind of writing and form, but if I read an imagist poet like Hilda Doolittle, I see crisp, strong writing which could easily be taken for a man's. So far, I don't think women have had all that much choice about what to write about, because of the narrowing process that takes place from puberty on which limits girls' choice of careers. The back of Penguins always used to say about male writers: 'he was merchant-seaman, bartender, carpenter', and it isn't really surprising that women have been inclined to write about domestic affairs since not very many have been foreign secretary, or in a position to observe life in a mill, or on the factory-floor; what can you describe if you haven't been further than school, marriage, children, a part-time job, except memories, childhood, a love-affair, and your domestic life? Often, I think women need to be far more gifted than men to transform something as prosaic and banal as childhood, school, a love-affair, which we have all had, into what they frequently do: marvellous, glowing works of fiction which actually help people to see life in a better way.

In the Basement
Sue Roe

I needed a change of mood to write this section. I just burst out of the house and sort of fell into the park. Out here in the street, there is a wonderful light over everything – the world seems charged, after concentrated hours at the typewriter. It is all green and yellow, and the wind is soft and strong and beautiful. Into the park, across the grass, past the tennis courts and all the little babies in their horizontal stripes, wriggling in the sand-pit, across the street and round by the houses. All the way, I am thinking, I want a bigger house, I want a garden. I think I'll put a fragment of the stories I have been writing about love into the *Notebook*. I want to go on and on writing about erotic love, and how it bathes everything in great shafts of light . . .

A baby has turned up in the basement again. This is always happening to me. Babies are always appearing in the basement. This one is rather more of a distraction than the one that lived in the basement of the house where I wrote *Estella*. To begin with, it has a certain fragile beauty, and some rather startling black hair. And its mother is superb. Her hair is spiked like a punk's, and when it rains she pushes the pram with its little white umbrella up, wearing a vicious-looking black shiny mac with padded shoulders, and some tarty-looking high heels. Just as you have got the measure of this idea of their separateness, the sun comes out and she comes up the steps wearing a stripey T-shirt, cradling the baby's head. If I am working at the window and I see them coming out together I just throw whatever it is I am working on across the room and go for a drive instead. If only I could paint properly, I could at least get rather dirty and be feeling my way round and through an object. Writing is too remote. The edge of a page could cut you – actually slit your skin – if you weren't careful. The paper is too dry. It is too late. I have spent too long out of the fray; have let it all go by . . . That kind of thing. (I hold that baby responsible for all this.)

I have never felt that the language I write in is a language forged by men. All I have felt – without, I think, fully realising it at the time – is that I dare not expose myself. I dare not give my voice full expression. Virginia Woolf is supposed to have felt this, and she used it as a device when she tried to write polemically, or to deliver speeches, but I am not at all sure that her problems with 'telling the truth about the body' had very much to do with the structures or shapes of the language itself – more with a highly personalised process of censorship which was to do, I think, with her being very careful not to release too many painful memories too soon.

Women writers. I think immediately of women who wrote of – or under – emotional and/or psychological distress, who re-crafted language to accommodate not only fine gradations of meaning, but also the notion of meaning in the act of being forged; meaning in flux; emotion in the process of being realised. H.D., especially, I think. And Jean Rhys, in her different way – a language which she spoke and heard spoken, a language of inflection, stripped of all pretension, all notion of performance. I wonder if this is true of male writers. I think of Beckett, Joyce, Conrad . . . This doesn't apply, in quite the way I mean it, to any of them. I think when we talk about 'women's writing' we are actually thinking about the business of writing about sexuality and the difficulty of bringing this experience into a state of realisation. H.D.'s writing is all about this, of course. As is, I think, Virginia Woolf's. Interestingly enough, when I read Henry James I feel he is extraordinarily good at *describing* this, but that he is not simultaneously experiencing its implications as he writes – painfully, painfully recalling and re-crafting it, in the very process of forging a sentence.

I think the notion of writing as being expressive of the body must on some level be important. I wonder whether women's writing tends to be questing, and questioning, rather than expressive of or working towards resolution. Behind some of the most powerful writing by women there is a desire to occupy the physical world in play; a desire to stop watching and become involved: this is very strong in Virginia Woolf's work; also in Jean Rhys's. But how? The women characters seem in some profound sense to be unqualified. There is always some obscure missing link – the heroines (I am thinking primarily here of nineteenth-century heroines, I have just realised) are never quite in command of themselves, and most 'serious' heroines are in agony for much of the narrative. Either in agony, like Lucy Snowe, or living obliquely, on some level pretentiously, at one remove, like Gwendoline Harleth.

Do male writers quite capture this state? I think immediately of the mother in Paul Bailey's *Gabriel's Lament*. Her actions depict this state wonderfully. Agonisingly. But Paul Bailey doesn't show it from the inside, in fact it is crucial to the development of the narrative that he does not do so. She is a fabulously tragic character, but we are given her tragedy in rather the same way as Dickens presents his female characters' tragedies: what we are arrested by, as a reader, are the gaps in the narrative; the silences. When Dickens comes up against a situation of great complexity, to do with questions of gender, he freezes the characters. Paralyses them. As with Miss Havisham and Estella. This is a fantastically effective way of writing. I am full of admiration, reading it. *Gabriel's Lament* I admire at least as much as, perhaps more than, anything else I have ever read. But it is not the *same* experience as reading a novel by, for example, Jean Rhys or H.D. There are definite technical differences. I don't have the space to examine them in detail here. And not all women writers write like H.D. and Jean Rhys, of course.

Writing always needs to reflect change; flux; brinks; turning-points. For our knowledge of such moments, such times, we necessarily reach back into ourselves and recall moments of crisis, shock, change. Is the 'crisis' of adolescence, for example, very different for women and men; do its 'traumas' manifest themselves differently? Surely the expectations which accompany such moments are profoundly – and historically – different. I sense that this is obscurely to do with the relationship between the body and the construction of the unconscious.

There is a great deal of writing about the connections between gender and writing. A lot of it is very repetitive, and borrows its insights – directly or indirectly – from the theories of psychoanalysis. I don't think there has been very much sheer speculation, very much allowing the imagination to run riot on this issue, since we are all so concerned not to be prejudiced, not to be sexist. I think it would be quite interesting to examine our prejudices on the subject.

Something else occurs to me: for women, during adolescence, there is a sense that a lot of things have got to happen and a lot of things have got to change. Often there is the feeling that there wasn't enough space, there wasn't enough time, to move things into their respective new places. A lot of things got stuck. When a thing gets stuck, you find yourself going back and back into it, time and time again . . . There must be somebody we can blame for this . . . (When there was a hurricane in Sussex last year, and whole trees were uprooted and complete slabs of pavement and cars and houses and parks were smashed to pieces and beach huts and caravans just concertina'd and the sea was the colour of old, stewed tea for weeks, my brother said, one of the reasons this feels so strange is that nobody's to blame.) We are in the habit of blaming somebody. Men. Women.

I wonder if the tragedy of life's inability to hold and sustain passion is obscurely satisfying to men (which may be why there are plenty of mistresses and not nearly so many 'masters'). I think it is appalling and anguishing for women – there is surely a fault, an accident, a missing link there somewhere. We feel that it is up to us to identify it. The sustained penalty of loving is eroding, distressing to women; resonant and moving and satisfying to men . . .? This makes me feel that it is unlikely that a woman could have written Shakespeare's tragedies. The transcendence and co-existence of such things as power, strategy, moral good, public honour, political gamesmanship, over passionate love, is not quite acceptable to me as a complete, an overall vision. I cannot imagine myself keeping all this in perspective. I think this must be because I experience power as being to do with that feeling that every pore of the skin, every surface, every sensual faculty, is open, whereas I don't think men experience power like that at all. I am profoundly bored by the idea of gamesmanship, but every very powerful man I know is inspired by this idea. They find it enormously satisfying to win (which necessarily means that somebody else loses), whereas I have a terrible habit of letting go of things because the idea of somebody else losing is so troubling to me. Yes, it sounds ridiculous, I know.

Perhaps we want to remember our discoveries, because they were always in some obscure measure incomplete and by remembering them we might perhaps retrieve and re-run them; make them more satisfying; more complete. Our innocence has value. I don't know if men feel the same about this, or what it would mean to a male writer to write about childhood (I wonder what Paul Bailey went through, writing about Gabriel). I think it would be interesting to talk to writers about their childhoods. It is interesting to see how many artists work gradually back to the imagery (if not the actual stories) of their childhoods – it is a starting point a writer often reaches only after years of crafting. The female childhood landscape . . . The male childhood landscape . . . But any comparison would be only a comparison between individuals. Rebecca West interests me, because as a novelist she has such an innocent voice, compared with her polemical voices.

I continue to be interested in the Modernist women writers, in whose work there is a feeling of walking in dread of some violent invasion – a form of takeover, but one which cannot happen – or, which they will not allow to happen – without creating a new way; a new vision: something they at once must and cannot resist wreaks violence, is forced through. And out of this comes a new way of seeing. I am thinking about H.D.'s fiction; about the feeling I have, reading it, that I am almost catching her breath, that I am poised, with her, on the edge of a moment of new insight or re-interpretation; that I am on the brink, with almost every sentence, of some anticipated change. There is a strong, sharp feeling that things cannot remain as they are, even for the duration of a moment; that the significance she has just discerned, has just grasped, is about to be removed. I always want to speak her lines, to read her work aloud; she writes on the edge of meaning, as though collapse might at any moment take place. And this is obscurely reminiscent, for me . . .

I think that when people think about the relationship between women and writing, or attempt to define 'women's writing', they often fail to ask enough questions. Women writers are very different one from another, though. A writer who is seldom mentioned in this context, but whose writing is very important because I feel she actually effects changes in the shape and structure of the writing because of her feminist insights, is Caroline Blackwood. Emma Tennant's writing is also very important in this respect. As with all great art, the writers must have suffered and changed in the process of producing it. I would want to think, when I think about 'women and writing', about the relationship between an artist and a powerful and demanding work of art. Only then would the question of gender difference really become interesting. The great artist is not thinking about how his or her work will change the world, or people's attitudes. The great artist has had to submit, as the work evolves, to a process of suffering and change.

Anybody's 'I'
Sue Stewart

The world of the imagination is genderless and, in this sense as much as any other, I sometimes feel it's more real than 'real' life. Some poems for instance, read countless times, can still astonish or overawe me: I feel the poem as a direct arrow from the poet's subconscious to mine, with language as the go-between. I do prefer the more lyrical poetry, that concerns itself with the subconscious or spirit, to political or social poetry, but this is not a rigid thing, and it's certainly no value judgement. I've been very impressed and moved by some political poems – whether feminist, left-wing or just plain angry – and there are plenty of people who will argue that poetry must live in the marketplace if it has to serve any function at all. I don't feel that way about it, I don't feel poetry needs a 'function' or needs to justify itself to any 'ism' or anybody. It just is.

When I began reviewing poetry I quickly gravitated towards women poets, partly out of a natural sympathy, partly out of positive discrimination. I feel this discrimination is almost as necessary now as it was a hundred years ago, but not because woman's poetic voice is necessarily different from man's: just less heard. My work is very different from that of the man I live with, but I don't think this points to a general rule: it's more a difference of personality than gender. I know many male poets whose work is softer than mine, more 'yin', and many women poets whose work is very 'yang' by comparison. Thankfully, there are now anthologies of women's poetry entering the market, and the variety of subject and style contained in them gives ample room for dissention. One group of poems would suggest a fundamental difference in the way women express themselves in poetry: that they were more honest than men, more personal, or suffered more. Other poems would suggest that women were more objective, restrained even: cool, classical poems that enlighten rather than give solace. For a historical sweep, I enjoyed *The World Split*

Open (The Women's Press) and *The Penguin Book of Women Poets.* And since 1985 there have been four anthologies, concentrating solely on twentieth-century poets, which have given me great sustenance: *Making for the Open* (Chatto), *The Bloodaxe Book of Contemporary Women Poets, The Faber Book of 20th Century Women's Poetry* and *Purple and Green* (Rivelin Grapheme Press). There may well be more, but these are the only ones I've come across.

When I'm writing I try to rediscover an early, untainted, childlike state, whilst keeping a watchful adult eye on what's going on, and making notes. I aim for a type of innocence, an openness and optimism. If I don't capture this feeling then the poem won't lift off at all, it'll be earthbound, a lead balloon. I don't mean that I only try to write celebratory poetry; rather, that even a dark poem still needs to have been made with great care. My aim is to make the reader feel the emotion, not to relive it myself all over again in the writing.

I also find that tact and diplomacy don't work on the page, so I try to be as honest as possible. I don't mean self-revelatory: the 'I' of the poem is not the same thing as the personal 'I'. I think of it as a 'supra-I', anybody's 'I', a pronoun looking for a person, a reader, to claim it. Imaginative 'knowing' might then lighten, contradict or complicate a tangible one. I like the creative tension that can operate where personal details earth the poem, imagination lifts it. The personal might then be transmuted, and the poem suggest at something other, something bigger than itself.

Writing as a Second Heart
Hélène Cixous

I am a woman, and this cannot be dissociated from my writing. The act of writing is not separate from my woman's being. I am a woman who writes.

Writing is a primary act. It comes from within. I feel it welling up inside me, growing out of me, transforming itself in language. The still dumb flow of writing passes through my woman's body, searching for words. I don't see how it could be separated from what has constituted it; it would be as if one were to ask me to separate my existence from the fact of being a woman.

I feel myself living, I live myself living, and it is the same thing for writing. And I am convinced that a male poet writes in an analogous way, feeling the inseparable relation between what he produces in language, and what passes in his body.

Why do I write? I could reply that I have moral reasons for writing, because I always write about things which seem to me urgent from a moral point of view. I write to save what would otherwise be in danger of disappearing. But this is already a justification for writing, and of course I don't write for this reason. This is what I write, but the fact that I write, its cause, lies elsewhere. I write because I have to. I need to write, like I need to eat, like I need to sleep, like I need to make love. It's like a second heart. I feel that by writing I continually renew myself and replenish vital forces. I need the incessant movement from body to symbol, from symbol to body; for me the two things are intrinsically linked.

If She Could Read Me Now
Jeannie Brehaut

The first girl I ever fell in love with was a twelve-year-old warrior. She and I spent one impossible year skipping junior high-school together. We lived in the leafiest, greenest suburb of Toronto so there were plenty of places to hide. Our favourite place was up on the hill where we sat and talked. I loved her and she let me. She was a girl and I was a girl. It was the beginning of my real life.

At the end of the school year we had a fight. I didn't understand what it was about. I wouldn't apologise and neither would she. Our friends couldn't help us. My love-affair with her was one big unrecorded secret. Then she was gone.

When her mother died I looked for her everywhere. The last thing I heard was that one dark night a man with a gold ring on every finger found her. She left with him because she wanted the one who loved her best to be a man.

I didn't and I don't. After she left I read every book in the young people's fiction section in our branch of the Toronto Public Library. There were no stories in there about my life.

Not finding anything to read about lesbians didn't mean I stopped being one. The secret unlived life of the lesbian child I was just went underground for a time. I didn't have these or any other words for what I was feeling. I missed my friend. I thought there was something wrong with me. I was very lonely. I didn't talk to anyone about my friend who left me and I took a long time to let go of her inside my head.

The time was Toronto in the mid-seventies but it might as well be present-day Britain. The Clause and Thatcher. Young people who think they may be gay need to be able to go into their local library and find books that address their experience and their feelings. It's in the interest of the entire community that young gay people feel good about themselves and get their needs met.

I'm now a part of this country's large community of gay writers whom the government is attempting to censor. Or, more effectively, encouraging us to censor ourselves. My work could be published and not go into any library or I could be prevented from giving readings because – by my very being – I am in violation of The Clause.

But I'm a writer. I live here. Between waitressing shifts I make up stories. Often I think, 'This is the sort of story I needed to find when I was a girl, and didn't.' I'm not writing happy endings at the moment but I believe they're very possible. I worry about the future implications of The Clause. I get angry. I write.

Coming Out of Limbo
Amryl Johnson

I did not feel confident enough to begin writing in Creole, dialect or as it is now generally referred to, Nation Language, until five years ago. I believe that in doing so, I reclaimed my identity. Prior to that, although I was not aware of it for some considerable length of time, I must surely have been in no man's land.

When I came to this country to join my parents, I was eleven. For the first twelve months, I would be the only black girl at the fee-paying school they sent me to in north London. And for the next four years we would be the only black family in the street. My parents – they went back a few years ago – spoke a mild Trinidadian dialect. Trinidadian Creole is, in any case, not as pronounced as the Creole spoken on some of the other Caribbean islands. Black visitors to the house had also been away from their island of birth a long time and their 'language' had, consequently, been modified. I spoke Standard English right through my school years and, naturally, wrote in Standard English also. English had always been my best subject at school; essays and short stories, my favourite period of any English lesson. None of those early stories show any sense of loss, of an identity being in danger. In fact, I don't think I came into them very much at all. They were largely objective. The main protagonist could well have been a blue-eyed blonde.

Nowadays, that would be extremely unlikely. My preoccupation is a cultural one. My inspiration is Caribbean and will continue to be Caribbean for some time to come. Having been starved of it for such a long time, I am rejoicing in and fascinated by the richness and vigour of the islands. During those early days in this country, however, it was a different story. Even after I became aware of Nation Language being used, reclaimed by black writers and performers in this country, it did not seem relevant to me. Later, a slow sense of recognition began to dawn. There was a longing, a hunger growing. A place where I felt I belong. I think racial prejudice is usually the first knife which starts to gouge. With this recognition came the urge to reclaim language. I did not feel confident, sure enough to attempt Creole in my writing. They were desperate times. I felt as if I was in a state of limbo. I had been away from the Caribbean for too long. It was no longer mine by rights. As a joke sometimes, I would put on a Trinidadian accent. It always sounded false. Most certainly, not in the least authentic. When I eventually plucked up enough courage to try writing in Creole, that also sounded false. The frustration I felt was coupled with a strange sense of guilt and shame. Neither on paper nor verbally did I sound like a woman from the Caribbean. Where did I belong? Who was I? Skin – that of other people's – has never bothered me. From my schooldays onwards, most friends have been white. During my schooldays, maybe, it was because I had no choice. Nowadays, it is a different matter. I accept people for what they are. I am guided by how I relate to the person and not if their skin happens to be the right colour.

During that period of limbo, my quest for an identity was not helped by people saying 'You're so English. You sound so English', or, 'Well, there's a surprise! Speaking to you over the phone, I would never have guessed you weren't English.' They usually meant it as a compliment. Poems of that period may have reflected the conflict but still seemed reluctant to hone-in on anything too specific.

MISSIONARY

You witnessed nothing
I hid it from
your apathy
When you turned your back
you should have
opened your eyes
but you walk like thunder
Cracks
span
your every space
I could not
follow
your lead

So you left me
lame
in your thoughts

> and rearranged
> trodden
> beneath your morality
> Before you reach the edge
> turn once
> and scan the sky
> The eagle
> with a broken wing
> will be me

from *Early Poems by Amryl Johnson*
(Sable Publications, 1982)

Things came to a head with the idea for a novel. As is often the case, that first attempt at novel-writing is autobiographical. The theme centered around a black woman living in this country, away from her country of origin for a number of years. In the novel, the main character has a recurring nightmare. In the dream, her ancestors demand that she takes stock. 'Where do you stand?' they ask her. 'Are you first of all black woman or are you an individual?' In order to get certain facts straight, it meant having to do some research into the slave trade. It would be inaccurate to say my growing sense of awareness was allowed to continue blossoming, gradually. It was as if every book I read on slavery simply went further and further into individual cases of brutality. Unbelievable! Unsurpassed! I became very depressed. Bitterly unhappy. Extremely morose. All white friends seemed in some way responsible. It was one of their ancestors who did the dastardly deed. It was a testing time for many friendships. Not all of them survived. My attitude was more than one or two could bear. So to them, I remain the unforgiven. I went through a strange metamorphosis. That period must surely have found me at the crossroads of my life. The novel was completed but remains unpublished. The fact that I finished it, in itself bears testimony to a courage I had never needed to test until that period of my life and I have never needed to summon since. More importantly, I answered the question I had, unwittingly, been putting in the mouths of my ancestors. Are you firstly an individual and then a black woman? Does the colour of your skin come before all else? Later, I came to understand that there was no conflict. We are the sum of our experiences. I was the sum of my experiences. My individuality is so closely bound up with being a negress that I could not possible separate the two. Nowadays, I would not want to. The two are fused.

Amryl Johnson is a black female writer motivated by things which demand recognition.

Some of my most bitter political poems were written during that period of initiation. I still regard this one as among my best.

MIDNIGHT WITHOUT PITY

Judas, take my hand
let us go from here
down into the valley
Keep your hood tight
about your neck
I do not want to see
your face
and if you still remember
the bitter taste
to know
you never stood a chance
or had a choice
against a destiny
which held you
manipulated you
rejected you
then teach me
teach me
teach me how
to count the silver
and forget the cost
and I am
Black
for I am
angry
my name
is
Midnight
Without
Pity

from *Early Poems by Amryl Johnson*,
(Sable Publications, 1982)

Despite this period and my parents having, by then, returned to Trinidad, it never occured to me to visit the Caribbean. The anger had drawn me towards an idea of self. It had not taken me any further onward in my quest for belonging. I had no place of my own. I had already spent more than two-thirds of my life in a country where I was not wanted. But where was home? I was afraid to regard the Caribbean as home. But the fact remained that I was most certainly in exile. A Trinidadian friend persuaded me to make the trip. Yet it took two years to pluck up enough courage to do so. 1982 found me on a plane bound for a six-week stay in Trinidad around Carnival time.

It gave me the courage to return the following year for a six-month stay on the islands. Those six months took me from Trinidad to Tobago, Grenada, Barbados, St Lucia, Guadeloupe and Dominica. My book of poems *Long Road to Nowhere* (Virago Press, 1985) and the travel-biography *Sequins for a Ragged Hem* (Virago Press, 1988) were inspired by those six months. They weren't easy. I had to come to terms with certain things about myself. Certain things betrayed me as someone who had been away for too long to fit in with the island way of life. The way I walk, the way I talk and my values. So, it wasn't simply a case of returning and celebrations all round. I was an outsider. I did not entirely belong. But it was this distancing effect which had me constantly questioning, examining, evaluating. Those two questions of years earlier would come back to haunt me. Indeed, had they ever stopped haunting? Where do I belong? How do I stand in all this? I was again in a state of limbo. But now I was ready to accept certain truths. If you do not harness it, and make it work for you creatively, sensitivity can destroy you. Instead of telling myself that I didn't belong to either culture, I reasoned that, if anything, I belonged to both. Writing in Creole as well as Standard English no longer presents a problem. It would have been insulting to draw on precise memories or shape certain inspirations which did not sound authentic. I am happily bi-lingual. I will be returning to the Caribbean for another six-month stay, visiting the islands from Martinique up to Jamaica. When I can afford to do so, I will buy myself a house on one of the islands. Part of the year will be spent there, the rest in Britain. I have enough ideas to keep me going for several years. Every one of these books has its roots in the Caribbean: that is where my inspiration is coming from; will be coming from. Tension and conflict are two words I no longer use when talking about my sense of belonging. I reserve them for plots in my writing and combine them with 'intrigue' to add flavour to my private life.

I said to someone the other day, 'I don't think black poets are going to be writing about daffodils yet awhile. There is a fire raging out there.

If we ignore it then we do so at our own peril.' Belonging and place are now everything to do with my mental state, how I see myself, my pride in being black. I hope to always recognise the mood and remain a sensitive barometer to change. Wherever I happen to be, physically, must always find me with all five senses sharpened and not dulled by comforts. I am a writer. I hope to remain a writer for the rest of my life regardless of my abode.

Writing With Men
*Sylvia Kantaris**

You could say I'm well on the way to becoming a poetic 'whore' in that I have already collaborated with two very different male poets and am contemplating collaboration with yet a third. I worked first with D. M. Thomas on a sequence called *News from the Front* (Arc Publications, 1983), the 'front' being the three-pronged battlefront of sex, religion and politics. More recently I worked with Philip Gross on a full-length book called *The Air Mines of Mistila* (Bloodaxe, 1988) which again – but very differently – confronts basic problems of our culture and the role of the poet (male, female and hermaphrodite) within it. A few separatist women have asked me, 'How *could* you collaborate with men? Surely they put you down all the time?' Well, the bald fact is that neither did, even though, in each case, I seemed to be almost expecting (worse, wanting) the male to take the lead, such is my preconditioning. Both my co-authors offered me genuine poetic friendship, and both treated me as an equal fellow practitioner, giving me astute critical feedback which I was slow to return in kind. It seemed to take me a long time to shed my deference, in both cases, but I managed it in the process of working so intimately with two such different craftsmen who proved to be quite as open to criticism as I am, and equally concerned to find a language in which to cross barriers.

Philip Gross reckons the fact of his gender is easily the least interesting thing about him, and I'm sure he means that (though I found his approach to poetry decidedly male in some ways, as I shall explain). Don Thomas has achieved notoriety, amongst separatist women, as an anti-feminist, yet reviewers of *News from the Front* all confessed to problems about deciding which was his voice and which was mine. We swapped voices in the course of our dual effort to explore communication gaps between male and female. Nevertheless,

*An embryonic version of 'Writing with Men' was published in *Stand*, Summer 1987.

there are differences. His contribution to the sequence is more 'formal' than mine, and he was far more daring about the sexual content. It took me a long time to dare to be almost equally daring, sensing in advance that I would be laying myself open to charges of sullying the purity and dignity of womanhood . . .

The liberation both Philip Gross and I experienced through collaboration was of a different order. We both learnt to write with a certain spontaneity and abandon such as neither of us had dared to do before. A case of responsibility shared being a responsibility halved, perhaps? But something of that spontaneity has carried over into work we have each written, separately, since. There was an extra bonus for me in that I now consider that I have quite as much right as a man to spread out and take up space, instead of huddling up small as women tend to on trains, buses and planes. (Whenever a man sits in the adjoining seat he seems to spread his legs wide and his elbows over the armrests, as if staking a territorial claim to half the woman's space as well as filling his own.)

I found it strange that most of the interesting characters in *The Air Mines of Mistila* are females and that the males tend to be caricatures. Philip was also puzzled, and challenged me to invent an interesting male. I tried, by having the Mistilan Women's Co-operative attempting to create a 'new Adam' who pronounced himself a feminist and a worshipper of woman, his 'Maker'. Unfortunately, in honour of his Maker, he ended up worshipping and adoring himself, and so had to be deleted as yet another botched job, though we incorporated the poems in the book. In retrospect, I think I was slyly prodding Philip in the ribs for having appropriated a character I'd invented and turned him into someone I didn't intend him to be simply because he (Philip) grew attached to his own poem about the boy – a poem I still consider to be one of his least successful. Philip seemed to have this extraordinary ability to invent the entire c.v. of a character while s/he was still in nappies, whereas I was wanting them to find their own direction (so long as I liked the direction . . .) My reactions were subversive and written into the texture of the book. Many of my poems are exaggeratedly down-to-earth commentaries on some of Philip's flights into the upper atmosphere.

I can hardly ignore the tendency of both my collaborators to try to *direct* the themes, to the extent that I had to sacrifice rather too many of my poems because they 'did not quite fit'. Neither male poet wasted much. I wasted at least half my *News from the Front* poems, largely because Don wanted clothes fetishism to be a central theme and I was more interested in other areas. Still, it is interesting that the male protagonist in the sequence is far more 'wooden' than his female counterpart. Don remarked, in his *Memories and Hallucinations* (Gollancz, 1988), that he has always been troubled by the problem of how to create male characters as sympathetic as his female ones.

In both collaborations, then, there were scratchy moments, but particularly during the writing of *News from the Front*, since it started as a confrontation, however playful. The exploration of the conditioning underlying the confrontation became the central theme of the book, and we provoked and challenged each other into retaliatory poems. It was almost sad that we became such good friends and fellow-conspirators in the process of writing and swapping 'voices' that we ended up tamely having to invent provocations *together*! But I could say of Don Thomas, 'How typically male to leave *me* to do the final arrangement of the sequence and then ask me to arrange it differently at the last moment!' Was it also 'typically male' on his part to be so easily persuaded that my arrangement worked best, I wonder? I could say of Philip Gross, 'How typically male to come up with a plan of an entire book after only twenty moves, as if it were a game of chess!' Was it also 'typically female' for me to insist on a few changes, I wonder? And 'typically male' of him to accede?

It occurs to me that I should mention the role of Philip's word-processor in relation to the 'deference' I referred to earlier. Philip could present me with drafts which looked so 'finished' and polished, and I find it difficult to criticise a ready-processed poem. I think my failure to give him as much feedback as he gave me may relate more to his word-processor than to him. This may be a sexist problem in itself. Solution: I should stop being lazy and *also* learn to use a processor? Belatedly, I am attending to the technology, but find myself conditioned to learn by a process of trial and error rather than allowing myself to be taught.

I think a lot of men and women would be a little afraid of 'exposing' themselves to each other in the act of creating and crafting poetry. Also, reviewers, readers and audiences often seem to be strangely disturbed by male-female collaborations. Reactions are strange. Even a feminist reviewer of *News from the Front* saw it as an attempt by D. M. Thomas to grapple with the problem of sexism by engaging with a female poet. I wonder why she saw *my* contribution as belonging to *his* development, since it worked both ways.

In an article in the *Glasgow Herald* about her collaboration with

Andrew Greig* Kathleen Jamie writes: 'You wouldn't believe the number of ways people . . . have couched the question, "Are you and Andrew Greig . . .Doing it?"' At least this is one problem I have not had, with regard to collaborations. At the time of writing this, *The Air Mines of Mistila* is still with the printer, but presumably no reviewer will speculate about whether Philip and I were 'doing it', considering that I am so much older than him. For once, there seems to be safety in age. However, I have certainly noticed how often women poets are reviewed in terms of speculations about their personal lives. It doesn't even stop at speculations. 'She should get herself a new lover,' advised one male reviewer, in the course of admiring my work, especially for themes of love and loss!

Collaboration in poetry seems to me a very wholesome activity, and not just as a way of avoiding AIDS, but because the people involved inevitably break down barriers between the sexes in quite fundamental ways. I obviously can't speak for collaborators of the same gender, but I assume that they also find benefits. My theme is the building of bridges across the gender gap. Men and women often come at poetry from such different angles that sometimes it looks as if we could never find a common language and craft. I am sure we can. Maybe poetry is more important than any of us know, yet, as a way of working across the supposed Great Divide. We could all moan ourselves mad about what's been done to us women (most of our centuries of poetry simply cancelled out), and we could even confuse moans with poetry, and often do. I suggest that engaging with 'the other' in the language of poetry is a way of healing the wounds of separatism, and certainly the best way I have ever found of approaching mutual recognition and trust.

We are all moulded by words – men and women. I see the poet's task to be one of continually breaking the moulds and remoulding in a different pattern, working towards the possibly unreachable ideal of a human family. I want a common language, informed, and respectful of our differences and similarities; and working together is the subtlest way I know of reaching understanding between the sexes – which is the primary task, to my mind.

*A Flame in Your Heart, Kathleen Jamie and Andrew Greig, Bloodaxe, 1986.

Many Rills, Will They Ever Run into One River, a River with Two Banks?
Nicole Ward Jouve

Susan asked, would I write something that had to do with writing and femininity, or writing and gender? I wanted to. For years now I have never written without the consciousness of being a female-who-writes, seeking, if not for a difference (for that would mean being second, in opposition to) at least for a specificity: a voice that would *also* be gendered.

I tried to formulate some general ideas and found that I could not. It was not for want of trying. I have spent a great deal of time and effort talking, teaching, lecturing, about language and gender, writing and femininity: only to find repeatedly that you can say, 'Yes, this is a feminine, or a female, or a woman's practice, yes, a certain inwardness, stream-of-consciousness, refusal of fetishism, fluidity of style, punning, subversion of logic, of phallogocentrism, re-vision, the re-writing of myths, and fairy-tales, deconstruction of gender-roles, silences, secrets, being-in-darkness, regressing, all that, one way or another, as well as certain subject matters, certain experiences that, for biological, social or economic reasons, only a woman could have, can all be called "feminine".' You can say that truthfully. But the proposition cannot be reversed. You cannot say, 'A feminine practice is intuitive etc., or will subvert . . .' Nor can you say that a woman will necessarily show her woman-ness by doing any of the above, let alone that she must, for that would be the beginning of prescription, the wolf forever at woman's door. You certainly cannot say, 'A man can or will do none of these things,' for you could almost instantly be shown some Romantics or Dadaists or Modernists or Surrealists who have done exactly what you have just described as 'feminine'. What you have *described*: not the *thing* that you have described. You could not find a male writer doing what Colette or Katherine Mansfield have done, which you may want to say is specifically womanly. But once you have analysed and labelled that specificity, and even more once you have theorised it, somebody will always be able to think of a man who has done just that, or something like it. Bet your boots. I've often played the game.

Yes, gender makes a difference to writing. Yes, that difference can be explored, words and rhythms can be sought to account for it. But no, that difference cannot be stated in universal terms, cannot be theorised. Perhaps that is just as well: universal statements do tend to be phallogocentric, to assume that human = male. There is no surer sign of a male-centred discourse than its assumption that it is genderless. The best thing seems to me to keep moving. From mould to mould? No, keep the flow going, for some gelatinous principle is for ever there, ready to make things set as soon as you stop. Write: that is indeed the way, the only I know, to make 'woman' come into (writerly) being.

I began to look for extracts from diaries that could be seen to have a relation to a piece of creative writing (fiction or otherwise) and to be woman-centred. I alighted on a series of notebooks that chrono-logically followed a novel that had to do with censorship, *L'Entremise**. I wrote it to get out of the field of fire which *Shades of Grey*** had created for me: my relations had been scandalised/horrified. Some would not forgive me for what they deemed I had done. I don't think that a man would have been so accused of impropriety, though I know the story about Proust who could not begin to publish *Remembrance of Things Past* till after his mother's death. The repression I imposed upon myself to be *bien vue* by my family, not to offend in *L'Entremise*, produced the need to be doubly improper elsewhere. I began a book about a murder committed by women. I wrote three notebooks, headed *Taboos* and *Unpublishables*: a red one about blood, a green one about sex, a brown one about shit. I dreamt of a book format that would have had more to do with female anatomy and in particular with female holes than the normal symmetrical one-two format. A book based on the number three, with alternating red, green and blue pages. But when I set about seeing how I could edit these notebooks for the present volume, I found it just couldn't be done. They *were* unpublishable. Not that they did not contain some bits of good writing, and some pretty interesting speculations. But I don't think the

---

*Editions des femmes, Paris, 1980.
***Le Spectre du gris*, Editions des femmes, Paris, 1977; (published as *Shades of Grey* by Virago, 1981)

reader could bear that kind of intimacy, and I couldn't bear to have people read some of the things I wrote.

Is it that censorship produces particularly strong effects in (some) women? Or was it just that as a cowardly female, highly processed by a Catholic education and permanently incapable of emancipating myself once and for all, I doomed myself to a perverse course, irrelevant and of no interest to other women?

Discovering the unreadable nature of my *Taboos* notebooks had the merit of making something obvious about notebooks in general. Which is that, unless you are much in the public eye – a famous writer or a politician or gossip-exploiter – you write notebooks, diaries, specifically as something *not* to be read by others, let alone published. I'm not trying for the old equation woman = private = home = secret, though to a large extent I'd say it applies to me. But it is true that the thrill of looking at a person's notebooks is that they were, when they were written, meant to be secret: modern literature has produced countless dramatisations of this. The fascination of the notebooks of a published book – the diaries of a Virginia Woolf, for instance – is that they seem to offer the secret of the book, its hidden or repressed history. This too has been much dramatised, from Gide's *Les Faux Monnayeurs* to Lessing's *The Golden Notebook*.

The Golden Notebook actually is a useful model for, as well as foil to, what I am about to offer. The idea, I take it, is that the 'golden' book in which Anna eventually writes is *the* solution to Anna's plight both as a woman and a writer. She ceases to be compartmentalised, to separate bits of herself into four notebooks. She becomes one, through and through, like gold. The golden notebook is also the sum total of the various texts – notebooks and narrative – that have made up the book which is about to finish. What I like about this is the various texts all adding up in the end, transformed into the substance of the one fiction. I would like that to happen to the family history upon which I embarked some time ago, and from which the extracts that follow are taken. I would like to find an overall form that would enable all the bits and pieces, the various modes of entry into writing, the public and the private, to flow into one. I used to think of my exasperating tendency to start all sorts of bits, to stop and start again, as fragmentation. I now optimistically think that this is the wrong image, that bits start as if the earth opened in yet another place and a rill of water began to flow; here the snow is melting, there a brook from an underground cave is forcing its way out. The perfect thing (but I may not be up to it, may not find the time and strength) would be for all the rills to find their way into a main river. Alas! there is more to it than finding the downward course.

What I do not like about *The Golden Notebook* is the artificial neatness of the four notebooks, the ease with which Anna knows how to consign politics to such a notebook, private life to another. I find that the reverse is true in my case. What is difficult is how to separate. The entries I have chosen from my pink notebook in particular are meant to illustrate the way in which everything – in particular the present – tends to invade everything else (there, the attempt to write the past). Yet it is because the writing of a book is fed by the present that it assumes the shape it does. The difficulty is to find a form, a voice, that can both make room for the past and live up to the questions and demands of the present – balance between the living time of writing and the time of memory.

One final word about readability-publishability. Of course, what follows is much edited, (though I have tried to keep close to what the notebooks contained). To start with I offer a translation: I wrote in France, and in French. Some passages are summaries, not translations, there to introduce and make intelligible later passages. Only a bearable number of entries have been kept from the pink notebook, which contains all sorts of data collecting and other attempts at fiction writing. Having it all would have made the whole thing too confusing, and uninteresting too, since some of the entries only made sense to me. I wanted the shape of two stories only to emerge from the bulk of material, and I have eliminated what would have dispersed attention too much. I wanted to show interferences at work between what was happening in the month of August, when all the following passages were written, and the past material on which I was working. For them to be visible I had to leave out others. What I hope does become perceptible is the phenomenal richness of life, the strands that go into any work in progress, which some writers know how to spin into a yarn. Here the strands, the rills, remain mostly separate. Yet in places you can see them beginning to twist. Or to join their courses into a larger rill.

One of the main tributaries has already found its way to the sea. Please God that I may one day be able to retrace its course.

From Pink Notebook. August 1987.
Translation/Adaptation

1. From the Journal *to the planned book. Journal called, 'Fous-nous la paix avec tes bondieuseries' (politely translatable as: 'Leave us alone with your religious mumbo-jumbo').*

Should I seek for an interesting 'angle' to this family history or should I just let myself go, have my pleasure, simply record the oral memories of those I have known? Must be confessed that it's arch-banal – family ranging from immigrant labourer to upper middle class – a cardinal here, a philosopher-Jesuit the friend of Valéry and of Bergson there, an aunt who helped Christian Dior create his fashion house – nobody really grand, nothing dramatic, most of them provincial middle-middle-middle and *barbotant dans le bénitier* – up to their ears in holy water. Would only be of interest to members of the family. And everything, I mean eveything, has been done, and superbly done. Family sagas galore [. . .] just about every novelist has produced one. Every family I know at it. We're ten a penny. Lucette Finas on how excited it made her to think of the *bodily* presence of her grandfather in 1870. That is part of the fascination. The bodies of your ancestors, which you touch through your parents' etc. flesh, make history real. You belong.

The feeling, religio/literary, gravestone, old mortality *e tutti quanti*, 'it is a duty not to let the dead disappear'. All the *conteurs* in the family – my grandmother, Mimi Marraine, Raymonde, Mizza – making stories, creating their lives through talk, now no longer there. There are millions of the dead. Each just as deserving to have their story written. If you wanted writing to 'save' life, it would become unreadable because each human being would have to become the potential (= saving) reader of thousands of millions of lives. If each of us tried to write them all, become the conduct through which the loved dead live again, none of us would have any time left to live. Perhaps each of us needs only one reader, as for a lot of old people one listener, intently listening (like that afternoon with Raymonde, something in both of us must have known she was going to die, and that is why she spoke, and I listened) – one listener is enough. So I should write for one reader only. Or just the family. And yet . . . I start thinking of the narrator's grandmother, in Proust, of Oriane

de Guermantes. The blue light of her eye. The light in the
bedroom in Balbec . . . Back with Art, capital letter. There is
something self-sufficient about talking yourself into other people,
younger people's memories, perpetuating through love and
speech. As soon as you *write*, other things are involved. Art etc.,
yes. So?

My mother's genealogical trees.

*   *   *

Another attraction is that, as the number of the people you must
write about multiply (as you look at the various branches), you
touch all layers of society, all modes of social diversification.
They have lived all over Marseilles, all districts, walked about
them, millions of footsteps. Lived all over the world. (Marguerite
Yourcenar saying that when we get to the Romans each of us
literally has millions of ancestors.) The thickness of it.

*   *   *

A perfect mix: it's fact, they all existed, I am trying to get at what
they call truth, be as exact as I can be. Yet it's fiction, for in order
to write, give life to, the abbé Brive or even my grandmother in
all that she was, before I knew her, and whilst I knew her, I have
to imagine, i.e. invent them. As you read Marguerite Yourcenar
on her ancestors, you can almost feel her getting hold of a meagre
story, a few facts – her mother dying at her birth, a great-uncle
riding through a forest – and, blowing (as Mallarmé's faun blows
into the drained grape-skin), she fills it out, she makes it luminous
again.

    She's got two sides. One book for her mother's family, one for
her father's side. I've got so many! Bricard, Jouve. Jouve, Brive.
Bricard, Perrault. Jouve, Vague. And so on. Swann's Way,
Guermantes' Way. For the first time in my life I've understood
what is so evident I never saw it, why Proust has two sides. Why,
at the end of *Remembrance of Things Past*, Gilberte Swann ends
up marrying Saint-Loup and producing the daughter who is the
coping-stone that enables the whole edifice to stand at last: Proust
reverses, he *inverts* what every bourgeois does but also every
aristo and every worker if not of parents unknown, when he/she
asks, 'Who am I?' by discovering his/her parents, then
grandparents, by bonding into the past, into history. And into the
future by producing children. The two sides, your mother, your
father, reach up above your head, they produce you, who are the
clé de voûte. Proust inverts this, he finds surrogate parents, alter

egos, people he's desired himself, Saint-Loup, Gilberte, to produce the daughter (*not son*). But in the future, something ahead of him. Then he can be born. Or he is born. Time is *retrouvé*. But then everything is finished. He's by-passed being a genitor. The Jewish artist, the *inverti*, refuses to enter History in the flesh, bond into society, he won't marry, won't have a child. The woman is born from his side during his sleep, like Eve from Adam. He is the matrix, the space of the cathedral. He is the only one who can get inside. He is woman-man.

*   *   *

5 August 1987. Louis in great form. Said something that startled me. (We arrived in Génolhac last night. The house. An inn once, belonging to an ancestor. House and garden built over what was a Charterhouse. They found lots of bones when they dug the swimming-pool. Delightful for this Protestant family to have so many monks beneath them. When Protestants were so persecuted in the Cévennes. Louis was chuckling. The plane trees and poplars magnificent. The wind has torn away a lot of the bark of the plane trees this year. Outside, Angèle, spread out in the sun, is our beach-rest, our placenta, our body. T. is typing. Louis engraving. I'm scribbling. Antoinette used to say, three are always four, like the three musketeers. (Three Brontë sisters create, the fourth child – Brangwen – is the placenta, the one that does not create, allows the other to be.)

Louis was talking about the bourgeoisie. The provençal bourgeoisie. (His lot, my lot.) The father. Powerful (Gaston, his own father, Mr Cordesse, my father). The fatherly power is offered to the son as a promise of inheritance, the inheritance of authority. The son (his brother Antoine, my brother Pierre) believes somehow that all he has to do is wait, that he will inherit. False, Louis was saying. All you can do is get out. Louis got out, he thinks Angèle and myself got out by marrying foreigners. If you get back in (Annette, Antoine, Pierre), you've been had. Annette burnt out. Pierre, who could have been an artist, broken.

I suddenly thought of Pierre's remark to my parents, what my mother was telling me. He said, 'I'm leaving my inheritance to my children, I'm going to make my will.' [. . .] – 'What inheritance?' my mother said (she still pays for his rent). For him to leave an inheritance my parents have to die first (a calculation my mother can't have relished). Then he has to disappear: suicide? Would he make a donation to his children? 'Whichever way you take it,' my

mother said, 'according to French law your children
automatically are your heirs, you can save on a solicitor's fee.'

What he meant: 'I didn't make it' (neither job nor degree, nor
can he make the films he wants to make – probably doesn't want
to make films any more; kept by his wife and parents; on the
brink of real depression). (He said, also, 'You have to take me as
I am.') Somewhere he is seeking for the place where he could be
God and father without being either, ideal father (how he plays
with his son) and ideal God without having to resort to the
abuses of power he so suffered from as a child, yet he wants to be
confirmed and comforted into the sense of self he's seen
embodied by his own father. 'As heir to the goods I can transmit
wealth in my turn, therefore I'm passing power on to my children,
yet I've removed myself, abstracted myself from the line of
descent. My "failure" has in no way diminished or impaired my
inheritance.'

Our great-grandmother and her shop of *objets de piété*
(religious objects, church supplies). The source of the family
wealth. Pierre found himself amidst Mimi Marraine's religious
bits and pieces, when his wife threw him out and he took refuge
in the apartment just vacated by death. There was a gilt statue of
a virgin crushing the dragon underfoot (that he gave to Tante
Denise), an ivory Christ which the dealer estimated was worth
2,300 francs and that he wanted to give me . . . He was
distributing the inheritance among the members of the family – he
was turning into the great-grandmother. 'Funny, crucifixes keep
their value. Missals, however beautiful, lose it,' he said.

*   *   *

What a strain between living (here, now) and the project to
recover the past. Which makes you into a vertical being, digging
through stratified rock.

Génolhac today.

Once upon a time there was a vaulted room at the bottom of a
house. The plaster was scaling off the walls and a bluey-black
cockroach hurried sometimes at night on the black and white
tiles. In the morning a horizontal light filtered through the leaves
of the great plane trees, spinning rainbows out of the water-spray
on the lawn. Quiet, in the black pool, the elongated brush of a
tuscan cypress. There were doric columns in front of the room,
supporting the terrace above. At the end of the garden, a wall of
lozes caught the sun, its flat top shining like a bar of silver. A

grasshopper had alighted on the torn corner of the jacket of
Carson McCullers' *Works*. A fly was rubbing its hands on an
empty spectacle-case. In the valley a cock was singing. You could
hear crickets too, and the beating of wings of some unidentified
insect, dry as the hollow hull of an autumn thistle.

2. Narrative
Title: *GARIBALDI* = 42

The telephone number was Garibaldi seventy-four eighty-four. It
seemed odd that a provincial bourgeois family that voted for the
Right and had built their big house thanks to the profit they made
out of religious goods should have a telephone number that
commemorated a foreign revolutionist. All the more so as
Garibaldi the *condottiere* had stormed the Vatican. An enemy of
the Pope, and it was by dialling his name that people called them!
Garibaldi the Red was the sesame that opened the cave of their
home.

But habit had made Garibaldi pink. [. . .] People said
'Garibaldi' as in Paris you would have said 'Danton'. Soon,
progress would get rid of these ghosts, as once the White Terror
had eliminated the Jacobins from the Pantheon; their corpses had
been dug up, thrown into the sewers. With wonder-working
simplicity, the conversion of the national telephone system into
numbers had reduced Garibaldi to forty-two. Danton had
become three two six. [. . .] It wasn't quite the camps, but those
matriculation numbers had effaced the last trace of those Reds
that the cities, in former times, had wanted to keep alive on their
waves and through their wires.

[. . .] The main door to the house was in a street that bore the
name of one of Louis XIV's mistresses. Very seventeenth century,
quite fitting the city that had given France Barrès and Maurras,
the royalists and Action Française men. The side-street, on the
other hand, dark and less smart [. . .] was called rue Auguste
Blanqui. It was only after years of history lessons, and many
reveries at a window overlooking the dark well of the street, with
the roof on the opposite side touched into its own pink shade by
the setting sun, that Françoise began to think for good about
poor Blanqui: he had spent forty-seven years of his life in gaol.
All for the sake of the Republic. [. . .]

To console poor Blanqui after his death, or to make it up to

him, they had given his name to an obscure provincial street.
Before, it had been called rue des Cyprès, which was nicer than
Auguste Blanqui, you had to confess, especially as there must
have been alleys of cypresses there at the time. Now there were
austere houses with shutters often shut, ajar in the afternoon over
windows which net curtains protected from the other side.
Nothing but tiny courtyards left from what had been all
countryside at the end of the eighteenth century, the hill covered
with convents and monasteries.

In the summer, the fig-trees in the courtyards smelt human.

The eruptions of the Left had covered the entire district, then
had grown cold. The bourgeoisie had reclaimed the ground, they
had clung to it, fed on all the chemical wonders of a loam sprung
from the inside of fire. The small owners of the area had bought
church lands during the French Revolution, built their houses
perhaps with the stones of the monasteries. That was how a
Delaud ancestor had got the land where their house now stood.

The entire city seemed bent on effacing all traces of its past.
When they had started excavating for a commercial centre near
the Stock Exchange they had discovered the remnants of a Greek
temple, a whole *agora* turned towards the sea. The promoters had
fought the archaeologists, won hands down. They'd surrounded a
few column stumps with a fence next to an underground parking
lot, and hastily built over the rest. More recently, when tunnels
had been dug for the underground, marvels had come up: bas-
reliefs, statues, capitals, who knows, perhaps mosaics and
frescoes: better than in Rome, it had been rumoured. Nobody was
allowed to say, nobody had been allowed to see. Remnants of the
Greek city that had stood up to Caesar, remnants from the
medieval city that had fought the Arabic invaders. Layer upon
layer, quickly dynamited or re-buried under galleries. [. . .]

3. *From another Notebook inside the narrative*

(All this, I'm sure, on account of Lanzman's *Shoah*, which I
haven't seen, but which all my friends have been telling me about
since I got to France in July. The methodical *acharnement* (fury?
obstinacy?) with which the Nazis not only exterminated the Jews
but did the least possible directly themselves, using some of the
Jews to do the work, and above all effaced the traces of the

massacres. Buried under, demolished, cremated, bulldozed, poured on lime, planted lawns over it all. If the Allied troops had arrived just a bit later in some of the camps there would have been nothing to see. How Nazis, the National Front in France, deny that any of it occurred. An entire race disappeared from Nature, melted away, was it a dream, who can tell when the dead are dead, bones gone? Rather like the elm trees have almost gone from Europe, faultlessly selected by the Dutch elm beetles. Trees fare better: our elm tree a stump in our Yorkshire hedge, but also stacked planks in our yard, tall-backed benches in the pub in Great Edstone. Nazi technology tried to make a species disappear as if it had been natural selection. (Invisibility to do with that word 'gas', gas fumes, gas chambers: you cannot see gas. Death was meant to strike as the Plague once struck Marseilles, brought in on board the ship which the Viceroy of Sardinia had seen in a dream, and not allowed to dock. She docked in Marseilles, Antonin Artaud recounts, my friend Artaud who lived not so far from where I grew up and was struck between the shoulder blades by an invisible knife near the Réformés church which I passed every Thursday on my way to the Canebière.)

What I'm after. Analogies, mistaken no doubt – mind hungry for analogies – how else do you understand? Between Marseilles, a city built layer upon layer, a port open for millenia to wave upon wave of colonists and immigrants, Phoceans, Greeks, Ligures, Romans, Arabs, later Italians, Armenians, Greeks, Turks, Corsicans, Spaniards, and the Germans of course, November 1942, later again Arabs, Pied-Noirs, more and more Arabs –

What I'm trying to get at however crude, let us dare, go on, is that there is in Marseilles, a port open to the sea, in which civilisations, buildings, are continuously being erected over the ruins or integration of others; a tendency – a *neurotic* tendency, expressed by its repeated production of fascist ideologies, like the National Front today, the vogue of Le Pen – to defend itself against upheavals by denying that they ever took place, or could take place: biologically, ideologically. Just look at the names of many of Le Pen's followers, they're all Italian, Spanish, Armenian, Corsican names – a lot of them anyway. 'We who are French . . .' They deny their own immigrant past, their own history, ever existed. You accuse others of being what you deny you have ever been: a foreigner, the one who threatens or dilutes national purity. There must be no other city in Europe with such fabulous underground remnants, so savagely ready to destroy them.

4. *Other entry, still interrupting the* Garibaldi = 42 *narrative*

I've seen it. Know which is the other side. Thinking about the war – Nazism – being here – made me see. Jouve etc. side/Cordesse Defferre side. Catholics/Protestants. Provincials/ eventual Parisians, operating at any rate on a national scale. One close-knit, repressive, patriarchal, right-wing Pétainiste family, the other liberal, left-wing, rebellious, aloof, stylish. They were in the Resistance.

My fascination, my enduring fascination for the Cordesse. What Louis has been to me. The custodian, through common memory, of childhood places; the dream of my youth, and my beyond. How he talks. Superbly inventive slang. Marseilles dialect.

The Cordesse-Defferre, over two generations, have been for the Jouve what the Guermantes are for Swann and the narrator. More splendour, and what looks like a superior ideology.

(Never realised before that Swann means swan. Swann's death, at the end of the Guermantes Way, and the red shoes of the Duchess.)

My patriarchal, neurotically tight father. When he needs his beloved trees cutting, he has to control every move, endless agonising about what is the best way, nobody allowed to intervene.

Here today. Génolhac. They're having their poplars cut, the neighbour waging war on them because the high branches beat on his roof tiles during the winter gales. A Mr Nicolas here, the village woodcutter. His father, Angèle tells us, got his elder daughter pregnant. Eleven children. Put the second daughter in his bed while his elder daughter was in hospital having his child. The elder daughter got them all out of it, got her mother, her sister out of it. Denounced him. [. . .] He got two or three years in jail. The two eldest sons took up the farm, developed a wood-cutting business. One Nicolas son today up the trees, climbing like a monkey, wielding a two-stage aluminium ladder, sending it higher up, then he's up it. Ropes are tied to the branch that's being cut, the men in the house all pull so it falls in the right

place. The Cordesse have turned the whole occasion into a
communal feast. Everyone is here, giving advice, pulling,
chopping wood, wheeling it away. [. . .] The Nicolas son lops
branches off with his chainsaw as easily as if it was a cake knife.

5. Resumption of narrative: Garibaldi = 42

The city was dedicated to the Good Mother. From her hill she
dominated the sea. A golden statue holding forth her child, a
serpent under foot, which she tamed like the treacherous
Mediterranean. A late nineteenth-century monument, the *marial*
nineteenth century, 'I am the Immaculate Conception', she had
assumed into heaven without the earth ever touching her body.
Pity in a way, unlike the Pharoahs we did not go for rich burials,
no longer believed that the underground as much needed to feed
on the good, the holy dead, as on sumptuous works of art and
food. We almost believed the reverse, that the earth would not eat
what was holy: it was a mark of sainthood that they should find
your body intact when years later they opened your grave. Death
where is thy victory? She was better than intact, the Virgin, not
even resurrected. Like a circus rider she had bounded through the
hoop of death, death had indeed been a paper tiger for her, he
had leapt and she was the one who had leapt through him. Had
the Virgin climbed into the stratosphere at the time when poor
Icarus had plumbed into the sea? 1957 was the year in which
Rome had proclaimed the dogma of the Assumption. Also the
year of the first sputnik: the Pope won, his astronaut had gone
much higher than those wicked Russians.

> . . . *Christ . . . aviateur*
> *Il détient le record du monde pour la hauteur . . .*
> (. . . Christ . . . airman
> He holds the world record for heights . . .)
>
> [Apollinaire's 'Zone']

Christ's mother had done even better, or he had made his mother
do better. The womb that had borne him had levitated
straightaway: had not known the darkness of the tomb.

The golden Virgin levitated, heavy and powerful, on the highest
hill of the town . . .

* * *

(P. 57) The Jouve ancestors had been royalists. They had
remained faithful to the Bourbons, the *légitime* branch. One

ancestor had corresponded with the extravagant Duchesse de
Berry, whose husband, the heir to the throne, had been murdered
shortly before his father Charles X's overthrow in July 1830. The
Duchess had given birth to the 'miracle-child', little Comte de
Chambord, born eight months after his father's death. She kept
trying to come back, get the people to overthrow the Orléans and
put her son on the throne. One moonless night the Jouve ancestor
would row her in his boat and help her land on one of the
countless pebble creeks along the bay. He would guide her
throughout Provence, introduce her to supporters. The Orléanist
police would eventually get her, hiding inside a huge stone
fireplace in a country mansion. She was with a male companion,
whether mere champion or lover Françoise's grandmother wasn't
sure, a gentleman at any rate, since she had had a pressing need
whilst the police went about their meticulous slow search, and he
had gallantly proferred his top hat as a chamber pot. The sound
had alerted the spies. They had raised the fireplace shutter, they
had seen the Duchess. Crouching, or standing with hoisted skirts,
Françoise had often wondered, staring at the metal shutters of the
fireplaces in the country house – you raised them one by one and
it made a sound a bit like the garage door in town. It always
seemed to her if she just raised them she would find a duchess
peeing in a top hat.

The Duchess had been courteously accompanied to the border,
or put on a ship back to England. In thanksgiving for services
rendered she had sent a Malines lace veil to the ancestor (was he
the gentleman, Françoise also wondered). Mamie, who kept it
wrapped in silk paper with letters from the Duchess among other
precious family relics, used to say, lifting a corner of yellow lace,
'You see, that is the veil of the Duchesse de Berry.' Françoise
imagined ancient weddings, the splendour of a court in faint
candlelight, a slightly vampirised court since it wrote with what
looked like weak tea, an ink so clarified by time that its *cursives*
and *jambages*, round like her grandmother's, were almost
invisible. It got mixed up with the Berri of George Sand's *La
Petite Fadette* and the 'ferrets' of Anne of Austria that were given
to gallant Buckingham, it made a world in which parchment was
lace, and lace, parchment. Everything the colour of pale *pipi*
(didn't Madame Augier say that babies' *pipi* was angels' *pipi*, and
surely Duchesses' *pipi* was as angelic as babies'?) – lace *pipi*,
angels' ink.

* * *

Round about the same period, on the Brive and Delaud side, there had been six orphans. Their uncle and tutor was a priest from the parish.

The eldest boy, perhaps under the influence of his uncle, but certainly looking to the Church for a sinecure (he must have been one of those seminarists so abominated by Stendhal's Julien Sorel), had eventually become a curate in a rich parish downtown, La Palud. The two elder sisters eked out a meagre living teaching as submistresses in a religious school down the rue des Cyprès. Same job as the Brontë sisters had had, same period, another country. Xavier, the young curate, a good-looking man, had quickly proceeded to take advantage of his position. 'Mademoiselle', he had asked one of his parishioners, a rich elderly spinster who came to him for confession, 'would you do a charitable deed? Would you lend my sisters, deserving young ladies, the funds for them to start a commerce?' 'Ah *mon Dieu*, you too, monsieur l'abbé,' she had replied, 'my nephews are forever borrowing money off me, and they never pay me back.' 'But my sisters will pay you back,' the abbé Brive had replied, 'and they will pay interest also.' The sisters had turned out to be such good *commerçantes* that they had not only paid the money back, interest and all, but paid it in two years. It was the eldest, Marie, who was the real business-woman, hardworking, astute and thrifty. The younger one, Louise, weaker, devotedly did whatever Marie said. The shop they rented, then owned, was round the corner from La Palud. They sold religious goods, rosaries, missals, cassocks, surplices, chalices, boys and girls' costumes for Confirmation ceremonies . . . In a few years' time they had made so much money that with the proceeds they had the initial house pulled down and built the five-storey family house in which, almost a hundred years later, their descendants still lived.

* * *

P. 73. It was God and his houses that Marie and Louise decked. God's men, bishops and priests. The statues of the saints. It was in front of God's altars that the real wax candles that were bought in Marie's shop burned. At home Marie and Louise saved up on candle-ends. Generous, magnificent even when it came to building for the family or endowing one of its members, Marie kept the same dress for years, re-used every bit of clothing for carpets and cloths, re-wound used bits of thread on a bobbin including that which had served as rough stitching. Black or white, they already had a knot at one end with a long tail, you pulled them out after the fine seam had been made, they served again, and again. [. . .] All life long Marie garnered, handling gold, ivory, incense, silk and lace, seeing to God's luxury by day, to the rigorous thrift of her house by night. [. . .] She was the purveyor of heaven – at home, she built for the future, for the large family she never saw, but which one day would fill the house she'd built with her earnings as God's caterer.

*   *   *

P. 91. It was the men, then, who eventually brought about the family's social ascent. Yet if you thought about it, it was the women who had had the real power. Rather like Tseu Hi, the Chinese Empress who so fascinated Françoise, wizened amid gold and satin; Françoise could hear the immense painted nails screeching on the lacquer of the throne, chop-stick nails at the end of the withered hands on which veins stood out as on her own grandmother's hands. Their power had served, sheltered behind, hidden under, the Male, the Imperial Throne: Marie had lived idolising her elder brother the abbé Xavier Brive – she'd built a villa on the hill for him when he'd been made vicar of a country parish, the presbytery house was too infra-dig for him – and then her son, another Xavier. Louise, Xavier's young wife, had idolised her handsome husband. Then when time and infidelities had driven them apart, she would worship her son André. Like Tseu Hi, she would against wind and tide preserve her Empire of the Middle against the eastern and the western barbarians, hold the family together inside the large bee-hive that her mother-in-law Marie had built.

*   *   *

P. 96. Yes, if you thought about it, until the last generation or so, that of the *caïds*, the *Arabes* as her mother called them, the macho men who had made it, moved centre stage, made wives and children into menials, satellites, it was women's figures that emerged as the powerful ones, even though they'd spent their lives propping up and serving men's images: God, Christ in his churches, his male representatives, the descendants of the apostles.

*   *   *

P. 102. It was the women. Françoise could not get over this, her youth had coincided with the rise of the men, her father, her uncle, to the zenith, she had always thought it was the men did it all. She'd been wrong. From the old *demoiselle* from the confessional who'd lent the money to the abbé Brive's sisters, to Marie and Louise and later to Louise her own grandmother and now (weird as it seemed) to her mother Marcelle who was quietly moving centre-stage, the hidden mover and visible mender and preserver, it was the women who'd made the house and made it live. Indoors, it was the statues of the Virgin that were the most charged with meaning, down to the Black Virgin that rather scared the child Françoise. Was she a satanic virgin, a virgin of caves and the night? A clay statue of Michelangelo's virgin once had tumbled down from some bookshelves and hit her grandmother on the head. There had been blood on her grandmother's scalp, and she had accused her grandfather of putting it there on purpose – he cared more about his broken statue than about his wife's skull. Perhaps indeed it was all that the men could do in that house, stick the pieces together, reproduce. It was to the women that the power of life and death belonged, the tasks that perpetuated life. That was perhaps the meaning of the multiple statues of the Good Mother at the corner of the houses that had been built in the nineteenth century, invaded what was left of the gardens, the church on the Mount where not so long ago shepherds had brought their herds to graze – the street that led up the steepest bit of hill was still called rue des Bergers . . .

Everywhere, practically on every street corner, there were statues of the Virgin. Sometimes alone, sometimes with her child. Or tramping the dragon underfoot. That was odd, because only very few of the houses could have been built by women like Marie, the rest had been the work of entrepreneurs, patriarchs . . . They too perhaps had recognised the power of that woman's image, or else they had imitated the structures they saw in the church, you said *l'église*, which was in the feminine mode, the bride of Christ, although it was led by men and only men could officiate in it and it was a male God whose cult was being celebrated although you said *la colombe*, feminine mode, for the Holy Ghost that was born of the love between the Father and the Son, you didn't say *pigeon*, you said, *colombe*. But it was all contained by the Church, aimed at the Church, went to nestle, procreate, inside the Church. That was perhaps what the countless Maries signified at the corners of the houses. Marie

Brive had provided the solid goods, money, stone for the human house, the furnishings of the divine house, Louise had had the maternal Authority, she had been the centre, centrifugal but also centripetal of all the love there was to be had, the moral Force, Queen Bee that she was inside the hive that Marie had built for her. There was a mystery there, Françoise felt.

Extracts from Green Notebook. Also August 1987. Also Translation/Adaptation

Génolhac, 7 August. Louis, Angèle & Co teaching me slang.

* * *

Sun, clouds. Huge plane trees. Cool water in the pool. Laurent makes a hell of a din with his guitar.

9 August. Chini (Louis's musician friend) here with his Swedish dancer wife and two lovely little daughters. 'Two little pink pigs,' Louis says.

* * *

Swedish cocks do *Kukluklu*. French cocks *Cocorico*. English cocks Cockodoodledoo. Italian cocks *Kikiriki*.
   German cocks?

* * *

Mme C. a Millionaire. Has no heating during winter. No longer goes to the restaurant. Angèle says she cannot bear to spend money that does not bring her an object, money that gets lost. She can spend five, seven thousand pounds for a picture, but she entertains her daughter in a frozen house, and even goes to spend part of the winter at her son's, which saves on expenditure. (Son just as mean as she is.) Louis says she's building her tomb in that house of hers. Accumulating works of art around her.
   The tombs of the pharaohs. Accumulation of treasures *under* the earth, serving no perceptible purpose. Trees need to have as many roots as branches. We no longer know the art of dealing with death, we're unbalanced. We bring everything back from the depths, instead of accumulating in and for darkness. We equate light (consciousness, publishing) with good. Psychoanalysis, etc. Fetishism of consciousness. Idiotic.
   (Write *for* darkness?)

12 August. Dream. Inside a bottle (wine, alcohol) with a quarter

of the liquid left there was a beast I wanted to get rid of. *Hanneton.* (The one I saw with my father, enormous; Guillaume's scorpion, that made his mother scream; large harmless insects from the *plateaux*, which Nicole T. showed me, long antennae, green and black stripes; Chacha's dress yesterday; green with a black belt; black slugs on the lettuce we picked yesterday.) (Clouds of gnats, as on a corpse, on the Cassini mountain yesterday; a hole at the centre – rubbish thrown there? the feeling of something rotten somewhere.) I tried to get rid of the beast, I shook the bottle, I don't know if it was going to spoil the liquid, it was unpleasant (tummy ache? Génolhac water should not be drunk, polluted by animals that piss in it, bulls, sheep, foxes). Finally I tipped the bottle. The beast came out and remained motionless. It should have been dangerous but bizarrely I was her friend, I remained looking at it. Alcohol had made it red, transparent, almost luminous and empty, like a chrysalis, all of a piece (wings part of the same carapace and body) – paralysed. I remained looking at it and it was going to become something else, something was going to happen, when T. said, 'Come into my bed.'

He scares me. I've never seen him so tired. And he drinks, drinks. Swims in the bottle.

Surely relates to my dream (instead of writing *rêve*, dream, I've just written *verre*, glass). Aiaiaiai Daddy Freud is even more transparent than my chrysalis. Am I slowly tumbling towards Kafka?

15 August. (Old Italian Rachel here, who used to be the cook.)

Very interesting discussion yesterday. We were talking about children in Greece and North Africa, little boys, six, seven, eight years old, called in to take *la goutte* (a drop, be suckled by their mothers) with their *goûter* (bread and chocolate). Rachel said she'd breast-fed a poor woman's baby (as well as her own) during the war: the woman had no milk and could not afford donkey's milk. South of Naples. No cows. End evening, someone started talking Albigensian crusades, Simon of Montfort, Louis in a bad temper said, '*J'en ai rien à têter*' (I've nothing to suck, it doesn't interest me). Chacha: '*Quand on dit ça c'est qu'on en a beaucoup à têter au contraire*' (when you say that it's that on the contrary you've got plenty to suck, you feel very concerned).

How the Cordesse have always fed me language.

20 August. Crises, crises . . . everything dreadful. [. . .] Is this family history just a pretext for burrowing back in?

*   *   *

21 August. Dreamt tonight I was in village hall. Almost no one there. Benches ¾ empty. We came in as a group. I was wearing a red dress (the one I put on last night to go to Jean-Marie's) [. . .]. Jean-Pierre comes and says he needs an actress extra. [. . .] (Jean-Pierre was trying to recruit us for a lecture he's organised for the village feast – [. . .] he's afraid no one will go, and was trying to make me go and participate in the discussion [. . .]). I don't want to go and act, but I realise if I say no all the others will also say no. Jean-Pierre tells me I have only one line: '*Morte, où es-tu allée*' ('Dead woman, where did you go?'), or, '*Morte, pourquoi viendrais-tu?*' ('Dead woman, why should you come?') – in short, something meaning I did not care about death. I say, 'Okay,' I go. I see the empty seats at the lecturers' table, Jean-Pierre's, mine. Suddenly I am in my old dream of the stage, I am about to go on and I realise not only do I not know my part but I don't even remember what the play is about so I can't improvise. Now I do not remember my line. Is it *Mort* or *Morte*? ('Death' or 'Dead woman?'). I try various formulae. '*Mort, où est ta victoire?*' (Death, where is thy victory?') But no, I'm quite sure, it was *Morte* ('Dead woman'). Louis told me this morning that it was the dream of one's own death, a transparent dream in which one becomes the *actor* of it. I don't know whether not knowing one's part is part of the standard dream. For that is where the anguish comes from. [. . .]

I wonder how Louis knows about that dream.

From the Blue Notebook

10 June 1988. Our closest friend, the man my own age whom I knew best after T., Louis Cordesse, died in the night of Wednesday 8 June of a generalised cancer . . .

It's the end of a life. It's more than the end of Louis's life.

*   *   *

Butterwick Yorkshire, 10 October 1988, I know now that if I ever write the history of my Marseilles, a family history, herstory, there will be two sides. Two ways. Two banks. Swann, Guermantes. Jouve, Cordesse.

- *Notes on Contributors*

Rosalind Brackenbury is a full-time writer, author of over nine full-length published works, as well as numerous short stories, articles and poems. She teaches creative writing in the extra-mural department of Edinburgh University, and is a regular columnist for the magazine *Resurgence*. Married for over twenty years, she now lives alone in Edinburgh as part of that city's large community of writers with her two children and visiting friends. She is currently involved in a project aimed at encouraging people to write.

Publications
A Day to Remember to Forget (fiction), Macmillan, 1971
A Virtual Image (fiction), Macmillan, 1972
Into Egypt (fiction), Macmillan, 1974
A Superstitious Age (fiction), Harvester, 1976
The Caolocanth (fiction), Harvester, 1979
The Woman in the Tower (fiction), Harvester, 1982
Sense and Sensuality (fiction), Harvester, 1984
Crossing the Water (fiction), Harvester, 1986
Telling Each Other It Is Possible (poetry), Taxus Press, 1987

Jeannie Brehaut was born in Toronto in Canada in 1963, and came to Britain when she was nineteen. She has worked as a waitress on and off since she was fifteen, and spends all her available time writing. Her first completed short story, 'The Eyes of the World', was published in *Aurora* magazine, and she is a regular reviewer for *The Pink Paper*. When she is not waitressing or writing, she enjoys reading, dancing, cycling, and painting her flat different colours. She lives in London.

Hélène Cixous has written over thirty books, including works of fiction, and plays for radio and stage. In recent years she has been involved in a collaborative writing association with the Théâtre du Soleil in Paris. She is Professor of Literature at the experimental University of Paris VIII-Vincennes, and is director of the Paris-based Centre d'Etudes Féminines which she founded in 1974. She was born in Oran in Algeria of French and German parents and lives in Paris. She has two children.

Publications

(Only a few of Hélène Cixous' texts are available in English. For a full list of her texts in French, readers are directed to the bibliography printed in *Writing Differences: Readings from the Seminar of Hélène Cixous*, ed. Susan Sellers, Open University Press and St Martin's Press, New York, 1988. The list of Hélène Cixous' available English translations is given below.)

The Exile of James Joyce (literary criticism), translated by Sally Purcell, John Calder, 1972

Vivre l'orange/To Live the Orange (bilingual edition; fiction), English text translated by Sarah Cornell and Ann Liddle, Editions des femmes, Paris, 1979

Angst (fiction), translated by Jo Levy, John Calder, 1985

Inside (fiction), Schocken, 1986

The Newly Born Woman (with Catherine Clément; feminism/literary criticism), translated by Betsy Wing, Manchester University Press, 1986

Marcella Evaristi was born in Glasgow and educated at the Universities of Glasgow and Edinburgh. At the age of twenty-five she won a major Arts Council bursary, and has worked as Playwright in Residence at St Andrews, Sheffield, Glasgow and Strathclyde Universities. Her plays include *Wedding Belles and Green Grasses* (Traverse Theatre Club, Edinburgh and BBC Radio 3), *Hard to Get* (Traverse Theatre and Granada television), *Terrestrial Extras* (Tron Theatre, Glasgow and Traverse Theatre), *Commedia* (Crucible Theatre, Sheffield and Lyric Theatre, Hammersmith; nominated for the Best New Play *Evening Standard* Award), and a BBC 'Play for Today' *Eve Set the Balls of Corruption Rolling*, which received the Pye Award for the Best Writer New to Television. She has also written and performed a number of one-woman plays, including *Dorothy and the Bitch* (Traverse Theatre), *The Works* (Traverse Theatre and BBC Radio 3) and *Visiting Company* (Tron Theatre). Her radio play, *The Hat*, was first broadcast on BBC Radio 3 in June 1988. The twins, Daniel and Gabriella, were born 25 November 1988.

Valerie Hannagan was born in 1953, and brought up in France. She came to Britain at the age of twenty to train as a teacher, and has worked in a number of schools. In 1982 she started part-time research at London University specialising in contemporary French women's writing. She has written a family history, several poems and short stories, and is currently working on a novel. Her short story, 'Una', was published in the August 1985 edition of *Spare Rib* under the pen-name of Vanessa Grey. She is continuing her research with a thesis on the French writer Monique Wittig.

Nicki Jackowska has four collections of poetry and three novels currently in print. Over the past fifteen years her poetry and prose have appeared in numerous publications, including Hutchinsons's *New Poetry* (volumes 6 and 8), *Bread and Roses* (Virago Press, 1983), *Angels of Fire* (Chatto and Windus, 1986) and *Dancing the Tightrope* (The Women's Press, 1987). She is also editor and a contributor to *Voices from Arts for Labour* (Pluto Press, 1985). She was a prizewinner in the 1985 Stand Short Story Competition, and has received a number of awards from the Arts Council and South-East Arts. She has worked as a tutor for the Arvon Writers' Foundation and the Regional Arts Associations, and in 1988 she held an extended residency at the Brighton Festival. She lives in Brighton with her seventeen-year-old daughter, Laura.

Publications
The House That Manda Built (poetry), Menard, 1981
Earthwalks (poetry), Ceolfrith, 1982
Doctor Marbles and Marianne – A Romance (fiction), Harvester, 1982
Letters to Superman (poetry), Rivelin Grapheme, 1984
The Road to Orc (fiction), Bran's Head, 1985
Gates to the City (poetry), Taxus Press, 1985
The Islanders (fiction), Harvester, 1985

Amryl Johnson was born in Trinidad and came to Britain when she was eleven. She went to school in London, and then to Kent University, and currently works as a creative writing tutor and occasional broadcaster. In addition to the publications listed below, her work has been included in a number of anthologies such as *News for Babylon* (Chatto and Windus, 1983), *Facing the Sea* (Heinemann, 1986), *With a Poet's Eye* (Tate Gallery Publications, 1986), *Watchers and Seekers* (The Women's Press, 1987), and *Let It Be Told* (Virago Press, 1988). She has recently completed a collection of poems and a book of short stories both of which are set in the Caribbean, and is currently working on a novel. She lives in Coventry.

Publications
Early Poems by Amryl Johnson, Sable Publications, 1982
Long Road to Nowhere (poetry), Virago Press, 1985
Sequins for a Ragged Hem (fiction), Virago Press, 1988

Sylvia Kantaris was born in 1936 in the Derbyshire Peak District. She studied French at Bristol University, taught in Bristol and London, and then spent ten years in Australia, where she taught French at Queensland University, had two children, and wrote MA and PhD theses on French surrealism. In 1974 she settled in Cornwall, and from 1976 to 1984 tutored a twentieth-century poetry course for the Open University. In 1986 she was appointed Cornwall's first Writer in the Community. She has published five collections of poetry, and her *Dirty Washing: New and Selected Poems* (Bloodaxe) is due out in July 1989.

Publications
Time and Motion (poetry), Prism: Poetry Society of Australia, 1975; reprinted Menhir, 1986
The Tenth Muse (poetry), Peterloo, 1983; reprinted Menhir, 1986
News From the Front (poetry), with D. M. Thomas, Arc, 1983
The Sea at the Door (poetry), Secker and Warburg, 1985
The Air Mines of Mistila (poetry), with Philip Gross, Bloodaxe, 1988

Medbh McGuckian was born in Belfast in 1950. She is author of five books of poetry, and her poems have appeared in anthologies such as *The Penguin Book of Contemporary British Poetry* and *The Faber Book of Contemporary Irish Verse*. Her first book, *The Flower Master*, won a Gregory Award, the Alice Hunt Bartlett Award and the Rooney Prize. In 1979 she won the National Poetry Competition. She has worked as a teacher of English, and as Writer in Residence at Queen's University, Belfast. She lives in Belfast and is married with three sons.

Publications
Single Ladies (poetry), Interim Press, 1980 (pamphlet)
Portrait of Joanna (poetry), Ulsterman Press, 1980 (pamphlet)
The Flower Master (poetry), Oxford University Press, 1982
Venus and the Rain (poetry), Oxford University Press, 1984
On Ballycastle Beach (poetry), Oxford University Press, 1988

Sue Roe was born in Leicester in 1956, and studied English at the

Universities of Kent and Sussex. Her poetry has appeared in *Pen New Poetry 1* (Quartet, 1986), *The Scotsman* and *Writing Women*. Her critical study *Writing and Gender: Virginia Woolf's Writing Practice* is due to appear in 1989. She is consultant editor to an academic publishing house, a regular reviewer, and currently holds the Creative Writing Fellowship at Reading University. She has recently completed a second novel, and is working on a series of short stories. She lives in Brighton.

Publications
Estella: Her Expectations (fiction), Harvester, 1982
Women Reading Women's Writing (ed.), Harvester, 1987

Carol Rumens was born 10 December 44 in South-East London. After winning a scholarship to grammar school, she began a degree in Philosophy at London University, but left half-way through her course to have a child. She is author of six published volumes of poetry and a novel, and works full-time as a writer and reviewer. She is divorced with two grown-up daughters, Kelsey (twenty-two) and Rebecca (twenty).

Publications
A Strange Girl in Bright Colours (poetry), Quartet, 1973
Unplayed Music (poetry), Secker and Warburg, 1981
Star Whisper (poetry), Secker and Warburg, 1983
Direct Dialling (poetry), Chatto and Windus, 1985
Selected Poems (poetry), Chatto and Windus, 1987
The Greening of the Snow Beach (poetry), Bloodaxe, 1988
Plato Park (fiction), Chatto and Windus, 1987

Carole Satyamurti was born in 1939. She studied at the University of London and did post-graduate work in the United States. She taught in Singapore and Uganda before settling in London, where she teaches at North-East London Polytechnic. Her poems have appeared in various magazines, including *P. N. Review, Encounter, London Magazine, Poetry Review, Literary Review* and the *Observer*. Her first collection of poetry *Broken Moon*, was published by Oxford University Press in 1987.

Nina Sibal lives in India and is a diplomat in the Indian Foreign Service. She has degrees in English Literature and Law, and chaired the United Nations commission which drafted the Convention on the Elimination of Discrimination against Women. Her first novel, *Yatra*, was published by The Women's Press in 1987. She is married with two children.

Sue Stewart was born in Lancashire in 1953, and moved South when she was eighteen. After working in Cambridge at a number of stop-gap jobs, she went to Kent University where she studied English and Art History. She then worked in London before moving to the Berkshire countryside. Her poetry has been published in the Phoenix Press anthology *Four Ways* (1986), and in a number of poetry magazines, including *London Magazine*, *Poetry Review* and *The Times Literary Supplement*. Her sequence of poems *Book of Hours* was illustrated by painter Celia Ward and exhibited at the National Poetry Centre and at the Maas Gallery, London, in 1987. She is a regular poetry reviewer, a member of the Poetry Society's 'Poets in Schools' scheme and the Arvon Writers' Foundation management committee.

Emma Tennant grew up in Scotland, and worked for a number of years as a freelance journalist and literary editor. She has written twelve full-length works of fiction, and is currently working on a feminist adaptation of Robert Louis Stevenson's *The Strange Case of Dr Jekyll and Mr Hyde*. She has a son and two daughters, and lives in West London.

Publications
Wild Nights (fiction), Picador, 1981
The Ghost Child (for children), Heinemann, 1984
Woman Beware Woman (fiction), Picador, 1984
The Crack (fiction), Faber, 1985
Black Marina (fiction), Faber, 1986
Hotel de Dream (fiction), Faber, 1986
The Last of the Country House Murders (fiction), Faber, 1986
Adventures of Robina: By Herself (fiction), Faber, 1987
Queen of Stones (fiction), Faber, 1987
The Colour of Rain (fiction), Faber, 1988
The House of Hospitalities (fiction), Penguin, 1988
A Wedding of Cousins (fiction), Viking, 1988
The Bad Sister (fiction), Faber, 1989

Alice Walker was born in Eatonton, Georgia, and has published four volumes of poetry, two collections of short stories and three full-length novels. Her third novel, *The Color Purple*, published by The Women's Press in 1982, won the 1983 Pulitzer Prize for Fiction. She is a consultant editor to the feminist monthly *Ms* and the black political quarterly *Freedomways*. Her essays have been collected in the volume *In Search of Our Mothers' Gardens*, published by The Women's Press in 1984.

Publications
Meridian (fiction), The Women's Press, 1982.
You Can't Keep A Good Woman Down (fiction), The Women's Press, 1982
The Color Purple (fiction), The Women's Press, 1983
In Love and Trouble: Stories of Black Women (fiction), The Women's Press, 1984
Horses Make a Landscape Look More Beautiful (poetry), The Women's Press, 1985
The Third Life of Grange Copeland (fiction), The Women's Press, 1985
Once (poetry), The Women's Press, 1986
Goodnight Willie Lee, I'll See You In the Morning (poetry), The Women's Press, 1987
Revolutionary Petunias (poetry), The Women's Press, 1988
Living by the Word: Collected Writings 1973–1987, The Women's Press, 1988
To Hell With Dying (for children), Hodder and Stoughton, 1988

Nicole Ward Jouve is French and has lived in Yorkshire for a number of years. She has published fiction in French and in translation, criticism in English, and a number of essays on bilingualism. Her study of the Yorkshire Ripper (*Un Homme nommé Zapolski/'The Streetcleaner': The Yorkshire Ripper Case on Trial*) was written and published in both French and English (Editions des femmes, Paris, 1983 and Marion Boyars, 1986). Her fiction has been published in English by Virago Press (*Shades of Grey*, 1981), and in *Bananas, Granta, Land, Writing Women* and *Numbers* magazines. Her study of *Colette* appeared with Harvester Press and Indiana University Press in 1987.